RONALD REAGAN

RONALD REAGAN

An Intellectual Biography
· · · · · · · · · · · · · · · · · · · ·

DAVID T. BYRNE

Potomac Books
An imprint of the University of Nebraska Press

⊗

Library of Congress Cataloging-in-Publication Data
Names: Byrne, David T., author.
Title: Ronald Reagan: an intellectual biography /
David T. Byrne. Description: Lincoln: Potomac
Books, 2018. | Includes bibliographical
references and index.
Identifiers: LCCN 2018027379
ISBN 9781640120037 (hardback: alk. paper)
ISBN 9781640121263 (epub)
ISBN 9781640121270 (mobi)
ISBN 9781640121287 (pdf)
Subjects: LCSH: Reagan, Ronald—Political and social
views. | Reagan, Ronald—Philosophy. | Reagan,
Ronald—Religion. | Presidents—United States—
Biography. | BISAC: BIOGRAPHY & AUTOBIOGRAPHY /
Presidents & Heads of State.
Classification: LCC E877.2 .B97 2018 |
DDC 973.927092 [B]—dc23. LC record available at
https://lccn.loc.gov/2018027379

Set in Janson Text LT Pro by E. Cuddy.

For my family

My country, 'tis of Thee,
Sweet Land of Liberty
Of thee I sing;
Land where my fathers died,
Land of the pilgrims' pride,
From every mountainside
Let Freedom ring.

CONTENTS

ACKNOWLEDGMENTS

All books are collaborative efforts, and this one is no exception. I would like to thank my agent, Joe Vallely, for finding this work a home, Tom Swanson for believing in this project, and all of the editorial staff at the University of Nebraska Press for their invaluable help.

INTRODUCTION

In his biography of Ronald Reagan, Lou Cannon calls him the "Rodney Dangerfield" of ideas. Even conservatives, notes Cannon, rarely value Reagan as an idea man. *The Conservative Bookshelf*, for example, examines the ideas of Pat Buchanan and Whitaker Chambers but excludes Reagan. In his work *The Conservative Intellectual Movement in America since 1945*, George Nash writes, "This book is about conservative intellectuals—those engaged in study, reflection and speculation; purveyors of ideas; scholars and journalists."[1] Nash continues that he does not study men like Ronald Reagan who are merely political activists. Liberals are reluctant to offer any intellectual abilities whatsoever to Reagan. The Democratic stalwart Clarke Clifford famously described Reagan as an "amiable dunce," and the notorious atheist Christopher Hitchens declares, "The fox, as has been pointed out by more than one philosopher, knows many small things, whereas the hedgehog knows one big thing. Ronald Reagan was neither a fox nor a hedgehog. He was as dumb as a stump."[2] One can more easily find scholarly intellectual treatments of men like Stalin and Hitler than of Reagan. I want to disprove the notion that Reagan was stupid and elevate him to the rank of an intelligent, thinking person. His ideas need to be studied.

This work was largely inspired by an intellectual biography of President Barack Obama published in 2012. The author of that book describes Obama as " very much an intellectual."[3] After reading that book, I realized a biography of President Reagan was needed too, because Reagan's thought is just as profound as that of Obama. Obama expresses no original ideas. Reagan, in contrast, took conservatism in a new direction because his thought was, in many respects, a rejection of the traditional conservatism proposed by the likes of Edmund Burke, Klemens von Metternich, and Russell Kirk. Reagan sought to bring radical, dramatic change to the world, specifically by spreading freedom to the people of Eastern Europe and rolling back parts of the Great Society. This was far more original than anything proposed by Obama. One biographer writes, "More so than any other American figure of the twentieth century, he endowed freedom with a conservative meaning, in the process appropriating for the right what had once been a liberal concept." The scholar Hugh Heclo contended that no twentieth-century president dedicated so much of his career contesting political philosophy. "To appreciate this significance, one must pay as much attention to Reagan's pre-presidential years as to his White House years. In that regard, Reagan belongs less to the twentieth century and more to the estimable company of Jackson, Madison and Jefferson."[4] In terms of ideas, Reagan trumps Obama.

Another task of this work is to explain Reagan to those who have spent so much time studying him. Reagan baffles historians. He was often called an enigma, even by those who knew him best. He authorized one biography as president, and it became one of the most controversial biographies of the twentieth century because in his effort to elucidate Reagan, the author, Edmund Morris, introduced fictional characters. Morris called Reagan one of the strangest men who has ever lived. Even most of Reagan's close friends and family acknowledge they never really knew the man who would became the fortieth president of the United States. Biographers have attempted to shine a light on Reagan, but with only limited success, maybe because they have employed conventional methods in order to try to understand an unconventional man. Former president Gerald Ford remarked that Reagan was one of the few leaders he had ever met whose speeches revealed more about him than did private conversations. Consistent with this, I am less interested in Reagan's personality, even less so in Reagan the president, and more so in his mind, or his cosmology. A traditional biography examines (usually chronologically) the personal and emotional life of a subject, and an intellectual biography may incorporate some of these methods, but this work analyzes Reagan's ideas by establishing a rationale for them. I place them in their historical and cultural context. In doing so I do not try to supplant other Reagan biographies but rather augment them by allowing readers to view Reagan through a different paradigm, one practiced by intellectual historians. An example of this is the fact that this work, unlike almost every other Reagan biography, excludes the most important person in Reagan's life, his wife Nancy. This is done because she did little to contribute to his political philosophy.

One other intellectual historian, John Patrick Diggins, attempted to study Reagan, but I found his work wanting. Despite its title, *Fate, Freedom and History* provides little analysis of how Reagan developed an ideology of freedom. Diggins contends that Reagan's core beliefs have their origins in the nineteenth century, particularly in Ralph Waldo Emerson and his idealism. He deems Reagan an "Emersonian president."[5] I agree with this, but I think Diggins's outlook is a bit provincial, since he reduces Reagan's intellectual sources to nineteenth-century America. I think we need to broaden our outlook and ask, What forces created nineteenth-century America? How was the American cultural landscape, and subsequently Reagan, shaped in the first place? Like all Americans, Reagan must be placed within the broader Western tradition. This requires us to venture outside of America history.

When asked why I study European history instead of American history, I answer that it is because America descended from Europe, just as a child descends from a parent. In order to understand American cultural history, one must understand its European roots. The Puritans provide an example. Most educated Americans recognize the Puritanical influence on American society—such as the Blue Laws that exist in parts of the United States today—but one must study European history to fully understand the Puritans. Similarly, in order to understand the American cultural values that shaped Reagan, one must study some European history.

Diggins, for instance, is right when he calls Reagan Emersonian, but where did Emerson get his ideas from? The answer is Plato. Plato was the first transcendentalist, arguing that the spiritual world transcends this earthly world. Reagan, like Plato, downplayed material things, instead favoring the spiritual. Plato was both an Idealist and an idealist, the former because he stressed the primacy of the mind and ideas, the latter because he believed in an ideal, utopian system of government. Both can be said of Reagan too. He lived in the world of ideas more than any other twentieth-century president. And Reagan, like Plato, advocated an ideal system of government, which he, like Plato, believed was universal. The casual reader may be surprised to learn that an ancient philosopher such as Plato could shape the thought of those who live 2,500 years after him and who probably have read very little of him! But ideas traverse eras and civilizations. Plato's ideas were transmitted to Reagan through Christianity. Plato's philosophy contributed to the Christian dualist philosophy, which shaped Reagan by minimizing the significance of the material world in favor of an extrasensory world.

Three specific historical forces shaped Reagan and produced a political philosophy that continues to exert profound influence across the country today, and none of them originated in the United States. The first of these are the same Christian values that have nourished Western and American cultural history, especially the concept of the Kingdom of God. Christians believe that God's eternal kingdom transcends any earthly value. This kingdom is universal; it is meant for all people, of all ages, and of all nations. Second, Reagan was shaped by the American emphasis on freedom and an aversion to a strong centralized government. Reagan wasn't a conservative; he was a liberal in the true sense of the word because he deemed freedom to be the highest political value, trumping equality, education, and sometimes even peace.

This belief in freedom has fundamentally shaped American culture since colonial times, but the intellectual origins of this belief, at least in modern times, lie in Western Europe. During the Enlightenment, philosophers argued that freedom was best achieved by minimizing the power of a centralized government, and this idea led to American revolutionary documents such as the Declaration of Independence and the Constitution. Enlightenment thinkers were the first "freedom fighters," from whom all other demands for liberty descend. Although today we consider Reagan to be a figure of the right, his notions of freedom are actually descended from Enlightenment thinkers. The Enlightenment gave birth to America, with its emphasis on freedom being the handmaiden. Significantly, too, most Enlightenment philosophers believed freedom to be universal, applicable to all people at all times.

The period between the two world wars, when Western powers acquiesced to—rather than confronted—Hitler was the third historical force that shaped Reagan. He used history as much as any American president to buttress his cosmology because he lived through one of the most catastrophic events in human history, World War II. Reagan could not escape the lessons of the appeasement era, when Western powers placated Hitler, allowing him to annex Austria and parts of Czechoslovakia. Reagan used the lessons learned from this era of appeasement to further his case that the United States needed to actively confront the Soviet Union. Reagan drew on the fact that extreme attempts at peace, negotiation, and compromise only strengthened Hitler, leading to the most deadly war in history. This spurred his activist foreign policy, which aimed at ending the Soviet Union, even if this policy seemed aggressive and confrontational to observers. Most of Reagan's baby-boomer critics emphasized Vietnam as their lesson. They used the debacle in Southeast Asia as evidence when arguing that the United States should not try to promote freedom to distant corners of the globe. Reagan, on the other hand, was a product of World War II. He looked at the world through a different prism.

My primary sources are Reagan's own writings. He was one of the most prolific writers in American presidential history. I suspect no other twentieth-century president, save Richard Nixon, spent as much time putting pen to paper as did Reagan. Reagan didn't write any books other than a couple of autobiographies, and this further explains why he isn't considered a thinker. From the dawn of civilization until the twentieth century, thinking people expressed their ideas in book form, or at least some sort of manuscript. But the twentieth century introduced new mediums, like television and radio, which allowed thinking people to postulate ideas outside of the published medium. Reagan was particularly deft at using the radio. After leaving Sacramento in 1974, he hosted a radio show on which he continued promoting his ideas. His handwritten notes for some of these speeches still exist. They, along with many of his letters, were brought to public attention by Kiron Skinner, Martin Anderson, and Annelise Anderson in the early 2000s. These writings revealed to the public a man engrossed in ideas.

Reagan's most famous early speech was given at the 1964 Republican National Convention and called "A Time for Choosing." It is a gold mine of political ideas, and it ignited my own interest in Reagan as an intellectual figure, defined as someone with significant ideas. It contains seeds of not just Reagan's philosophy and presidency but also, to some degree, the contemporary American conservative movement. Anyone interested in American history should read it. Reagan delivered countless other speeches during the 1950s, 1960s, and 1970s. As governor of California, he routinely spoke out on national and even international issues. And unlike modern politicians, he wrote his own speeches before becoming president. With a few exceptions, I refrain from using any of Reagan's presidential speeches, as it is not always clear whether these came from Reagan or from his speechwriters (although these men and women maintain that their greatest source was Reagan's earlier writings, and Reagan always made adjustments to important speeches before he gave them).

All of Reagan's writings and speeches contain an ethical philosophy, a theory about how the good life can be achieved, and this can be summarized in one word: *freedom*. How do we make the world a better place for future generations? Spread and maintain freedom. What is immoral? Denying freedom. These writings reveal that in accordance with our modern era, where earthly affairs dominate our life and thought, Reagan tried to bring freedom to earth. This is not to say he abandoned faith in a theological heaven on earth, but rather he expanded this notion with the idea that freedom could be brought to earth. Combining the Christian and Enlightenment traditions, Reagan believed in a Kingdom of Freedom. He reconciled the dominant idea of the Middle Ages, the Kingdom of God, with the most powerful idea of our era, the concept of freedom. Reagan blended traditional Enlightenment notions with Christianity. He felt that all of our efforts must be invested in spreading freedom, because if we lose, hell will reign on earth. The process may be a titanic struggle, but ultimately we will win. Good will conquer evil. This synthesis did not originate with Reagan, but no president in history had made this the central theme of his presidency. Where presidents before Reagan tried to protect freedom, Reagan audaciously sought to spread the Kingdom of Freedom around the world. By using this paradigm to understand Reagan, we can begin to make sense of his mind, something at which few people, whether friends or foes, have succeeded.

Specifically Reagan sought to expand and protect freedom through ideas like reforming social security, shrinking government, reducing welfare spending, promoting free trade between nations, lowering the top marginal tax rate, and increasing defense spending. These ideas continue to exert influence in American politics today, and not just on the Republican side of the aisle. It was a Democrat, Bill Clinton, with some support from his party, who signed NAFTA and welfare reform into law. Today both sides agree that social security needs fixing. Furthermore Reagan's tax cuts, decades later, still have faced no serious efforts to repeal them, even during times when the Democrats controlled Congress. Reagan's foreign policy ideas live on in the minds of neoconservatives. He insisted that America had a moral obligation to overthrow tyranny and spread democracy to the farthest reaches of the world because democracy is a universal value, not a Western one. Before Reagan, containment, which accepted the existence of dictatorships in places like Eastern Europe, was the dominant theme in American foreign policy. Reagan rejected this, insisting that America could and should end tyranny, an idea that is one root of the Iraq and Afghanistan conflicts. Was Reagan an inchoate neocon? I will explore this contention.

I would like to respond to a couple of criticisms I anticipate. Critical readers will point out inconsistencies between Reagan's thought and his presidency, or between what Reagan said and what he did. But no historical thinker can claim perfect consistency. Describing contradictions in his thought does not weaken my argument that Reagan is a significant intellectual figure in American history. Marx, Newton, Freud, and Descartes, all have their indefensible inconsistencies, which their contemporaries noted. Jefferson, the man who penned the words "all men are created equal," owned slaves. Describing these inconsistencies is a worthwhile endeavor, but it does not render these people's thoughts meaningless. Intellectual historians do not play the "gotcha" game, in which inconsistencies mean intellectual futility. If all thinkers were required to be perfectly consistent and completely intelligible, intellectual history would be void of figures.

Likewise, arguing that Reagan was not original in some of his ideas does not weaken his position as a significant thinker in American history. He was, in fact, a derivative thinker whose thought was influenced by others positing similar philosophies, from Enlightenment philosophers to our own founding fathers. For that matter, Freud was not the first to discuss the existence of the unconscious; Newton did not discover gravity; Darwin did not discover evolution; and Marx was by no means the first socialist, communist, or materialist, or even the first to suggest class struggle. Jefferson was not the first to suggest that men, by nature, are free and equal. An intellectual biography of any of these men must include a mention of their predecessors. They were all great synthesizers; they wove together diverse ideas into a comprehensive cosmology that influenced Western thought and culture. In fact a detailed analysis of the thought of Marx, Freud, Darwin, and Newton will reveal that their intellectual insights were the result of their ability to synthesize what, at least until their time, had been distinct and unrelated currents of thought. This describes Reagan. He wove together various themes of American cultural history—such as its egalitarianism, its belief in a divinely sanctioned mission, its religious tradition, and its emphasis on freedom—and created a comprehensive cosmology that continues to dominate the American political landscape. He was influenced by a host of thinkers that spanned centuries, from Adam Smith to James Burnham, from St. Augustine to Milton Friedman.

Some skeptics may question Reagan's intellect entirely. There is a natural human tendency to deem different people inferior, and this is just as true in the intellectual realm. Intellectually debasing "the other" is an unfortunate occurrence but completely normal. The reasoning goes something like this: I am intelligent. Therefore people who think like I do are intelligent, while those who think differently than I must be less intelligent, because if they were intelligent, they would believe what I believe. In Reagan's case, this could be applied to ask, How can an intelligent person believe that increasing military spending promotes peace? Or, How can creating favorable policies for the wealthiest Americans in any way benefit the downtrodden? This is ludicrous. No intelligent person could believe this. Therefore Reagan can't be intelligent. I contend this way of thinking is flawed. We naïvely believe that our political and philosophical opinions derive from our intelligence, when in fact most people develop an ideology at a relatively young age. People don't become educated and then develop a political or religious ideology; rather they adopt a value system in their teens or early twenties, and then become educated. Lou Cannon, after describing Reagan's intelligence as an "enigma," uses the ideas of psychologist Howard Gardner to understand Reagan's intellect. Gardner argues for "multiple intelligences," and Cannon contends that Reagan lacked the type of intelligence usually associated with politicians, professors, and lawyers but ranked very high in "interpersonal intelligence." This may explain why Reagan succeeded in his meetings with Gorbachev; ultimately Reagan got what he wanted.

Finally, Reagan's cosmology made him who he was. Those who study his personality are left confused because his personality didn't define him. Instead, his ideas did. In the Platonist tradition, Reagan believed in the power of ideas. These included ideas about

freedom, ideas about democracy, ideas about government intervention in the economy, ideas about the transitory nature of communism, ideas about confronting the Soviet behemoth, and ideas
about abortion. Reagan was an idea man. For my purposes, whether
one agrees or disagrees with his ideas is irrelevant. Most historians
don't agree with and can find serious fault in the ideas of Marx, but
he remains a salient intellectual figure because of the influence his
ideas have exerted on Western history. I am not a Marxist, but I go
to great pains to explain to my students the principles of Marxist
philosophy because of its significance for the modern world. For
the same reason, even if you aren't a Reagan supporter, his philosophy remains important for anyone curious about the world.
Reagan, like all American presidents, was a polarizing figure, and
I urge the reader to briefly suspend your opinions in order to gain
insight into him. That is the goal of this work.

RONALD REAGAN

1
. . .

Religious Roots

I, in my own mind, have thought of America as a place in the divine
scheme of things that was set aside as the promised land. . . . I
believe that God in shedding his grace on this country has always
in this divine scheme of things kept an eye on our land and guided
it as a promised land.

—REAGAN, "America the Beautiful"

Reagan's ideas emerged from a Christian context. Like so much of
Western thought, his political and ethical philosophies are inter-
twined with his religious cosmology. Religious influences permeate all Westerners because we have been shaped by our pasts, at
both cultural and intellectual levels. Reagan's branch of Christianity
provided the foundation for his domestic and geopolitical philosophy. This will be described in more detail throughout this work.

Reagan's childhood was materially poor but rich in spirit. His
mother, Nelle, taught him her religious beliefs, which were a Protestant form of Christianity. She schooled him in Christian doc-
trine and lived a Christ-centered life. One of her friends recounts,
"Many of us believed that Nelle Reagan had the gift to heal. She
never laid on the hands or anything like that. It was the way she
prayed, down on her knees, eyes raised up and speaking like she
knew God personally, like she had lots of dealings with him before.
If someone had real troubles or was sick, Nellie would come to

their house and kneel and pray."[1] Nelle's granddaughter Maureen said Nelle made you feel like you could change the world. Reagan's father, Jack, was an alcoholic Irish Catholic, but Nelle's Christian beliefs shaped her son. She imbued him with optimism too. He recalled, "While my father was a cynic and tended to suspect the worst of people, my mother was the opposite. She always expected to find the best in people and often did."[2] This optimism endured throughout Reagan's life, infusing not just his personality but his political beliefs as well.

Nelle belonged to the Disciples of Christ, an evangelical brand of Protestantism, which can be traced to the Second Great Awakening that began in the United States in the early 1800s. Politically charged, this Great Awakening paralleled the rise of modern democratic politics. Its leaders insisted that Christian principles should be applied to political and social issues because religion provides us with answers to ethical questions and politicians create laws that foster ethical behavior. Politics and religion can never separate, just as modern-day ideologies can never be separated from politics. How can any ethical system be separate from the field that tries to create a just society? This Great Awakening contributed to the abolition movement in the nineteenth century and, later, women's suffrage and temperance movements.

The Second Great Awakening was also a reaction against the Enlightenment notion that if God exists, He created the world and then left the scene, like an absentee landlord. This deism promotes the image of a distant God who has no concern for His creation, but evangelicals insist that God intervenes in the world and in our lives. God inspires people, evangelicals believe, and all of our success in the world is due to God's divine will. For an athlete, this means that every victory is achieved with God's help; for an author, it means that every book that author writes is shared with God; and for the president of the United States, it means that every bill signed into law contains God's grace. For those unfamiliar with this religion, these may be notions that smack of messianic arrogance, but devout evangelicals believe that they achieve nothing on their own because God's hand guides everything. We are merely His agents.

Besides relying on Scripture, evangelicals draw inspiration from Christianity's greatest philosopher, St. Augustine. Augustine reconciled Platonic philosophy with the teachings of Jesus. Plato divided the world into two: the world of forms (ideas) and the world of appearances. The latter, he held, were cheap, meaningless representations of the true and perfect forms. All truth and goodness, according to Plato, could be found in the universal, permanent, immaterial forms. Augustine continued these ideas by arguing for the existence of two worlds: this earthly, material, temporary world, and the next world, the universal, permanent, immaterial world of God. One day the Kingdom of God will descend upon the entire world, engulfing all nations. God never distinguishes between nations, races, and cultures. As Nelle Reagan wrote, "Those who have turned against missions have turned against everything Christ taught—and the very last words he uttered, 'Go ye into all of the world and preach the gospel to every creature.'"[3] Like any good Christian, Reagan was taught the universal nature of his values and that he must spread them.

Reagan prayed to this providential Creator regularly. Prayer is central to Christians because it brings them closer to God and allows them to recognize His grace. It strengthens their relationship with God. Although prayer can be a laundry list of wants, it can be more than that. Reagan always prayed before taking off in an airplane, as many people do, but while a secularist might presume that Reagan prayed that he would survive each flight, he actually prayed that he would accept whatever God had in store for him. Reagan believed that God had a plan for him.

This deference to God does not mean that modern evangelicals believe human beings have no agency in this world. Providence should not be equated with fatalism. Nelle introduced a young Reagan to the book *That Printer of Udell* by Harold Bell Wright, a work that stresses human ability to change the world. Reagan cites this work as one of the most important influences on his life and thought. He writes:

[The book] had an impact I shall always remember. After reading it and thinking about it for a few days, I went to my mother
and told her I wanted to declare my faith and be baptized . . .
and I was baptized several days after finishing the book. The
term "role model" was not a familiar term in that time and
place. But I realize I found a role model in that traveling printer
whom Harold Bell Wright had brought to life. He set me on
a course I've tried to follow even unto this day. I shall always
be grateful.[4]

Udell is a Christian story about a hardworking man named Dick
who sees the world as a struggle between right and wrong. Seeking to apply Christian principles to his own corrupt world, Dick
helps those in need. *That Printer of Udell* insists that some of our
fate lies in our own hands. In modern times we take for granted
the idea that individuals can influence important events, but this
sentiment was less common in the Middle Ages, when God was
seen to be the ultimate cause of most historical events. Human
agency dominates our modern world, however; we control everything, our society tells us. Reagan, like other modern devout evangelicals, believed that God controls events, but human beings too
can mold the world. This unifies Christian thinking and its belief
in an omnipotent God with our modern feeling that individuals
matter. The medieval Christian chanted, "Let the Kingdom of
God come," but the modern Christian chant, as uttered by the
nineteenth-century German philosopher G. W. F. Hegel, is "May
the Kingdom of God come, and our hands not remain idle."[5] We
can help bring the Kingdom of the Lord to the earth. We are not
helpless because we have free will.

Udell inspired a new religious faith in Reagan. As a young adult
he joined a Christ-centered ministry called Christian Endeavor, a
group that taught the Bible to young people and promoted spiritual strength among its members. Reagan even taught classes for
the organization, and he seemed to have had a flare for making the
Bible come alive.[6] His activities as a young man were not merely
spiritual, however. He also thrived in the secular world. In high

school he played a variety of sports, participated in drama, worked on the yearbook, and was student body president. Despite what his detractors contend, these are the typical high school activities of a highly intelligent person. Still, Reagan's religious beliefs were never far from his thoughts. His high school commencement speech cited John 10:10, where Jesus tells his followers, "The thief comes only to steal and kill and destroy; I have come that they may have life, and have it to the full."[7] Christianity affirms eternal life. No other religion offers so much to believers; arguably, all a Christian needs to receive this eternal life is faith. It is very seductive.

Reagan's evangelicalism must be contrasted with the "hellfire and brimstone" approach preached by those who insist humanity is (mostly) damned. The latter descends from Calvinism, but Reagan's evangelicalism explicitly rejected many Calvinist doctrines, including the total depravity of man, the belief that all human beings are completely separate from God, and the theory that we have no free will. Reagan's Christianity was optimistic, open, and hopeful. In a 1950 interview he said he didn't believe in hell: "I can't believe an all wise and loving father would condemn any of his children to eternal damnation."[8] It's not that those who don't believe in God will burn forever in the netherworld. Everyone will always be loved by God. Rather, they will be separate from God, a fate worse than any physical torment because they will be separate from all that is good and just. In his classic work, *The Great Divorce* (1945), which Reagan certainly read, C. S. Lewis asserts, "A damned soul is nearly nothing. . . . Good beats upon the damned incessantly as sound waves beat on the ears of the deaf, but they cannot receive it."[9] The damned, those who reject God, don't suffer; they just feel nothing. This is the opposite of life.

Reagan, like Lewis, believed in free will: "Nor do I believe that God can be blamed for all the tragedies in the world. The tragedy of war, for instance. If we each lived according to the rules of the Bible, if we loved our neighbor and did unto others as we would have others do unto us, how could war ever be? The responsibility is in our hands alone. And our lives are in our hands. I'm not a fatalist."[10] Evangelical, anti-Puritan ideas could not be better expressed. Reagan believed that a close relationship with God was, in fact, obtainable in this lifetime, for everyone, at any age. Reagan descended from this Christian faith, and although Scripture played a key role in his faith, Reagan, like other evangelicals, did not bow only to Scripture, as did the Puritans and Calvinists. Reagan's brand of Christianity was a little more liberal. This does not make it any less Christian.

Some of Reagan's biographers find his version of Christianity paradoxical. One writes, "The nature of Reagan's religious beliefs is baffling. He seemed to offer Christianity without Christ and the crucifixion, a religion without reference to sin, evil, suffering or sacrifice."[11] This is true, but Reagan's brand of Christianity represented the Protestant view that no specific acts (rituals) are necessary for the good life. This was at the heart of the Protestant Reformation. For Catholics, activities such as confession, attending mass, and receiving communion are required. Protestants may practice these activities in one form or another, or they may not. Just because Reagan didn't express any outward or public manifestations of Christianity doesn't mean he was less religious or Christian. Protestant Christianity is a relationship with Jesus Christ. For Protestants, all that is technically required is faith in Christ. The good life is built on that. A more solid foundation cannot exist.

As a committed Christian, Reagan did believe in God, Christ, the Resurrection, and, of course, salvation. Salvation played a dominant theme in his life, although the application of salvation often differed; some applications were personal, others were political. When analyzing the young Reagan almost all Reagan biographers refer to the following story he told of himself as an eleven-year-old boy: "I came home to find my father flat on his back on the front porch, and no one there to lend him a hand but me. He was drunk, dead to the world. I stood over him for a minute or two . . . seeing his arms spread out as if he were crucified, as indeed he was—his hair soaked with melting snow, snoring as he breathed."[12] Reagan saved his father by dragging him into the house but never told him about the event. Salvation can be a private phenomenon. Or it can be public. As a teenage lifeguard, he allegedly saved seventy-seven people from a river so turbulent, the city prohibits swimming there today. The local newspaper touted Reagan's feats and made them front-page stories. Reagan called lifeguarding his favorite job.

Experiences like these, combined with his Christianity, led Reagan to view himself as a savior, although, as he writes in his memoirs, few recognize they need to be saved. "I would have been fine if you'd left me alone," maintained most swimmers whom Reagan saved. Even during his movie career, with one exception, he played the good guy. The one exception, *The Killers* (1964), in which he slaps Angie Dickenson, bombed at the box office, suggesting that even years before his presidency, many Americans preferred Reagan as the good guy. This theme of Reagan as savior shaped him into the popular cold warrior he became when he attempted to save America from communism.

Secularists may scoff at Reagan's notions about salvation, but salvation has been so fundamental to the Western intellectual and cultural heritage that modern Western ideologies remain steeped in the concept. Environmentalists, for example, seek to save the earth from the effects of sinful human activity. Animal rights activists view mankind as innately sinful, living with no regard to animals, whom they seek to save. These ideologies, too, seek to perfect a world writhing in sin. Environmentalists and animal rights activists seek a purity that is religious in nature. It involves abstinence (e.g., vegetarianism or minimizing one's carbon footprint) in the name of salvation. This is not a coincidence. Salvation is a central part of the Western heritage, one that secularism hasn't expunged.

Reagan was a mama's boy, and he learned about salvation from her. Something he learned from his father was a tolerance for different ethnicities and races. Jack Reagan, born in 1883, was a second-generation Irish American whose parents arrived in the United States, like so many other Irish immigrants, around the time of the Civil War. Changing the family surname from O'Reagan to Reagan helped with assimilation. However, this didn't limit the discrimination that they, along with several million other Irish immigrants, faced in the late nineteenth and early twentieth centuries. Because of this personal experience, Jack Reagan hated discrimination. He refused to let his children see *Birth of a Nation* for the way it portrayed the Ku Klux Klan. One night the Reagans stopped at a motel that did not allow Jewish guests. Instead of patronizing the business, the Reagan family slept in the car. Likewise, at the peak of his acting career, Ronald Reagan ended his membership with a popular country club in the Los Angeles area because they denied Jewish members. Reagan was particularly sensitive to America's immigrant and ethnic history because his family epitomized it.

After graduating from high school, Reagan did something fewer than 10 percent of high school graduates did in the 1920s: he went to college. He was the first one in his family to do so. His parents never even finished high school. In 1928 the future president started at Eureka College, a private Christian school with roughly 250 students. Reagan later said these were the best times of his life. He played football, was on the swim team, joined a fraternity, was on the student senate, worked myriad jobs to make ends meet, and achieved average grades as an economics major. Like many college students, Reagan's intellectual curiosity peaked later in life. The most telling event of Reagan's college career had nothing to do with academics; it occurred his freshman year when he was chosen as a spokesman for his class regarding a dispute between administration and faculty. Reagan's peers trusted that he could advance their cause. It was a harbinger of things to come.

The primary goal of Eureka College was to promote and instill biblical values. The Bible was the word of God for everyone at Eureka, and it was required reading for all students. Reagan believed that the Bible held the answers to all of the world's problems. Though sometimes nameless, the authors of the Bible were great thinkers. Even those who disagree with the Bible's tenets—those who deny its validity—have been influenced by its ideas. It remains fundamental to Western culture and civilization. The Bible's most popular book, the Book of Revelation, contributed to Reagan's cosmology, as well as that of many secular thinkers, by describing life as a great struggle between good and evil. It promises victory for the righteous, but only after titanic conflict. The book was composed around the time of the reign of the Roman emperor Nero, when Christianity was in its infancy and struggling against the Roman yoke, so the Book of Revelation gave Christians reason for hope, even in a time of deepest despair. Revelation promises the defeat of evil, followed by the utopian Reign of Saints, but only after a titanic conflict known as Armageddon. This religious paradigm can easily be applied to the cold war, as well as contemporary American struggles against Islamic extremists. For the secular, the Book of Revelation is fiction, but for many evangelicals, like Reagan, it explains both the present and the future.

This helps to explain Reagan's optimism, one of his most enduring traits. After all, according to the Word of God, the righteous will be rewarded. "All in all, as I look back I realize that my reading left an abiding belief in the triumph of good over evil," said Reagan.[13] This became psychologically satisfying during times of despair, such as the Great Depression, which hit just as Reagan graduated college. Whereas the 1930s were trying times for many Americans, Reagan succeeded, finding work as a sports broadcaster in Iowa at one of the most powerful radio stations in the Midwest, who. This testifies to his rhetorical skills, since when he earned this job, the national unemployment rate was over 20 percent. All jobs were in demand. The *Time* magazine correspondent Hugh Sidey, who listened to Reagan as a young boy, recounts that during the Depression, Reagan "managed to give us the feeling that things wouldn't always be that way, that they would get better."[14] Reagan conveyed his optimism to his listeners.

Reagan succeeded during the Great Depression because he was not deterred. Life is never easy, but the Bible maintains that the good will prosper. A Christian can believe in the imminence of a better age, even in times of crisis. Some interpret Christianity pessimistically for its belief in the sinful nature of man, but one can also use the Bible as a lens through which to optimistically view the future, extolling the age when heaven and earth are reconciled and when the righteous will join the Lord. One view is pessimistic, the other optimistic. These two types of Christians are sometimes contrasted as "Good Friday" and "Easter Sunday" Christians.

Good Friday Christians are generally pessimistic, focusing on man's sinful nature and emphasizing Christ's suffering and persecution. Easter Sunday Christians celebrate the resurrection of Christ and look forward to the Second Coming, when the righteous live. Reagan epitomized Easter Sunday Christians. President Jimmy Carter, his opponent in the 1980 presidential election, was a Good Friday Christian. Carter was, in many respects, a better Christian than Reagan; he attended church more regularly, knew the Bible better, was open about his born-again experience, and even participated in overseas missions. Yet Reagan received more votes from southern evangelicals. How can this be? This can be attributed to Reagan's optimism. Carter's most famous speeches chastised the American people, describing their innately sinful nature, as exemplified by excessive oil consumption. His outlook for America was gloomy. Reagan, on the other hand, promised that something better awaited us. Which message would you vote for? The majority of Americans went with the positive.

Broadcasting not only allowed Reagan to express his optimism, it allowed him to use his greatest intellectual gift: his imagination. Sports broadcasting requires imagination because the broadcaster tells stories, trying to create something as real as possible for the listener. Reagan's first audition in Iowa required him to broadcast a live imaginary football game, complete with the sights, the sounds, the players, and the action. Reagan had to create an entire football game, play by play, in his mind. That audition earned him his first job in broadcasting. Reagan eventually graduated to Major League Baseball, broadcasting Chicago Cubs games from Des Moines, Iowa. Sometimes the radio station lacked the funds to send him to Wrigley Field, so he verbalized accounts of the game, relying on telegraphic reports that came to the radio station. If a Cubs player hit a home run, Reagan described it in vivid detail, despite lacking visuals. Once, the telegraph wire went down, forcing Reagan to improvise. He recalls, "I knew of only one thing that wouldn't get in the score column and betray me, a foul ball. So I had Augie [the batter] foul this pitch down the left field line. I looked expectantly at Curly [the producer]. He just shrugged helplessly, so I had Augie foul off another one, and still another; then he fouled one back into the box seats. I described in detail the redheaded kid who had scrambled and gotten the souvenir ball."[15] Foul ball after foul ball after foul ball. This went on for nearly seven minutes. One of his regular listeners was a teenager who became a Hall-of-Famer, Bob Feller. Feller contends that Reagan creatively tapped the mike with a pencil to signify a hit. A *Sporting News* poll ranked him as the fourth-most popular baseball announcer outside of a major league area.[16]

Reagan parlayed his radio success into a highly successful career in Hollywood. His first trip to California came during the Cubs' spring training in 1937.[17] By this point Reagan was already a minor celebrity. He met with a talent agent in California who arranged a screen test with Warner Brothers. Shortly thereafter, in the midst of the Great Depression, the twenty-six-year-old Reagan signed a contract for $200 a week. Goodbye Midwest, hello California. He was typecast in many of his earliest acting gigs as a radio announcer. And he continued to use his imagination since actors must create environments for themselves. They must leave everyday life and enter one created by their imagination. By the late 1930s, Reagan had moved to Los Angeles with his parents and become an active member of the Hollywood Beverly Church.

Success again followed Reagan: by the end of the decade he had appeared in nineteen films. He had a reputation as a responsible, serious actor who usually got along with his fellow performers. In 1942 he starred in quite possibly his best film, *Kings Row*. His most memorable line comes when, after noticing his legs are gone, he shrieks in disbelief, "Where's the rest of me?!" This line would be the title of his first autobiography. Shortly after the movie was released, he departed for military service, but he never saw any combat due to his poor vision.[18] Upon returning home, he became more active in Hollywood politics, even rising to the position of president of the Screen Actors Guild (1947–1951, 1959). Political issues seemed to have been Reagan's passion, even at the peak of his Hollywood popularity. Jane Wyman, Reagan's first wife, recalls that Reagan was always more passionate when discussing political and current affairs than when talking about his current script.[19]

From the late 1930s through the mid-1940s Nazism, not communism, was America's worst enemy. America and the Soviet Union cooperated in the fight against the Nazi threat during World War II, so, at least temporarily, the Soviets were our brothers in arms. The United States even funded its future adversary. (A similar event occurred four decades later, when the United States funded Iraq in its war against Iran. In each instance, the country America funded seemed to be the lesser of two evils.) Anticommunist sentiment in America waned at this time. For his part, Reagan spoke far more critically of fascism than of communism during this era, because fascism seemed like a greater threat to the world. This era of good feeling was fleeting, however, and so was Reagan's naïveté about communism. The overt origins of the cold war lie sometime between 1945 and Stalin's blockading of Berlin in 1948. In between, Stalin consolidated his control of Eastern Europe, reneged on his promise to President Franklin D. Roosevelt of democratic elections, and kidnapped and sent to labor camps almost anyone who seemed to disagree with him. So within a span of three years the Soviet Union transformed from our brothers in arms against the Nazis to our new world enemy. This new enemy, like the old one, was inherently expansionist, because the paranoid Stalin equated territory with security; the more of Europe he controlled, the safer he felt. For its part, the United States helped economically to rebuild Western Europe and joined the North Atlantic Treaty Organization (NATO), the first peacetime alliance the country had ever joined, and stationed troops in West Berlin and West Germany. If Western Europe was to remain free and democratic, it would need America to act as a buffer. Reagan learned this lesson in the late 1940s, and he never forgot it.

It was during this time that Reagan first encountered communists in Hollywood. Reagan was part of a host of Hollywood organizations, such as the Americans Veterans Committee, the Screen Actors Guild (SAG), and the Hollywood Independent Citizens of Arts, Sciences, and Professions. Communists infiltrated these organizations and managed to make their influence far stronger than their numbers suggested. Reagan resisted communism, not just for political and religious reasons but for its disingenuous tactics. Communists routinely claimed to be representing the majority even when they were clearly a minority, a method that did not begin in 1940s Hollywood. Consequently when Reagan became SAG president in 1947 (he was nominated by Gene Kelly) and refused to participate in some communist-supported strikes, he became one of their biggest enemies. In the late 1940s no issue was more important to Reagan than limiting communist influence in Hollywood. He supported a resolution that denied any self-identifying communist the position of officer in SAG, for example.

Like Reagan, communists sought to promote freedom, but the two sides' ways of achieving freedom differed. For one side, freedom could exist only in relation to God; for the other, freedom was achieved by eliminating religion. In the West, freedom and Christianity have developed a complex relationship. Enlightenment philosophers, some of the architects of the modern secular Western mind, viewed religion and freedom as antagonistic. Eighteenth-century thinkers like Voltaire, David Hume, and Condorcet saw organized religion as a threat to freedom, stifling critical inquiry and limiting personal freedom. Hume, for example, writes, "As to ecclesiastical parties; we may observe that in all the ages of the world, priests have been the enemies of liberty."[20] The atheist Holbach wrote, "True toleration and freedom of thought are the most proper instruments for the destruction of religious fanaticism."[21] Holbach reasoned that Christianity denied people their freedom by enslaving them to the clergy. People couldn't live freely, he believed, in a religious society where morality came from an elite who claimed justification from an immaterial God. For modern secularists who embrace these Enlightenment sentiments, religion and freedom clash: where religion flourishes, freedom suffers, and the more religious a society, the more starved for liberty that society becomes.

Marx augmented these arguments by contending that capitalists (the ruling class) promoted the falsehood of religion in order to maintain control of the masses and dupe them into ignoring the harsh realities of their lives. Those living in capitalist countries, he proclaimed, were deceived by the bourgeoisie, the false prophets of freedom. Subsequently communists in the Soviet Union confiscated church land; desecrated church property and relics; rigidly secularized education; banned religious weddings, funerals, and baptisms; and executed many religious leaders. At roughly the same time a young Reagan was first learning Christian principles, Soviet children (including Ayn Rand) were encouraged to turn in anyone, even adults, who preached about God. The Soviet Union practiced what some secularists still preach: that eradicating religion improves humanity. According to this belief, progress correlates with secularism. The aim of the Soviet government was to ensure that the material needs of its people were met in preparation for the glorious age of communism, a classless final stage of history, devoid of religion, when man would return to his pristine state. They too tried to bring their own version of heaven to earth, where freedom would reign supreme.

Christians like Reagan view things differently. In the Gospels, freedom is achieved when one finds God, as in Luke 4:18: "The Spirit of the Lord is upon me, for he has anointed me to bring Good News to the poor. He has sent me to proclaim that captives will be released, that the blind will see, that the oppressed will be set free." When Paul employs this concept in Scripture, he usually juxtaposes it against or compares it with Jewish law, which early Christians like Paul believed enslaved Jews, as opposed to Christ, who sets us free. Paul declares in Galatians 5:1, "So Christ has truly set us free. Now make sure that you stay free, and don't get tied up again in slavery to the Law." Christianity is a liberating philosophy because Christ frees us from our sinful state and past religious traditions. According to this philosophy, freedom is achieved when humankind is liberated from the extensive laws detailed in the Mosaic Code (Torah) and is fulfilled through Christ. In other words, Leviticus tells us what we cannot do, but Christ frees us from these restraints. Christ frees us because through Him we find God and the good life. Christ frees us from our sins.

For Reagan, freedom couldn't be separated from God because it was a gift from God, so any nation that lacked knowledge of God also lacked freedom. This is based on 2 Corinthians 3:17: "Now the Lord is that Spirit; and where the spirit of the Lord is, there is Liberty." Reagan asserted, "All men and women yearn for the freedom that God gave us when he gave us free will."[22] Furthermore, he said, "God meant America to be free because God intended each man to have dignity and freedom."[23] For Reagan it all boiled down to the fact that "where the spirit of the Lord is, there is freedom."[24] The French president François Mitterrand claimed, "[Reagan] has two religions: free enterprise and God."[25] In no way did Reagan replace the Christian emphasis on the spiritual with the American emphasis on freedom; he merely combined the two ideas. For Reagan, the two concepts were actually just one, because he believed that God and freedom are inexorably bound.

This is an important part of the American cultural tradition. Believing the relationship between freedom and religion is a zero-sum game ignores the fact that a puritanical zeal coupled with a love of liberty produced the young American republic. America's Founding Fathers loved liberty, but they were not completely secular. They were indebted to America's religious heritage. Two months before signing the Declaration of Independence, the minister and founding father John Witherspoon preached,

> A good form of government may hold the rotten materials together for some time, but beyond a certain pitch even the best constitution will be ineffectual, and slavery must ensue. On the other hand, when the manners of a nation are pure, when true religion and internal principles maintain their vigour, the attempts of the most powerful enemies to oppress them are commonly baffled and disappointed. . . . He [God] is the best friend to American liberty, who is most sincere and active in promoting true and undefiled religion, and who sets himself with the greatest firmness to bear down prophanity and immorality of every kind.[26]

Alexis de Tocqueville remarked, "In France I had always seen the spirit of religion and the spirit of freedom marching in opposite directions. But in America I found they were intimately united and that they reigned in common over the same country."[27] Democracy in America is different from democracy in Europe. The uniqueness of American civilization—what separates it from its European heritage—is the enduring link between freedom and religion. Christianity was the backbone of European civilization for one thousand years and was brought to America by its first overseas immigrants, who sought religious liberty. This began the time-honored connection between American religion and American freedom. America has no history of religious wars and oppression, so to Americans there seems to be no conflict between religion and freedom.

Reagan's ideas conformed to the American heritage. He spoke the American cultural language most fluently. America has always been the most religious nation in the West (defined as Europe and the United States) and the primary defender of freedom. During the 1920s and 1930s, when European nations were experimenting with more secular and totalitarian systems like communism, socialism, fascism, and Nazism, America stubbornly maintained its liberal-democratic political system. Even today socialist, communist, and proto-fascist ideas gain more traction in Europe than in the United States. But for Reagan, as for most Americans, these political systems were exercises in futility because they meant more government control, at the expense of liberty.

Reagan believed America was the defender of good, "the shining city on the hill" that must lead the fight for freedom against atheist darkness. American cultural historians may cite John Winthrop's sermon "A Model Christian City" as the progenitor of this idea, but the notion really goes back to Scripture. The prophet Isaiah, writing as Jerusalem was on the verge of destruction by the Babylonians, predicted that a resurgent Jewish Kingdom would rise from the ashes, becoming a beacon of light for all nations of the world. A New Age would dawn. Christ's Sermon on the Mount preaches, "You are the light of the world. A city set on a mountain cannot be hidden. Nor do they light a lamp and then put it under a bushel basket; it is set on the lampstand, where it gives light to all in the house. Just so your light must shine before others, that they may see your good deeds and glorify your heavenly father."

Reagan saw America as this light, a light that leads all other lights in the cold war. As the leading defender of freedom in the world, America bore a moral responsibility to confront and eliminate the forces of evil. Reagan insisted in 1952, "I, in my own mind, have thought of America as a place in the divine scheme of things that was set aside as the promised land. . . . I believe that God in shedding his grace on this country has always in this divine scheme of things kept an eye on our land and guided it as a promised land."[28] It was America's anointed destiny to lead a crusade against the evil empire. These ideas help us understand Reagan's seemingly aggressive cold war policies, even in light of the Vietnam debacle. He saw the cold war as a holy war, and he knew that God was on our side. With His help, Reagan believed, we could not lose.

This belief that America has a divinely appointed mission predates Reagan and exemplifies the cultural tradition that Reagan epitomized. President Woodrow Wilson proclaimed, "The stage is set, the destiny is closed. It has come about by no plan of our conceiving, but by the hand of God that led us this way. We can only go forward, with lifted eyes and freshened spirit, to follow the vision. It was this that we dreamed of at our birth. America shall in truth show the way."[29] Reagan quoted from FDR's fourth inaugural address when he declared, "The Almighty God has blessed our land in many ways, so we pray to Him now for the vision to see our way clearly."[30] And John F. Kennedy stated, "We are by destiny, rather than choice, the watchmen on the walls of world freedom."[31] It is thus not those who assert American providence that run counter to the nation's cultural tradition but rather those who deny it.

America's historic moral position is to defend liberty around the world because America was "born modern," meaning that unlike older nations such as France and England, America has only one tradition, and that is a tradition of liberty, individual rights, and equality. Furthermore freedom is not just a tradition in America but its raison d'être. Less burdened by her past, America can look forward.

And it wasn't just Reagan's conservative ideology that emerged from the broader Western religious landscape. Political ideologies can never be separated from religion, even among people who fashion themselves as secular. Modern political ideologies evolved out of religions during the eighteenth and nineteenth centuries. That's when new values, like freedom, justice, environmentalism, equality, education, health care, and human rights, emerged. These values and cosmologies attempt to replace Christianity as a way to interpret reality, and they prescribe how to live the good life. Nonbelievers get judged, damned, and even hated. Although these movements may seem void of religious concepts, they also are fundamentally ethical movements with their own conceptions of good and bad, saints and sinners, and sacred beliefs, which seem like truths to devout believers. They too seek to gain adherents through conversion. Each explains worldly misery and promises a better world if the proper values are adopted. Punishment and despair await those who resist.

Cultural anthropologists insist that certain patterns of thinking cannot be eliminated from society because the human mind needs some sort of structure to help it understand the world. Even radical ideologies like Nazism and Marxism are frameworks through which to understand the world, and they each provide solutions to problems that beset society. In fact, most ideologies, including Christianity, Islam, and Judaism, insist that although the world is sinful now, hope exists—as long as we act properly. But if we lose faith, we are doomed. In sum, in the West ideology cannot be separated from religion because religion provides the foundation for Western civilization and culture. Even when a snake sheds its skin, it still maintains the same vital organs. Our world may look very different now than it did during the Middle Ages, but closer inspection reveals that our minds are not all that different from those of our medieval ancestors. There are never any complete breaks in history, just evolutions. Some Christians may see themselves as distinct from the Greco-Roman era from which their faith emerged, yet deeper analysis of Christianity finds evidence of ancient Greece and Rome, as seen in the Catholic Church's patriarchal and hierarchal nature. Just as Christian thought could never escape its Greco-Roman past, neither can modern culture, despite some secularization, escape its Christian past. It is therefore not a coincidence that the Age of Ideology eclipsed the Age of Faith; ide-ologies become new faiths, only cloaked in new nomenclature. In the United States today the ideals of our civil religion include lib-erty, equality, democracy, and freedom of speech. Christianity may have waned among some intellectuals as Western culture focused less on the next life, yet sacred values persist. Reagan's freedom-centered philosophy, must be placed in this context.

2
...

From Liberal to Conservative

We can lose our freedom all at once by succumbing to Russian aggression, or we can lose it gradually by installments. The end result is slavery.

—REAGAN, "Losing Freedom by Installments"

Reagan returned to civilian life after World War II, critically examined the society to which he returned, and was not happy: "Like most soldiers who came back, I expected a world suddenly reformed. I hoped and believed that the blood and death and confusion of World War II would result in a regeneration of mankind, that the whole struggle was simply the immolation of the phoenix of human liberties and that the bird of happiness would rise out of the ashes and fly everywhere at once."[1] The post–World War II era was still sin-ridden. Sacrifice, death, violence, and destruction didn't improve humankind, as it was supposed to. This frustration is what led Reagan to enter politics. He maintains in his 1965 autobiography, "I would work with the tools I had: My thoughts, my speaking abilities, my reputation as an actor. I would bring about the regeneration of the world I believed should have automatically appeared."[2] Reagan says he joined a host of political organizations in the wake of World War II, as he was "hell-bent on saving the world from Neo-Fascism."[3]

Part of Reagan's frustration may have stemmed from the realization that his best acting days had passed, even though he was only in his forties. The war curbed Reagan's momentum toward acting immortality, which up to that point had been a realistic ambition. In a 1941 "Stars of Tomorrow" poll, he finished second to Early Flynn and ahead of James Cagney as one of Warner Brothers' most likely future stars.[4] By any standards, Reagan was an acting success. Some of his detractors denigrate his career by calling him a "B actor," but this is misleading. He played roles in B movies, but he also starred in major films, like *Knute Rockne, All American*. He routinely worked with A-listers such as Eddie Albert, Humphrey Bogart, Pat O'Brien, and Shirley Temple. He signed a million-dollar contract in late Depression-era dollars; his acting skills made him a wealthy man. He earned a star on the Hollywood Walk of Fame in 1960, before any of his political success. During his lifetime he was a celebrity, but the type of celebrity that is forgotten. New men, future immortals like Marlon Brando, Charlton Heston, and Rock Hudson, moved in and ascended to the heights to which Reagan aspired. Reagan's career resembled that of a professional baseball player who played in the major leagues for ten years, even made a couple of All-Star games, yet was not quite a Hall-of-Famer.

Reagan's time in Hollywood wasn't over, however. He still had an important role to play, just not on the big screen. His election as SAG president meant that now he could butt heads with the studio execs, like Jack Warner, who had denied him the A-list stardom he felt he deserved. As president of SAG, Reagan negotiated on behalf of actors during labor disputes. During his time in this role, he gained some critical concessions for actors, including residuals for film actors when their movies appeared on television. Big-screen movies had begun to be shown on the small screen, and film actors felt they were being deprived of compensation. When actors demanded residual payment and producers declined, Reagan led a Hollywood strike. This was the first major strike in showbiz history, and it worked: studios agreed to pay actors deserved residuals. Furthermore these events honed negotiating skills that served him well as president. (Reagan once declared that it was easier working with Gorbachev than with Jack Warner.) This would not be Reagan's last time at the center of a strike.

By the late 1940s the future president was so politically engaged it contributed to the breakdown of his first marriage, with Jane Wyman. (The fact the couple lost a child roughly one year earlier must have played a strong role too.) During the divorce proceedings, she complained to the presiding judge, "In recent months my husband and I engaged in continual arguments on his political views. . . . Despite my lack of interest in his political activities, he insisted I attend meetings with him and be present during discussions among our friends."[5] Reagan routinely had parties at his home in the Hollywood Hills where political ideas bounced around the room.

Reagan's initial leanings were liberal. He blamed Republicans for the Great Depression, voted for Franklin Delano Roosevelt all four times, and supported the New Deal. He considered FDR a demigod who saved America, both from fascists abroad and Republicans at home. His attitude toward FDR mirrored the attitude many conservatives have toward Reagan today. FDR's death in 1945 did nothing to change Reagan's political passions. He campaigned for Harry Truman and Hubert Humphrey in 1948. In one campaign address, Reagan states:

> I remember listening to the radio on election night [in 1946].
> Joseph Martin, the Republican Speaker of the House, said very solemnly and I quote, "We Republicans intend to work for a real increase in income for everybody by encouraging more production and lower prices without impairing wages or working conditions," unquote. Remember that promise: a real increase in income for everybody. But what actually happened? The profits of corporations have doubled, while workers wages have increased by only one-quarter. In other words, profits have gone up four times as much as wages, and the small increase workers did receive was more than eaten up by rising prices, which have also bored into their savings.[6]

Two years later, he campaigned for Helen Gahagan Douglas in her high-profile Senate race against Richard Nixon. Los Angeles Democratic leaders even deemed Reagan too liberal to run for

Congress. Lou Cannon suggests that Reagan was not as liberal as he portrayed himself in his memoirs, and this may be true, but he was certainly a staunch Democrat. Truman lambasted communists, despised Stalin, and provided material assistance to those threatened by communists, so one could plausibly loathe socialist variants and still support the Democratic Party. Truman even signed an executive order that allowed the FBI to determine if any federal government employee had communist ties. The divide between Republicans and Democrats on the issue of communism was narrow, at least during the late 1940s. This would change soon. And so would Reagan.

Between 1948 and 1952 cracks appeared in Reagan's political philosophy and in America that still reverberate today. Like many Americans, Reagan always opposed Nazism and fascism, but he claims naïveté to the true nature of communism until the late 1940s, when he realized that communism posed the same threat that Nazism did, because both encroached on freedom. In one of his first political overtures in 1947, after being described by the interviewer as a liberal who cared about freedom, the thirty-six-year-old Reagan stated, "[America's] highest aim should be the cultivation of freedom of the individual, for therein lies the highest dignity of man. Tyranny is tyranny, and whether it comes from right, left or center, it's evil. I believe the only way to save our country from all of the extremists is to remove conditions that supply for the totalitarian fire."[7] When Reagan said these words, one could describe him as liberal, proclaiming freedom as his highest value. But a new movement, a left-wing movement, was fomenting in United States, and it seemed to threaten freedom, at least economically. By 1948 communism seemed aggressive, and Reagan, for the first time, viewed it as the new enemy: he began associating Nazism with communism, deeming both evil movements that denied freedom to humankind. Reagan began to pivot, shifting from one end of the political spectrum to the other, in the name of freedom.

As the 1947 interview continued, however, Reagan said that he was not in favor of banning the Communist Party, reasoning that if the American people knew all of the facts, they would never support communism anyway. He insisted before Congress, "As a citizen I would hesitate to see any political party outlawed."[8] Reagan had faith in the American electorate.[9] A real populist, he wasn't cynical about the American people or the democratic process, unlike socialists and communists in the 1940s. Despite legitimate fears about communism, he never believed democracy should be usurped to stop it. Reagan questioned the American government, but not the American people.

The communist threat after the war seemed even greater than the Nazi threat, because the Nazis didn't have the technological capacity to detonate an atomic bomb, which the Soviets did, partly thanks to communist spies working in the United States, like Klaus Fuchs, who in 1950 admitted that he was a Soviet spy. Neither did the Nazis have groups within the United States (the fifth column) working to promote revolution. The situation grew dire in October 1949, when the People's Republic of China was proclaimed, even as Americans offered material assistance to its enemies. Now the world's two largest countries were communist. Marxist predictions about the inevitable victory of the proletariat seemed real. The paranoia that gripped the nation during the 1950s was not irrational. The deadliest war in human history had just ended, yet another one seemed imminent. And this one could be nuclear.

As Reagan's son Michael recounts, "The year 1949 was a terrible year for Dad. He had already lost his wife and his children. That year he also broke his leg in an amateur baseball game. . . . He had stopped making movies for a time and was going through the worst dry spell of his career. He carried a gun because of threats against his life."[10] In academic lingo, 1949 was Reagan's *annus horribilis*. He lost a newborn baby (Christine) a day after her birth in 1947, and his wife filed for divorce in 1948.[11] This devastated Reagan, and he was grieving. One way people cope with pain is with anger. And politics provides a way to release that anger because it's socially acceptable to hate political figures and ideas. It's easier to release anger against political figures and ideas than friends, family, neighbors, or coworkers, although they may become targets too. Communism and those who didn't share his political opinions were about to bear the brunt of Reagan's frustrations. Like millions of Americans today, Reagan cast his personal frustrations, fears, and desires onto political figures and political ideas. A new American leader was born.

Reagan's extreme anticommunism accordingly emerged in the late 1940s. Next, he needed intellectual sources to provide him with ammunition to confront the perceived enemy. Today liberals and conservatives learn from people who have similar views. Sources of this information include Fox News, MSNBC, *Huffington Post*, Rush Limbaugh, Michael Moore, and many social media sites. Each of these sources provides fuel for the ideological war. Reagan didn't have Fox or Limbaugh, of course, but there were plenty of conservatives he could draw upon as he developed his new conservative views. Some were even former communists. One example is Arthur Koestler, author of *Darkness at Noon*. Koestler's work allegorically describes Stalin's purges in the 1930s, tacitly showing similarities between the Soviet and Nazi totalitarian regimes. Koestler's story also appears in *The God That Failed* (1949), another book Reagan read. It contained a collection of stories from six writers and thinkers who left communism, each for his own reasons. "The only link, indeed, between these six very different personalities," the work states, "is that all of them—after tortured struggles of conscience— chose Communism because they had lost faith in democracy and were willing to sacrifice 'bourgeois liberties' in order to defeat Fascism. Their conversion, in fact, was rooted in despair—a despair of Western values."[12] This shows how the rise of communism and fascism were, at least to some degree, consequences of declining faith in Judeo-Christian values. More so than people in other Western nations, Americans like Reagan held onto their past.

Maybe the most important intellectual influence from this time was Whittaker Chambers, another former Communist Party member who busted the communist chains in the late 1930s because they suffocated religion. Chambers's 1952 work, *Witness*, is a story of a young communist and his disillusionment with the movement.

It remains high on conservative must-read lists. In his explanation of his own rejection of communism, Reagan cites Chambers's conversion to Christianity and break with communism: "Chambers marked the beginning of his personal journey away from communism on the day that he was suddenly struck by the sight of his infant daughter's ear as she ate breakfast. He realized, he said, that such intricacy and precision could be no accident, no freak of nature. He said that while he didn't know it at the time, in that moment, God—the finger of God—had touched his forehead."[13] This "intelligent design" argument has been propounded by Christians for centuries. The argument runs that random chance could never explain something as magnificent as the ear or eye, as evolutionists suggest, and therefore they must have been created by an intelligent and providential Creator, or God. Interpreting atheist communism and Christianity as two antagonistic faiths struggling against each other for supremacy, Chambers, a melancholy and pessimistic figure, believed that communism was the wave of the immediate future but decided he would rather lose with the righteous than side with evil.

Whereas Chambers was pessimistic, James Burnham was optimistic about American cold war prospects. Like many young intellectuals in the 1920s, Burnham, who was born in 1905, was seduced by the Marxism-Leninism that waxed after the Bolshevik Revolution in 1917. The Great Depression of the late 1920s and 1930s did nothing to dissuade him and thousands of other Marxist intellectuals. However, the Stalin era divided Marxists into those who supported Stalin, and those, repulsed by his brutality, who mostly gathered around Leon Trotsky. Burnham was in the latter camp, even coediting the Trotskyite journal, *New International*. He now mingled with all leading Marxists.

Burnham changed his political allegiance during World War II, when he took the heretical stance of renouncing dialectical materialism.[14] Partly prompted by the Hitler-Stalin pact in 1939, Burnham began viewing communism and Nazism in a similar light. In *The Struggle of the World* (1947) he defines communism as "a worldwide, conspiratorial movement for the conquest of a monopoly of power in the era of capitalist decline. Politically, it is based on terror and mass deception; economically it is, or at least tends to be, collectivist; socially it is totalitarian."[15] He continues by arguing that communism and fascism are different only as two boxers competing for the heavyweight championship are different; they look different on the surface, but they both share the same means and ends. Burnham demanded a hardline policy against the Soviet Union that would undermine the First Socialist Society. He rejected containment for moral reasons, for how could the United States be passive when so many inside the contained region perished?[16] Would containment have thwarted Nazism? His *The Coming Defeat of Communism* (1950) is a sort of "What Is to Be Done?" for anti-Marxists. Burnham lambasted containment for being defensive. He asserted, "Containment, however, cannot be the end objective of a policy. More generally, a defensive policy—and containment is a variant of the defensive—can never win."[17] The United States must seek liberation, by force if necessary.

There have always been noninterventionist conservatives (Donald Trump successfully earned the votes from this crowd in 2016), and Burnham tried convincing them that America must take an active role against communism abroad. All conservatives opposed the spread of any sort of socialism or communism at home, but that didn't mean that the United States should lead the crusade fighting communism abroad. Burnham insisted that the fate of humanity was at stake. He can be classified as an early neoconservative, among those who seek to spread democracy. The final chapter of his work is "The Inevitability of Communist Defeat." Insisting that there are enough determined men in the world with the resolve to fight communism, Burnham believed the victory of democracy was inevitable. Reagan cited Burnham as an influence and awarded him the Presidential Medal of Freedom.

Another critical work published in 1953 was Russell Kirk's *The Conservative Mind*. Kirk can best be described as a traditional conservative, in the mold of Edmund Burke, whom Kirk discusses in the second chapter of his work. Like Burke, Kirk believed in the rule of law and real permanent morality, not the type that changes every few generations as new intellectuals emerge, each seeking to establish an independent identity. Like Burke, Kirk distrusted those who tried to construct the ideal society based on human intellectual principles. Burke's target was French philosophes who sought an ideal society based on reason. Kirk refuted Marx, who insisted a perfect communist could and would emerge from the ashes of capitalism. Accepting the Christian idea about the inherently flawed nature of man, Kirk believed that humanity can never be perfected, at least not by human minds in this world. Therefore external restraints like government are needed, sometimes strong external restraints. Like Burke, Kirk argued that change should not always be passively accepted as inevitable. Vestiges of the past should be preserved because they contain wisdom. (For Marxists, the communist stage in history discards all elements of the backward bourgeoisie-capitalist era in history.) Kirk writes, "Conservatives respect the wisdom of their ancestors. . . . They are dubious of wholesale alteration."[18] That is not the same as saying that most change is bad. Burke and Kirk accepted change, but cautiously.

From the twenty-first-century conservative perspective, the third chapter of Kirk's work is the most interesting. It is titled "John Adams and Liberty under the Law." Kirk calls Adams the father of American conservatism. Kirk conventionally places Alexander Hamilton alongside Adams. Their opponent was Thomas Jefferson. Kirk favored the strong central government that curbed short-term populist impulses. He distrusted the masses. Freedom was good, but it was worthless outside the context of Christianity because "political problems, at bottom, are religious and moral problems."[19] Politics, religion, and morality can never be separated. He even critiqued modern-day capitalism, insisting that if it's taken too far, without any restraints, it weakens traditional bonds between man and man. Kirk supported capitalism, but not the extreme laissez-faire that he associated with the early days of the Industrial Revolution. His brand of capitalism opposed the libertarian model that many conservatives espouse today.[20]

Political events in the United States, specifically trials, further created a New Conservatism. Chambers was a key figure in the Alger Hiss case, an important event in forging the modern American left and right. Chambers showed the House Un-American Activities Committee that Hiss was a communist spy. Hiss swore under oath that he had never been a communist or Soviet spy, but when Chambers produced evidence he kept hidden in a pumpkin (where else would one hide sensitive documents?) Hiss was exposed and found guilty of perjury in 1950. The Hiss trial not only brought Richard Nixon to national prominence, but it fundamentally altered American public opinion. Whereas most conservatives sided with Chambers, in this case many leftists sympathized with the alleged communist. A second notorious accusation of espionage that altered the American political landscape, and therefore Reagan as well, was that levied against Julius and Ethel Rosenberg. They were accused of giving atomic secrets to the Soviets. The Rosenbergs were found guilty of espionage and ultimately sentenced to death. Their trial in 1951 further divided the American public, with the left mostly supportive of the Rosenbergs, whereas conservatives presumed guilt. A new political landscape burgeoned in response to communism.

These events and writers like Kirk, Chambers, and Burnham helped launch a new American conservatism that emerged in the wake of World War II and helped create Ronald Reagan. These voices and many others were amplified by the new periodical, *National Review*, started by William F. Buckley in 1955. Reagan was an early subscriber and read it regularly for three decades. *National Review* and *Reader's Digest* were his favorite magazines. At *National Review*'s thirtieth-anniversary dinner Reagan said, "The man standing before you was a Democrat when he picked up his first issue in a plain brown wrapper; and even now, as an occupant of public housing, he awaits as anxiously as ever for his biweekly edition."[21] *National Review* urged political activism against liberalism and war against communism. It contained articles by virtually all of the twentieth century's leading conservative voices, including the ones analyzed in this work and even Reagan himself. Burnham and Kirk were editors. Reagan would have read articles by

Burnham. For example, in his contribution to the July 18, 1956, edition, Burnham wrote:

> And as they rolled over Polish bodies the Communist tanks flattened also the soft rhetoric of our George Kennans and Stewart Alsops, our experts and smug journalists, who have been telling us how the Soviet regime has come to be accepted by its subjects, how (in Kennan's servile words) "there is a finality, for better or worse, about what has occurred in Eastern Europe." The people of Poznan, clasping hands as they faced the tanks demanding food and decent working conditions and an end to Moscow's rule, and the soldiers who joined them instead of firing on them: these in one day communicated more of the truth about the Soviet Empire than a decade's dispatches by correspondents and diplomats.[22]

Arguing for big-tent conservatism, the magazine published voices from across the conservative political spectrum. Paleoconservatives, neoconservatives, Zionists, isolationists, Christians, libertarians, Jeffersonians, and Madisonians have all used the *National Review* as a sounding board.

One attempt to unify these disparate voices came from Frank Meyer, another regular contributor to *National Review*. Meyer can best be described as a libertarian. He believed government should exist only to protect freedom. Rejecting the traditional conservatism of Kirk and its emphasis on tradition and order, Meyer argued for individualism. This should not be confused with the objectivism of Ayn Rand, however. Meyer believed that the individual was the highest good, but not the only good. The individual exists within what Meyer called an "organic moral order" that taught virtue and required nourishment. Rand disagreed, insisting that man exists only for man. Meyer retorted that God and objective morality exist. His philosophy sought to reconcile Kirk's traditional conservatism with the new, more freedom-centered conservatism that emerged in the wake of World War II. Occupying a middle ground between Kirk and Rand, Meyer tried to unify Christianity with freedom:

The principles which inspire the contemporary American conservative movement are developing as the fusion of two different streams of thought. The one, which, for want of a better word, one may call the "traditionalist," puts its primary emphasis upon the authority of transcendent truth and the necessity of a political and social order in accord with the constitution of being. The other, which, again for want of a better word, one may call the "libertarian," takes as its first principle in political affairs the freedom of the individual person and emphasizes the restriction of the power of the state and the maintenance of the free-market economy as guarantee of that freedom.[23]

His philosophy came to be called fusionism, and it still plays a critical role in twenty-first-century conservatism. There has been no truer political fusionist than Reagan, maybe because he understood both sides better than anyone else. At a political conference for conservatives in March 1981 Reagan told his audience, "It was Frank Meyer who reminded us that the robust individualism of the American experience was part of the deeper current of Western learning and culture. He pointed out that a respect for law, an appreciation for tradition, and regard for the social consensus that gives stability to our public and private institutions, these civilized ideas must still motivate us even as we seek a new economic prosperity based on reducing government interference in the marketplace."[24]

Differences existed among all of these conservatives, but they were bound together on one principle: an unequivocal opposition to communism. Communism is the right's version of racism: it is the scourge of the earth, and every semblance of it must be eradicated in every degree, for moral reasons. The further we move away from communist ideas, the better the world becomes. Any policy that contains a whiff of communism, according to the right, or racism, according to the left, must be opposed. There are different degrees of both, from the extreme and obvious (less common), to the more subtle brands (more common). The latter are almost ubiquitous, often coded, peering around every corner, on the verge of ruling society, unless the strong and morally righteous remain vigilant. Sometimes exaggerated, political opponents melt into this awful extreme. To the right, those who support government-run health care are communist; to the left, those who seek to build a wall to curb illegal immigration are racist. Many on both sides of the political spectrum ascribe the worst possible human instincts to the other. This may be a secularized version of the Christian idea that man is innately sinful and fallen. The left-wing and right-wing minds share much in the way they perceive racism and communism, respectively, because both minds evolved out of the broader Western tradition.

Reagan also began encountering new economic theories that emerged in the wake of World War II. They attempted to explain the Great Depression and Nazism. In his economic thinking Reagan drew upon three twentieth-century classical economists: Ludwig von Mises, Friedrich Hayek, and Milton Friedman. These men embraced the orthodox Enlightenment economic philosophy as propounded by Adam Smith, the baron de Montesquieu, and David Hume, as opposed to the greatest government interventionist of the twentieth century, John Maynard Keynes. The latter was by no means a Marxist, but he riled classical liberals with his advocacy of drastic government interventionist policies in times of economic despair, like the Depression. Keynes reasoned that monetary flow drives the economy, from patron to business, from business to employee, so the more money flowing through the economy, the better the economy. The Great Depression, Keynes believed, was caused by a lack of monetary flow as people hoarded money in fear. Government must therefore lubricate the movement of money by pumping it into the economy. Expensive? Yes, but the government can recoup what it spends during economic upswings by raising taxes. Although subsequent conservative economists like those described below have refuted Keynes, he was more of an economic centrist because he accepts many classical economic positions, such as the idea that lowering taxes promotes economic growth. Keynes was a pragmatist who contended that sometimes the ends justify the means.

Keynes's ideas spurred myriad responses from those who argued that government policies are ineffective and impinge upon freedom. Mises provides one example. Like thousands of other German intellectuals in the 1930s, Mises fled Nazi Germany for the United States, but unlike many other German intellectuals, he was an ardent capitalist. He attempted to refute socialism by arguing that centralized planning led to tyranny. In *Planning for Freedom* (1952) he wrote, "Tyranny is the political corollary of socialism, as representative government is the political corollary of the market economy."[25] You can't control the economy without controlling the people. Political and economic systems aren't distinct. Based on his firsthand experience in the 1920s, Mises argued that nothing ruins a nation more thoroughly than national debt (Keynes accepted debt during economic crisis) and that the best way to limit debt is to limit spending. Everyone knows that Germany's attempts to repay reparations by merely printing more money led to economic and political calamity, but why did Germany need to print so much money? Because of its debt. All government expenditures must be repaid. By curbing spending and limiting debt, Mises argued, governments ward off totalitarianism.

His friend Friedrich Hayek agreed. In his "The Use of Knowledge in Society" (1945) Hayek argued that government planning promotes prosperity less efficiently than does the private sector because the architects of a centrally planned economy can never understand the needs of society like the private sector can. Marx argued that capitalism will collapse, partly due to its inherently uncoordinated nature. Hayek countered that the free market, although technically uncoordinated, does coordinate people's actions in a (mostly) rational fashion and directs them in a socially constructive way. Hayek defended the free market, even in the wake of the Great Depression. Moreover, he believed that government should be feared in times of peace because the larger the government grows in size, the more restrictions it will impose on personal freedom, whether it be of the left or of the right.[26] Many consider Nazism and communism to be two antagonistic movements since they conventionally are placed at two ends of the political spectrum. Hayek early recognized the practical totalitarian outcome of both ideologies due to their collectivist natures.

In *The Road to Serfdom* (1944), Hayek reduced economic theorists to two groups: individualists, like himself, and collectivists or totalitarians. Nazis and communists demonstrated collectivism because both argued for a state-centered economy designed to promote the greater good, like society and the nation. Hayek insisted that this only paves the way for totalitarianism: "The authority directing all economic activity would control not merely the part of our lives which is concerned with inferior things; it would control the allocation of the limited means for all our ends. And whoever controls all economic activity controls the means for all our ends [and] must therefore decide which are to be satisfied and which not. This is really the crux of the matter. Economic control is not merely control of a sector of human life which can be separated from the rest."[27] Again, you can't control the economy without controlling the people. Moreover, Hayek explained that socialism never arrives overnight. Instead it is an evolutionary process as government (with the support of many intellectuals) takes control of one sector of the economy after another, or creeping socialism.

Another freedom-centered economist who fueled Reagan was Milton Friedman, hailed by the *Economist* as the most influential economist in the second half of the twentieth century. Originally a disciple of Keynes, Friedman moved away from Keynesian government activism, fearing these policies would lead to inflation and low growth rates. To some extent he was right: the Great Society years of the 1960s were followed by a period of rapid inflation and a sluggish economy. Friedman consistently stressed the advantages of a free market, not just economic but social. In contrast to the ubiquitous Soviet bureaucracy, he stressed that a free society must have a free economy, for how could one freely challenge the system if everyone was economically dependent on it? Friedman was not an economic libertarian who wanted to banish all government; he argued that government was needed to ensure that everyone played fairly, but he feared the expansive American government that emerged in the wake of the Great Society.

Friedman's interpretation of the Great Depression appealed to conservatives like Reagan because it contended that the federal government's monetary policy caused the calamity, not laissez-faire economic policies. Friedman argued, "The Great Depression in the United States, far from being a sign of the instability of the private enterprise system, is a testament to how much harm can be done by the mistakes on the part of a few men when they wield vast power over the monetary system of a country."[28] Too much power in one institution means when that one institution fails, the consequences arc widespread. (Many on the right used these same arguments when they maintained that the inept Federal Reserve Board policies of low interest rates, not conservative economic policies, led to the housing crash of 2008 and the subsequent recession.) Friedman's theories appealed to Reagan, who had initially blamed the Depression on Republicans. Friedman allowed Reagan to interpret the most traumatic event of his youth with a new conservative twist. Laissez-faire economic policies did not lead to the misery that directly hurt Reagan's family, but rather too much government control. Friedman later served in the Reagan administration.

Hayek, Mises, and Friedman are all on the Mount Rushmore of American conservative economic theorists, but one lesser-known figure whom Reagan regarded highly was the great Muslim fourteenth-century philosopher Ibn Khaldun. One of Islam's foremost intellectuals, Ibn Khaldun stated over six hundred years before modern conservatives that eventually taxes will become so high that they will become burdensome. When this happens, "the interest of the subjects in cultural enterprises disappears, since when they compare expenditures and taxes with their income and gain and see the little profit they make, they lose all hope. Therefore, many of them refrain from all cultural activity. The result is that the total tax revenue goes down, as individual assessments go down. . . . The costs of all cultural enterprise are now too high, the taxes are too heavy, and the profits anticipated fail to materialize.

Finally, civilization is destroyed, because the incentive for cultural activity is gone."[29] Conservatives too can rationalize that civilization will perish if their values aren't supported. It's no wonder Reagan liked Ibn Khaldun. He preached what Reagan wanted to hear.

In modern times the theory that high taxes can lead to less productivity and therefore less tax revenue was argued by Arthur Laffer, another hallowed conservative economist whom Reagan followed. Laffer conceptualized the advantages of a capitalist system with lower tax rates. The reasoning of the Laffer Curve is this: We can all agree that a tax rate of 0 percent brings no money to the federal treasury, so how can the government collect money without taxes? The controversial side of the Laffer Curve theorizes that a tax rate that is too high, say 100 percent, will decrease worker productivity, leading to declining incomes and therefore less government revenue. Higher taxes means less tax revenue because workers will have no incentive to work since all of their earnings will be taken from them. Individuals will have less incentive to be creative and productive since they will receive none of the fruits of their labor. Fewer people working hard and fewer people making money lead to less government revenue. The Laffer Curve is by no means scientific, but conservative adherents, including Reagan, maintain that government tax revenue can be raised by reducing taxes, and tax revenue can be decreased by raising tax revenue. This defies conventional wisdom, which holds that the more government taxes, the more money it accrues. Reagan was no economist, but he was familiar with all of these ideas. He wrote in 1977 that economists like Laffer, Paul McCracken, and Arthur Burns "have each made it clear that government can increase its taxes and create the jobs we need without inflation by lowering the tax rates for business and individuals."[30]

Reagan's own domestic activities also contributed to his burgeoning conservatism. When seeking to understand Reagan's evolution from liberal to conservative, many biographers cite his experiences at General Electric (GE), which he called a "postgraduate course in political science": "I was seeing how government really operated and affected people in America, not how it was taught in school."[31] Before becoming president and even before becoming California's thirty-third governor, Reagan honed his political philosophy in speeches, television appearances, and radio shows while promoting GE. From 1954 to 1962 he criss-crossed the country as a spokesman for GE, an experience he believed gave him the ability to understand the political needs of the common man. Reagan estimated that as a GE spokesman, he met with 250,000 employees, "and with speeches sometimes running out fourteen a day, I was on my feet in front of a mike for almost 250,000 minutes."[32]

Reagan's mentor at GE was Leonard Boulware. Notorious for his tough stand against labor unions, Boulware encouraged his employees to read conservative economic writers, such as Henry Hazlitt.[33] Hazlitt can best be described as a popularizer, someone who introduced nonspecialists like Reagan to many of the economic experts mentioned earlier. In any field, outsiders have difficulty digesting the works of experts due to nomenclature. This is especially true in the hard sciences, partly true in the soft sciences like economics and psychology, and even true in the humanities, in fields like philosophy and history. All great thinkers have popularizers. Hazlitt was one of the great conservative economic popularizers in the post–World War II era. A friend of Ayn Rand's, his most important work is titled *Economics in One Lesson*. Based on the ideas of Hayek and Mises, the work encourages free trade and low taxes. In a chapter titled "Taxes Curb Production," Hazlitt contends, "These taxes inevitably affect the actions and incentives of those from whom they are taken. When [a business is heavily taxed] its policies are affected. It does not expand its operations, or it expands only those attended with a minimum of risk. People who recognize this situation are deterred from starting new enterprises."[34] Hazlitt also spread the classical liberal economic philosophy through his time at *Newsweek*, the *New York Times*, and the *Wall Street Journal*.

Although GE hired Reagan to promote their products, he spent much of the time discussing political issues with ordinary middle-class Americans. His biographers suggest these years turned Reagan from an opponent to an advocate of big business and corporate America.[35]

Thanks to his time at GE and the thinkers analyzed above, by the late 1950s Reagan feared not only expanding communism but also expanding government. He began arguing that excessive tax rates curbed production and therefore hurt the little guy. He testified before Congress in 1958 as a representative for the Motion Picture Industry Council, "The high tax rates and limitations imposed by the capital gains [tax] structure tend to make futile the capital investment required in the production of a motion picture. . . . An even greater deterrent to the motion picture industry in this county is the reluctance of high income earners in the talent field to make more than 1–2 pictures a year [due to high taxes]. Good story material has always been scarce. It is double so when successful writers curtail their output because of diminishing returns due to excessive surtax rates."[36] This, in turn, hurt everyone who worked in production. Reagan claimed, "The result is unemployment in our industry, and it is also a loss of tax revenue to the government."[37] He began believing that higher taxes lead to declining tax revenue. The more the government intrudes in the economy, the less prosperity there is for the people.

Reagan feared the growth of government that continued with the support of President Eisenhower, who expanded social security and raised the tax rate in 1956. In a 1958 speech titled "Business, Ballots and Bureaus," Reagan said, "If I had to choose one salient characteristic of the revolution of our times, the word would be collectivism—the tendency to center power of all initiative in one central government."[38] Reagan even began critiquing Social Security, fearing that government would have to rely on excessive taxation to pay future recipients. This, of course, meant socialism. He stated in the same speech, "We must recognize that socialism through taxation may be slower, but it arrives at the same end as outright nationalization of industry. . . . This entire theory of progressive tax was spawned by Karl Marx more than 100 years ago. He gave it as the necessary basis for a socialist state. Karl Marx said that the way to impose statism on a people, socialism on a country, was to tax the middle class out of existence." A 1959 headline for GE's *Schenectady News* read, "Reagan Sees a Loss of Freedom through a Steady Increase in Taxes."[39]

Reagan was reared by his father to be skeptical of big business, but this was changing. Before his employment by GE, Reagan viewed the federal government as a positive force for society, but after his time at GE he viewed business much more favorably. His second wife, Nancy Reagan, maintained that the experiences he had traversing the country for GE were pivotal in shaping his values, particularly his fear of government intrusion. Cannon agrees.[40] Reagan himself writes in his second autobiography that one day in about 1960 he told Nancy, "You know something just dawned on me: All these things I've been saying about government in my speeches . . . all these things I've been criticizing about government getting too big, well it just dawned on me that every four years when an election comes along, I go out and support the people who are responsible for the things I'm criticizing."[41] Some may see this as the time period when Reagan first became a front for the bourgeoisie.

The struggle against communism became personal for Reagan, because during the 1950s communists began infiltrating Hollywood. Communists believed they could alter American culture through movies since they provided a way to educate the masses or, in Marxist lingo, "raise class consciousness." As president of the Screen Actors Guild, Reagan was on the front line during a contentious period in American history. He received numerous death threats and even bought a license to carry a concealed weapon. Despite these personal threats and despite his anticommunist passions, however, Reagan's biographers agree that he was no McCarthyite. He lamented that some of his liberal friends were unjustly accused as communists. As Edward Yager notes, Reagan "opposed Communist activity in Hollywood without the extremism of Joseph McCarthy."[42] He successfully steered a moderate course among conservatives: he hated communism, yet he wasn't reckless in his accusations. Usurping civil rights had no place in his ethical philosophy; the ends did not justify the means. Upon testifying before the House Un-American Activities Committee (Nixon had no questions for him), Reagan refused to name names. "I do not believe the communists have ever at any time been able to use the motion picture screen as a sounding board for their philosophy and ideology," he said.[43] At the same time, Reagan warned actors that if they offended public opinion to such a degree that movie studios refused to hire them, they wouldn't have his union's support. He was not completely innocuous when it came to modest coercion in his fight against communism; Reagan was an FBI informant, and he fell for the Republican line that communists were infiltrating America. He was influenced by the mass hysteria, just not to the same degree as many other conservatives. He didn't see communists everywhere, for example, and he believed suspects were innocent until proven guilty. When informed that a member of SAG was a communist, he carefully studied the evidence against him or her before making a judgment. This allowed him to navigate around the political landmines of the era.

These events in the late 1940s and 1950s contributed to Reagan's shifting allegiances, not away from communism, as he never supported that cause, but rather away from the Democratic Party. Reagan actually maintained that he did not leave the Democratic Party but rather the Democratic Party left him. During the 1930s and 1940s thousands of leftist German intellectuals escaped Nazi Germany for the United States, helping to change the Democratic Party, forging a New Left. Largely the brainchild of ex-communists, the New Left recognized the futility of authoritarian and highly centralized political systems, such as that which existed in the Soviet Union. Whereas Mises and Hayek reacted by embracing free-market capitalism, New Left writers just rejected communism. They were socialists or democratic socialists. They sought to change American society by introducing more secularism and economic equality, but through peaceful democratic politics, not revolution. The Soviet experiment had shown them what a left-wing society looked like when taken to the extreme. Besides some form of socialism, they adhered (like all German leftists of the time) to some Marxist principles, including class distinction, secularism, and an aversion to nationalism. Herbert Marcuse, Max Horkheimer, and Theodor Adorno are quintessential examples. They ascended intellectually and added a new vein to American liberalism that would expand under subsequent left-wing luminaries such as C. Wright Mills, Abbie Hoffman, Noam Chomsky, Bill Moyers, Howard Zinn, and a host of other scholars and writers. Politically maturing in the 1960s, they rallied around causes like fighting Jim Crow laws and protesting the Vietnam War. As neo-Marxists they shared a more cynical attitude toward American capitalism, history, and religion than did pre-1960 Democrats like Roosevelt, Truman, and Kennedy. By the 1980s these intellectuals had obtained powerful academic positions in the humanities and media that allowed them, to some degree, to rewrite American history in accordance with their values. (All groups write and rewrite history in accordance with their beliefs.) For them, America was never a shining city on a hill, a beacon for the downtrodden. How could it be? It was the most capitalistic nation on earth, ripe with inequality and oppression.

Herein lie the origins of the "culture wars." They can largely be reduced to a clash between conservative Christians and neo-Marxists—the former, the most powerful intellectual and cultural force the Western world has ever seen; the latter, the second-most powerful. Neo-Marxism is newer, of course, and some of its adherents believe this gives it precedence, a fact that is demonstrated by their progressive thinking. Marx believed that history moves in a linear fashion, as we grow toward a more secular and socialist society. More socialism and secularism is considered progress, even for almost all leftists today.

The neo-Marxist influx into the Democratic Party means Reagan spoke truthfully when he stated that he did not leave the Democratic Party, but instead it left him. The Democratic Party changed in composition during the 1950s and 1960s, welcoming baby-boomer leftists who were more secular at the expense of traditionalists like Reagan and other conservative Democrats. The latter were marginalized. The germs of the social chaos of the 1960s, even within the Democrat Party, emerged. The times were changing. The

Reagan who was too liberal to run for Congress in the early 1950s campaigned for Nixon in the 1960 presidential election, the same man he had campaigned against in 1950. A letter Reagan wrote to Nixon in the midst of this presidential election demonstrates this new conservative cosmology:

> Unfortunately, he [Kennedy] is a powerful speaker with an appeal to the emotions. He leaves little doubt that his idea of the "challenging new world" is one in which the Federal Government will grow bigger and do more and of course spend more. I know there must be some short-sighted people in the Republican Party who will advise that the Republicans should try to "out liberal" him. In my opinion this would be fatal. . . . One last thought—shouldn't someone tag Mr. Kennedy's bold new imaginative program with its proper age? Under the tousled boyish haircut is still old Karl Marx—first launched a century ago. There is nothing new in the idea of a Government being Big Brother to us all. Hitler called his "State Socialism" and way before him it was "benevolent monarchy."[44]

Consistent with modern-day conservatism, by 1960 Reagan began conflating (sometimes correctly, sometimes not) left-wing economic theory with Marxism. This became common in Reagan's post-1960 writings and speeches and was a direct result of studying Mises, Hayek, and other writers.

The inaccurate association of liberals, socialists, and communists (those on the left make the same mistake when they equate conservatives with racists and fascists) was partly also inspired by Barry Goldwater's *Conscience of a Conservative*, published in 1960. Deeply influenced by Hayek, Senator Goldwater from Arizona united everyone on the left wing of the political spectrum by calling them "collectivists." He declared, "The collectivists have not abandoned their ultimate goal—to subordinate the individual to the state—but their strategy has changed. They have learned that socialism can be achieved through welfarism quite as well as through nationalization. They understand that private property can be confiscated as effectively by taxation as by expropriating it. They understand that [the] individual can be put at the mercy of the state—not only by making the state his employer—but by divesting him of the means to provide for his personal needs from cradle to grave."[45] Government enslaves those who become dependent on it. The final goal, for all socialists and communists, is the enslavement of man. Therefore, for Goldwater, all of their ways must be rejected, including the creation of the welfare state. Goldwater's *Conscience of a Conservative* influenced Reagan by inspiring in him a sense of economic urgency. *Conscience* didn't much necessarily teach Reagan much since he had already expressed many of the same concepts, but it could only heighten Reagan's belief that America was going to hell because the welfare state was growing so rapidly in the post–World War II era.

Reagan projected these ideas in 1961 in a piece he wrote for *General Contractor*, a trade magazine, titled "Losing Freedom by Installments." Reagan argued, "We can lose our freedom all at once by succumbing to Russian aggression, or we can lose it gradually by installments. The end result is slavery. Professor Schlesinger says 'The political argument for the welfare state is that the welfare state is the best insurance against revolution.' This just isn't true. Our defense against [communism] is individual freedom and our free economy."[46] Reagan was referring to the American historian Arthur Schlesinger Jr.'s *The Vital Center* (1949), which argued that in order to ward off communist totalitarianism, the American government had to take an active role in promoting a welfare state. Otherwise the poor and downtrodden would revolt, duplicating the 1917 Russian Revolution. This made as much sense to conservatives as arguing to liberals that we should adopt slightly right-of-center policies in order to ward off far-right candidates (although Schlesinger insisted his policies were centrist). Reagan continued, "Under high flown phrases 'freedom from want,' 'human rights,' we see the federal government laying its hand on housing, health, farming, industry and education."[47]

Reagan worried about the same creeping socialism that Hayek had warned about. He explained in 1962, "Our friends seek the answer to all of the problems of human need through government.

Freedom can be lost inadvertently this way. Government tends to grow; it takes on a weight and momentum in government programs that goes beyond the original purpose that caused their creation." Expanding New Deal programs meant more government encroachment, at the expense of liberty.[48] Reagan makes these ideas the centerpiece of his famous "A Time for Choosing" speech.

3

...

Fostering Freedom at Home

You can't control the economy without controlling the people.

—REAGAN, "A Time for Choosing"

In 1964 California was the American dream. It was the center of the technological and cultural world. With hundreds of families moving there every day, it replaced New York as America's most populous state. It also boasted the world's sixth-largest economy. There was tremendous intellectual ferment too. In 1964 Mario Savio was leading student protests at UC Berkeley as the New Left first appeared on the political stage. Just south of San Francisco one of the great cultural icons of our lifetime, Steve Jobs, was beginning to make sense of the world around him. Nearby, the man most responsible for the personal computer, Steve Wozniak, was entering his formative years. By the end of the decade data were being transmitted electronically from Los Angeles to Palo Alto, inaugurating the age of the internet.

The Republican Party, on the other hand, was in disarray. Barry Goldwater was trounced by an FDR protégé, Lyndon Baines Johnson, in 1964, and Democrats took a whopping sixty-eight of the one hundred Senate seats. As government was expanding under the auspices of the Great Society, the Republican Party was shrinking. California and the GOP seemed to be moving in two different directions—one successful and optimistic, the other possibly destined for oblivion. Reality, however, was different. California's governor Pat Brown, another FDR disciple, believed that government existed to do good. During Brown's stewardship, taxes were raised and new government works program like the California aqueduct and thousands of miles of freeway were built. But by 1965 California's coffers were nearly bare and its citizens—not for the last time—resisted tax increases.

Enter Ronald Reagan. "When I first became aware of Ronald Reagan in the 1960s," says longtime aide Martin Anderson, "I was struck by how much I agreed with what he was saying. It all seemed reasonable. No other political figure came close to laying out a blueprint that fit my personal convictions. When he talked about the Soviet threat, the danger of communism, the proper role of government, the need for low taxes, the greatness of our country, I just said to myself—'yes, yes, yes.' I don't think I became a Reagan conservative. As best as I can remember, I always was one. . . . When he spoke, he spoke for me."[1] Anderson sums up the core principles of Reagan's philosophy: the danger of communism, the need for low taxes, and the greatness of America. Reagan indeed spoke for millions, if not tens of millions, of Americans, many of whom traditionally identified with Democrats more than Republicans.

Reagan made his last film in 1964. Hollywood had turned him into a famous and wealthy man. He had achieved the American dream, but he wasn't satisfied. He had political ambitions. His foray into national politics, like most of his efforts in life, was a smashing success. Possessing the natural gifts of a storyteller, he found that his acting skills and name recognition paved the way to a rise to national prominence as a political figure. In 1964 Reagan became a political star.

The Goldwater campaign needed a jump start. Many, including Goldwater himself, were ambivalent toward Reagan because some of his ideas seemed radical. Furthermore, he was a Republican neophyte, having officially changed his party affiliation only in 1962. But by 1964 Reagan's conservative convictions were sincere, so he was given roughly thirty minutes of airtime to defend conservatism, in hopes of saving the Goldwater campaign. "A Time for

Choosing," the name subsequently given to Reagan's speech, was given before a live studio audience. Reagan began by stating, "The sponsor has been identified, but unlike most televised programs, the performer hasn't been provided with a script. As a matter of fact, I have been permitted to choose my own words and discuss my own ideas regarding the choice that we face in the next few weeks." The speech gave Goldwater a temporary boost, and *Time* called it "the one bright spot in a dismal campaign."[2] It marks the birth of Reagan as a national political figure.

"A Time for Choosing" is Reagan's most important pre-presidential speech, in terms of both its significance for him and its content. It reveals that Reagan had serious reservations about American society. Nothing less should be expected. Most political, religious, and intellectual figures are a bit alarmist in nature, often conveying the message "If you don't support my ideas, we will continue upon this treacherous course." No ideology gains adherents by extolling the status quo. Whether it be political figures running for office or intellectuals, those hoping to inspire followers must advocate for some sort of change. As the Russian historian Adam Ulam explains the attraction of Marxism to intellectuals, "They must not promise more of the same, but an entirely different and marvelous world."[3] The members of the intellectual class must not perpetuate what already exists, or their intellectual talents will be wasted. They must propose something new or they will be indistinguishable from the morose masses. At the height of the cold war, American intellectuals critiqued American consumer capitalism while their Soviet counterparts, the dissidents, critiqued Soviet socialism, the most equal society the modern Western world has ever seen. Accordingly, despite the overwhelming triumph of Western capitalism over Soviet socialism, despite the fact that capitalism has become the dominant economic system of the age, the most vocal critics of this system are intellectuals. The question for these intellectuals is this: How can they establish themselves as independent thinkers if they believe what the masses believe? How can they identify themselves as true intellectuals if their ideas are mundane?

This model describes Reagan. Like all thinkers, he was a little alarmist and contrarian. He declared, "This nation has never been in greater danger. Yes, our defenses are approaching second best to Russia—yes, inflation has virtually driven us from the world markets we must have. Yes, government has a permanent structure—a bureaucracy so huge and firmly entrenched that it has the power to override the decisions of our elected representatives."[4] Reagan's rhetoric rings like that of a revolutionary. Before establishing their own versions of utopia, thinkers first must argue that what already exists needs to be destroyed. All advocates of change must convince people that the existing world needs changing, and they do that by condemning the existing world. Only then can we create the New Jerusalem.

The faulty foundation, for Reagan, was the result of LBJ's Great Society, an effort to promote social and economic equality in America. It descended from FDR's New Deal, which to adherents was never an attempt to impinge on freedom but rather an attempt to expand freedom, including freedom of speech, freedom from want, and freedom from fear. "There can be no freedom for the common man without enlightened social policies," insisted Roosevelt.[5] Most historians agree that after the Great Depression, the post– World War II economic boom in America was the largest the world had ever seen. It brought unprecedented wealth to Americans. Yet by the early 1960s over 20 percent of Americans still lived below the poverty line, creating a need for even more economic change, led by the government. Johnson declared a "war on poverty" and created a new federal agency, the Office of Economic Opportunity, which was designed to administer federal funds to the needy. Unprecedented federal government expansion into fields like education and health care characterized the Great Society. Whereas the New Deal attempted to save the impoverished middle class during a time of economic crisis, the Great Society attempted to enrich the poor during a time of prosperity.

Reagan warned of the potential problems inherent in a system with too much government control, specifically the lack of freedom and the oppressive nature of bureaucracy: "Today, there is hardly a phase of our daily living that doesn't feel the stultifying hand of government regulation and interference. We are faced with a collection of internal powers and bureaucratic institutions against which the individual citizen is powerless." Government programs grow in size, creating a larger bureaucracy against which citizens helplessly flail, like a fly caught in a web. Reagan equated social programs with totalitarianism: "You can't control the economy without controlling the people, so we have come to a time for choosing. . . . I suggest that there is no left or right, only an up or down: Up to the maximum of individual freedom consistent with law and order, or down to the ant heap of totalitarianism, and regardless of their humanitarian purpose, those who would sacrifice their freedom for security have, whether they know it or not, chosen this downward path."[6] Government control leads to socialism, and this spawns totalitarianism, Reagan believed, because socialism, by definition, means government control of the economy, and the economy is simply a conglomerate of individuals, so the more the government controls the economy, the more the government controls the people.

Reagan lambasted government programs such as welfare and social security. This became commonplace in the 1990s, but it was a new way of thinking in the 1960s. It was the way welfare worked that was the problem, Reagan believed. Every government program has administrative costs, and the larger the program, the larger the costs. Government programs tend to have high overhead and administrative costs because the bureaucracy must be paid and fed. And there are other basic costs, such as rental space, travel costs, and costs for vehicles and supplies. This doesn't include the inevitable "government waste" that accompanies all programs, even those favored by conservatives, such as military spending. Reagan contended, "Welfare spending [is] 10 times greater than in the dark depths of the Depression. We're spending 45 billion dollars on welfare. Now do a little arithmetic, and you'll find that if we divided the 45 billion dollars up equally among those 9 million poor families, we'd be able to give each family 4,600 dollars a year. And this added to their present income should eliminate poverty. Direct aid to the poor, however, is only running about 600 dollars per family. It would seem that someplace there must be some overhead."[7] Only a portion of the intended aid ever reaches those in need due to the high costs of administering the program.

Moreover Reagan argued that welfare spending merely perpetuated poverty. He said in a 1967 speech, "We are a humane and generous people. . . . But we are not going to perpetuate poverty by substituting a permanent dole for a paycheck. There is no humanity or charity in destroying self-reliance, dignity and self-respect."[8] Reagan anticipated the views of the social scientist Charles Murray. Like Reagan, the scholar argued that welfare spending promotes poverty by fostering an underclass. In his work *Losing Ground: American Social Policy 1950–1980* (1984), Murray noted that government expenditures on the poor had increased dramatically over the past thirty years. The consequence? The American poor had become reliant on government, thereby limiting initiative. Providing for the poor didn't alleviate poverty, Reagan and Murray believed.

Reagan challenged any sort of government-run health care system because he believed government-run health care paved the way for socialism: "One of the traditional methods of imposing statism or socialism on a people has been by way of medicine. It's very easy to disguise a medical program as a humanitarian project. Most people are a little reluctant to oppose anything that suggests medical care for people who possibly can't afford it."[9] The road to totalitarianism is paved with good intentions. Reagan feared that a government-run health care system would erode individualism via a bloated bureaucracy, taking American society one step closer to collectivism. He viewed proposed health care reforms with cynicism, believing the motives for such measures were socialist and, ultimately, communist. The corresponding left-wing idea is that securing America's borders is actually a tool for racism. Expanding health care and strengthening border security seem innocuous enough, but the true malignant intentions must be unveiled. It is easy, maintained Reagan, to support such seemingly humanitarian goals without realizing their implications. Yet by creating a

new class of government employees, we create an enlarged, ineffi-
cient government that erodes individual freedom. Reagan despised
government-run health care because he opposed attempts to minimize individual freedom that will inevitably ensue as our taxes
are raised and our government expands. In response, California's
governor Pat Brown called Reagan an enemy of all social progress. Nevertheless Reagan believed that socialized medicine paved
the way for real socialism (taking us even closer to communism)
imposed upon the unsuspecting masses, who would be seduced by
the tenets of "health care for all."

Even social security, the "third rail" of American politics, felt
Reagan's wrath. The first major political figure to question the
long-term solvency of social security, Reagan stated:

> There is no fund, because Robert Byers, the actuarial head,
> appeared before a congressional committee and admitted that
> Social Security as of this moment is 298 billion dollars in the
> hole. But he said there should be no cause for worry because
> as long as they have the power to tax, they could always take
> away from the people whatever they needed to bail them out
> of trouble. And they're doing just that. . . . A young man, 21
> years of age, working at an average salary—his Social Secu-
> rity contribution would, in the open market, buy him an insur-
> ance policy that would guarantee 220 dollars a month at age
> 65. The government promises 127. He could live it up until
> he's 31 and then take out a policy that would pay more than
> Social Security. Now are we so lacking in business sense that
> we can't put this program on a sound basis, so that people who
> do require those payments will find they can get them when
> they're due—that the cupboard isn't bare?[10]

Whereas FDR envisioned social security as a way to expand freedom to older needy Americans, Reagan argued that it was another
unnecessary government program that had morphed far beyond
its original intent into something that was so entrenched that fixing it became more difficult with each passing day. How do we fix
social security? Reagan toyed with the idea of private accounts in

the 1970s.[11] Private accounts allow more power for citizens, limiting the authority of the central government and enhancing individual freedom.

Education too bows to freedom. Reagan argued, "Control of education should remain, as much as possible, at the level of the local school boards and unwanted unification should not be imposed from above, but should only take place if it represents the will of the people directly involved. Increased autonomy should be granted to our state colleges and universities and the management of the people's affairs should be kept, as much as possible, at the local level."[12] Reagan promised to abolish the Department of Education if elected president, believing it had little real impact on improving the lot of teachers and students. Like social security, the Federal Department of Education, which had just been created in 1980, was another government-run program that Reagan felt impinged on freedom.[13] Conservatives—an exception being President George W. Bush—pushed for state-centered funding for education because by reducing federal programs, we maximize freedom, since every dollar taken from the Department of Education can be given back to the people or sent to local school officials who can spend the money more in accordance with their needs. Ideally, important decisions should be kept as local as possible, finding their greatest expression when the individual chooses for himself or herself. This empowers people because it reduces the unequal power government exercises in the field of education. Foreshadowing conservative ideas about school vouchers by decades, Reagan stated in 1976, "Parents have a right—and a responsibility—to direct the education of their children. This should include the choice of school their children attend."[14] Reagan argued that education should be in the hands of parents, not the government. School vouchers provide more power to poor and middle-class parents, at the expense of the government or school boards.

These notions premise a states rights philosophy whereby programs such as educational initiatives are the domain of the states, leading to programs that are smaller in size since they are used by fewer people at the state level. Reagan asserted, "This isn't to deny the rightful place of the federal government; but states' sovereignty is an integral part of the checks and balances designed to restrain power and to restrain one group from destroying the freedom of another. We can do more by keeping California tax dollars in California than we can by running them through those puzzle palaces on the Potomac only to get them back minus a carrying charge. Federal help has neither reduced the size of the burden of our state government, nor has it solved our problems."[15] Reagan didn't oppose all education spending; he just sought less government control of education.

Reagan was not a radical libertarian seeking the destruction of the federal government. Sometimes people create a false characterization, such as suggesting that Reagan wanted to eliminate the entire federal government, or that Obama is a communist who seeks government control of all aspects of society, or that Trump is like Hitler. Philosophers call these exaggerations building a straw man because it creates a mischaracterization that can easily be torn down. These (mis)interpretations of reality make people feel right, a feeling that can be empowering. Conversely, feeling wrong can lead to guilt and embarrassment. Creating false representations avoids the reality that Reagan, Obama, and Trump have done beneficial things for society because this thought causes anxiety. Our emotions, or desire to avoid emotions, lead us to create false realities. Sometimes in politics (and in life) we believe things not because they are true but because we want them to be true because it soothes anxiety and fear.

Reagan never attempted to eradicate everything FDR accomplished. He always insisted that he opposed Great Society bureaucracies, not the New Deal. As Frank Leuchtenberg shows in his *In the Shadow of FDR*, one can paint a portrait of either a pro-FDR Reagan or an anti-FDR Reagan, depending on which conflicting bits of evidence one chooses to focus on.[16] Biographer Stephan Hayward explains, "Reagan delighted in annoying New Deal fans with reminders that he cast his first vote for FDR in 1932, but he really infuriated liberals with his assertion that it was he, rather than modern liberals, who was the legitimate heir to Roosevelt's legacy. To be sure there is a studied ambivalence and ambiguity to Reagan's relationship to the New Deal, which was expressed with his oft-recalled remark that fascism was the basis for much of the New Deal."[17] Reagan supported the broad principles of the New Deal; he merely opposed their expansion by Roosevelt protégés like LBJ and Brown.

One may wonder how someone who lived through the Great Depression and voted for FDR four times could become so conservative. Reagan is often portrayed as FDR's antagonist: one man viewed government as a way to solve the nation's problem, while the other condemned government as the nation's problem. Yet Reagan and FDR were not as antagonistic as they first appear. They may be treated as opposites, but there is also concordance. Such ambivalence is common in the history of ideas. Aristotle was Plato's pupil, but he rejected key parts of his teacher's thought. The same can be said of Descartes and Spinoza, Freud and Jung, and Marx and Hegel. Jung, Spinoza, and Marx all started new intellectual movements, but they cannot be separated from their heritage. Is Jung a critic or a disciple of Freud? The answer is both. Jung disagreed with Freud in key details, but Freud set the terms of the debate. The presidential historian Richard Neustadt deemed Reagan a "New Deal Republican."[18] Reagan was a disciple of FDR's but believed the New Deal had limitations. Alterations were needed in order to maximize success. Government programs had expanded since the days of Roosevelt, and as far as Reagan was concerned, it was time for contraction. The New Deal was intended to provide temporary relief to victims of the Great Depression, as it did to Reagan's family, not to become a way of life. Reagan wanted to make the New Deal more amenable to the contemporary world, not overthrow the system.

The Aid to Families with Dependent Children (AFDC) program provides a paradigmatic example of a government agency that morphed far beyond its original intentions, fostering government dependency. Originally part of the New Deal, the program was intended to bring relief to poor single mothers at the height of the Depression, in 1938, when 250,000 American families received support from the program.[19] Despite the end of the Depression and the relative economic prosperity of the 1950s and 1960s, by 1974 the number of families receiving assistance from the program had ballooned to 10.8 million, mostly under the auspices of the Great Society.[20] This is what bothered Reagan. He believed that the families who received public assistance during the Great Depression, like his own, needed and deserved the aid; now, however, families were exploiting the system, necessitating a drastic overhaul and cuts. The New Deal expanded government services to those who really needed them, yet the Great Society merely promoted reliance on government. FDR's New Deal saved American capitalism. Now American capitalism needed to be saved from LBJ's Great Society.[21]

The relationship between Roosevelt and Reagan resembles that between Thomas Jefferson and John Adams, who were ideological adversaries in the first presidential campaign in American history, each having their own vision for America. Antagonisms, both personal between Adams and Jefferson and ideological between their respective parties, were every bit as intense as the conflicts between modern-day Republicans and Democrats. Does that mean Adams and Jefferson were complete opposites? Yes and no. Despite intellectual (and at times personal) hostility, and despite the intense animosity between their two parties during the elections of 1796 and 1800, today the two men are grouped together among the Founding Fathers. Both of these men favored a Republican form of government, a radical idea at the time. And on the big issues of the day, there was concordance between these two giants in early American history. Similarly, even many eighteenth-century French thinkers whom we today classify as Enlightenment philosophers would have been horrified to be grouped together. Intense divisions and rivalries existed among the likes of Rousseau, Voltaire, Turgot, and Diderot. In their minds, they were not concordant. One day Roosevelt and Reagan may be viewed as complementary figures who successfully promoted capitalism and democracy in times of despair. The New Deal, after all, was an effort to save capitalism, an effort that in itself drew the ire of some far-left critics who believed Roosevelt blew a golden opportunity to overthrow capitalism. (James Burnham, before his disassociation with communism, provides one example.)

Closer analysis of the New Deal reveals that Reagan may not be quite the anti–New Dealer that many make him out to be. The only New Deal programs Reagan routinely criticized were the Tennessee Valley Authority and social security. Furthermore, to be fair, the social security program that Reagan criticized in the 1960s and 1970s was far more expansive than anything FDR intended. Although some conservatives continue to question social security, there has been no serious political effort by Reagan or his disciples to repeal the Federal Deposit Insurance Corporation or the Fair Labor Standards Act, or any of the other core aspects of the New Deal. Reagan never criticized most of these programs. Some aspects of the New Deal saved American capitalism, while others were wasteful.

Reagan certainly wanted to reduce some government programs, but this doesn't mean he sought to destroy government. Reagan never saw himself as someone who sought to overthrow the New Deal. Most of the New Deal was erased during World War II because unemployment was nearly eliminated. Roosevelt didn't intend for the New Deal to be a permanent feature of American life anyway. Reagan liked to quote one of Roosevelt's national addresses, in which FDR declared, "The lessons of history, confirmed by the evidence immediately before me, show conclusively that continued dependence upon relief induces a spiritual disintegration fundamentally destructive to the national fiber. To dole out relief in this way is to administer a narcotic, a subtle destroyer of the human spirit. The Federal Government must and shall quit this business of relief."[22] Reagan contended, "As smart as [FDR] was, I suspect he didn't realize that once you created a bureaucracy, it took on a life of its own."[23]

Reagan did not oppose FDR and the New Deal. Rather, he opposed the new Democratic Party that was emerging in the wake of World War II. He especially loathed the burgeoning Democratic hyperemphasis on class because he never saw the world in terms of class. Class is a social construct. It became critical in the nineteenth century, after the hereditary and religious concepts that were previously used to define people broke down. So central was class for Marx that he argued raising class consciousness was a necessary precondition for the imminent workers revolution; the oppressed classes must be taught they are exploited. Many left-wing writers continue to assert the importance of identity politics, arguing for the saliency of class and race, but class, like race, nationality, religion, or sexual preference (the last two are identities that matter for some contemporary conservatives), did not define people for Reagan. Some Americans believe that in an ideal world, race, sexual orientation, and religion won't matter. Include class, and Reagan would agree. Even today many of Reagan's critics argue that he didn't do enough for the lower classes. This may be fair, as long as those who argue this recognize that they are using their own values. It's no different from a Republican judging Clinton and Obama unfavorably because they raised taxes. Reagan believed we should neither discriminate against, judge, nor favor people for their race, religion, gender, or class. Instead, he envisioned a class-blind society.

Reagan wasn't the only one attempting to create a brave new world in 1964. Another group at the other end of the political spectrum yearned for change. A generation younger than Reagan, they were hell-bent on saving America from racism, war, and corporatism. When compared to Reagan, the similarities are just as striking as the differences. Like Reagan's "A Time for Choosing" speech, the "Port Huron Statement" (1962) equally mixes desperation and social criticism in a clear and simplistic manner. It was a manifesto of the Students for a Democratic Society, written primarily by Tom Hayden, a student at the University of Michigan. The document declares

> We are people of this generation, bred in at least modest comfort, housed now in universities, looking uncomfortably to the world we inherit. When we were kids the United States was the wealthiest and strongest country in the world; the only one

with the atom bomb, the least scarred by modern war, an initiator of the United Nations that we thought would distribute Western influence throughout the world. Freedom and equality for each individual, government of, by, and for the people— these American values we found good, principles by which we could live as men. Many of us began maturing in complacency.

As we grew, however, our comfort was penetrated by events too troubling to dismiss. First, the permeating and victimizing fact of human degradation, symbolized by the Southern struggle against racial bigotry, compelled most of us from silence to activism. Second, the enclosing fact of the Cold War, symbolized by the presence of the Bomb, brought awareness that we ourselves, and our friends, and millions of abstract "others" we knew more directly because of our common peril, might die at any time. We might deliberately ignore, or avoid, or fail to feel all other human problems, but not these two, for these were too immediate and crushing in their impact, too challenging in the demand that we as individuals take the responsibility for encounter and resolution.

While these and other problems either directly oppressed us or rankled our consciences and became our own subjective concerns, we began to see complicated and disturbing paradoxes in our surrounding America. The declaration "all men are created equal . . ." rang hollow before the facts of Negro life in the South and the big cities of the North. The proclaimed peaceful intentions of the United States contradicted its economic and military investments in the Cold War status quo.[24]

Whereas Reagan's vision was for an America with less government coercion, less socialism, and less secularism, the early New Left sought to save America from war, racism, and corporate influence, all in the name of change and moral righteousness. Other topics that the New Left came to embrace were gay rights, legalization of drugs, and access to abortion.

How do we understand these calls for change by both sides of the American spectrum at the same time? Calls for change are inevitable because each new generation needs a way to establish its identity. Bringing change to the world helps us feel special and important. Reagan recognized this when he said in 1967, "Each generation is critical of its predecessor."[25] If I live and nothing changes, I have no significance. Calls for change from both sides of the political spectrum therefore will persist, ad infinitum, as long as human values rule society. All groups want change until their values are adopted, and then they become rigidly conservative and shout "Stop" in the name of righteousness. How many American liberals seek to change American abortion laws—ever? Once their values are adopted, adherents resist change, making them conservative. There is nothing intrinsically conservative about any ideology, because all ideologies believe in something and try to spread these views through change. Today's Christian missionaries, for example, try to bring change to the societies they encounter. When analyzing the seeming conservative nature of Reagan, one biographer wrote, "The most conservative expressions of society are ordinarily religious. Attitudes toward the divine tend to be stable, as their object is thought to be."[26] Yet early Christians desperately tried to bring change to the Roman Empire by replacing the polytheism that had dominated Western civilization for thousands of years with monotheism. They sought radical social reform. All current proponents of social change walk in their footsteps. Even in the twenty-fist century Christians and Muslims around the world try to bring change. At the other end of the spectrum, archsecularists like Leonid Brezhnev of the USSR, Erich Honecker of East Germany, and Nicolae Ceausescu of Romania resisted any change to their secular societies. It only seems like religious people resist change because traditionally their values have ruled society, so naturally they resist changes to this. But if socialist and/or secular values ever reign supreme (as they did in the USSR), their leaders too will resist change.

In 1966 Reagan increased his chances for bringing change by declaring himself a candidate for governor of California. He had name recognition, and his 1964 speech for Goldwater solidified his conservative credentials. Still, he seemed to have little chance in the general election against the popular two-term incumbent Brown, a man who had legitimate presidential aspirations. However, social disruptions in California, including the riots in south-central Los Angeles and anti–Vietnam War demonstrations, plagued Brown in 1966. He didn't help himself when he tried to criticize Reagan by reminding California voters that an actor had killed Abraham Lincoln. Reagan secured 58 percent of the popular vote, winning in a landslide.

In 1967 the political scientist James Q. Wilson analyzed Reagan and southern California culture in his essay "A Guide to Reagan Country." It appeared in *Commentary* magazine a year after Reagan was elected governor of California. Wilson argued that Reagan succeeded in California because he epitomized its culture: Reagan was Protestant, had small-town Midwestern roots, enjoyed the outdoors, and had his own home and car. People in southern California had freedom but not complete anonymity because everyone could see what they were doing, how much their houses cost, how well their lawns were kept, and what the outside of their houses looked like. This encouraged individualism, argued Wilson, because everyone wanted to have a unique house and car. Since southern California had so many transplants, each with his or her own unique background, the area was less collectivist in nature. The populace didn't identify in groups, such as "Irish Catholics" or "WASPs." Wilson, who grew up in Orange County, insisted that he had never even heard the word "ethnic group" until he reached graduate school. This contrasted with San Francisco, where, as on the East Coast, people bonded with their ethnic groups, lived in apartments, and used public transportation. San Francisco was more Catholic than southern California as well. Wilson insisted that Reagan was a national political force who had to be reckoned with.[27]

Reagan's two terms as governor were quite eventful. He enacted ideas he had preached, like 1971 Welfare Reform Act. This act tightened eligibility requirements for recipients of AFDC, which had become such a popular program that roughly one in every thirteen Californians was receiving assistance.[28] Over the next several years the number of recipients of aid dropped from roughly 1,566,000 to 1,330,000.[29] Reagan's ideas would eventually be implemented on the federal level.

But like his presidency, although his rhetoric was usually on the far right, his policies weren't, especially when it came to spending. In fact Reagan had right-wing critics during the 1960s and 1970s whom he merely deemed ultraconservatives. Reagan's inability to completely fulfill all right-wing dreams was partly because during his sixteen years as chief executive, his party never controlled the lower chambers, so he had to compromise. For example, although he confronted university protestors at the height of the Vietnam War, and despite his critiques of government involvement in higher education, higher education funding increased by 136 percent during his tenure as governor.[30] Another example comes from the Department of Mental Hygiene. Reagan initially cut spending for this department, laying off 2,600 workers. Two years later, however, after public outcry, he changed his mind and significantly increased the department's budget, so that state expenditures for the Department of Mental Hygiene increased by almost 25 percent after his first three years in office.[31] Reagan also signed legislation that raised taxes in order to combat California's budget problems (when the state's budget issues improved, he cut taxes, effectively giving the money back to the taxpayers). Even his environmental record was liberal.[32] Most significant, he signed a bill that liberalized abortion in California. His attempt to reduce backroom abortions backfired, however, because of the bill's language: it maintained that abortion was permissible whenever the mother's physical or mental health was at risk. What Reagan didn't realize until later was that a doctor could use "health risks" to justify almost any abortion. The number of abortions in California skyrocketed from 518 in 1967 to an average of 100,000 a year.[33]

Abortion was not one of Reagan's favorite topics before he became president. Less than 1 percent of his speeches and writings analyzed abortion. Reagan addressed issues like communism, socialism, health care, defense spending, the Soviet Union, taxes, national defense, and even balanced budgets far more frequently than abortion. Reagan was pro-life, but ending abortion was not his highest priority, unlike other elements of the right. Reagan maintained, "I can find no evidence whatsoever that a fetus is not a living human being with human rights."[34] However, he accepted abortion when the life of the mother was at risk or if the pregnancy was caused by rape, for example. He said in a radio address from about 1974, "In our Judeo-Christian religion we recognize the right to take life in defense of our own. Therefore an abortion is justified when done in self-defense. My belief is that a woman has the right to protect her own life and health against even her own unborn child. I believe also that just as she has the right to defend herself against rape, she should not be made to bear a child resulting from the violation of her person and therefore abortion is an act of defense."[35]

Reagan also liberalized divorce laws when he signed the California Family Law Act of 1969. This bill made "no fault" divorce the law of the land, so anytime one party wanted to dissolve the marriage, that party could easily do so under the guise of "irreconcilable differences." No longer did an aggrieved party have to prove that specific actions like abuse, imprisonment, or adultery had been committed. Michael Reagan, the adopted child of Reagan and his first wife, Jane Wyman, lamented the social changes wrought by this law: "The problem is that we have made divorce too easy in our society. . . . And do you know who is responsible for making divorce too easy? Would you believe—Ronald Reagan?"[36] Considering the fact that as governor of California Reagan raised taxes, liberalized abortion, and facilitated divorce, one wonders if he would be conservative enough to capture the Republican nomination for the presidency today.

4

. . .

Understanding Reagan

What do we want for ourselves and our children? Is it enough to have material things? Aren't liberty and morality and integrity and high principles and a sense of responsibility more important?

—REAGAN, "The Value of Understanding the Past"

Reagan's disregard of class and his demands to reduce some government programs designed to help the poor, combined with his Christian faith, has led opponents to ridicule him. Christ helped the poor, his detractors point out; Christians are supposed to help the poor, but conservatives oppose government programs intended to help the poor. How can their apparent apathy toward the American poor be reconciled with their alleged Christianity? Even many of Reagan's biographers and friends could not comprehend how such a compassionate and Christian man could cut federal funds aimed at helping poor people. Many assumed that Reagan lacked compassion and empathy. Mario Cuomo said, "At his worst, Ronald Reagan made the denial of compassion respectable."[1] Biographer John Diggins wrote, "Once he was in public office, the religious duty of benevolence was no part of [Reagan's] public policy."[2]

This reasoning is too simplistic, however. A deeper examination of Reagan's thought and Christian principles reveals that he never rejected the teachings of Jesus; rather they were the inspiration for his entire cosmology. Reagan's class blindness did not reject Christianity; it descended from it. The denial of the significance of material things is concordant with Christian heritage. Arguing that Jesus insisted that we help the poor and yet Reagan ignored the material needs of the poor, so therefore his philosophy can never be reconciled with Christianity builds another straw man. The criticism is valid only if one interprets Christianity materially, emphasizing the parts of Jesus's teachings that conform to a materialistic philosophy. In the twenty-first century this may make sense, since we live in such a materialistic age. However, by suspending our materialistic biases and treating Christ's mission as spiritual, as most Christians historically have, Reagan's ideas make more sense.

The Roman Empire of Jesus's time resembled in many ways the United States today: it was strong, rich, diverse, and possessed both great wealth and extreme poverty. Equally important, Rome possessed a vast bureaucracy and an efficient (though deeply unpopular) tax-collection system that ensured the emperor was never short of funds. Yet Jesus never demanded that the Roman emperor or any earthly ruler alleviate the sufferings of the poor. The materialist Kingdom of Caesar shared nothing with the eternal immaterial Kingdom of God. Jesus did not tell the tax collectors they should tell their bosses to share their wealth. Instead he encouraged individuals to privately do good works: "When you give to someone in need, don't do as the hypocrites do—blowing trumpets in the synagogues and streets to call attention to their acts of charity! I tell you the truth, they have received all the reward they will ever get. But when you give to someone in need, don't let your left hand know what your right hand is doing" (Matthew 6:2–3). Helping the poor is, in the Christian worldview, a private affair. Reagan put this into practice: he regularly gave money to charities and even wrote personal checks to the needy during his tenure in the White House.[3] The individual, not the government, must help poor people.

And the Bible is explicit about how much we should help the poor. Reagan wrote in 1961, "For an illustration of the difference between proportionate and progressive tax, we can look to the

Bible. There [tithing] is explained as the economic basis of our Judaic-Christian religions. The Lord says you shall contribute one-tenth and He says, 'If I prosper you 10 times as much you will give 10 times as much.' That is proportionate but look what happens today when you start computing Caesar's share. A man of average income [who] suddenly prospered 10 times as much would find his personal tax increased 43 times."[4] Reagan associated a progressive income tax (whereby the rich pay a higher percentage of their earnings than the poor) with Marxism. The Bible, at least for Reagan, demands a flat income tax.

Anyway, Christianity downplays the significance of this material and fallen world. This world means little because it is so brief compared to the eternal duration of our next lifetime. Those who spend their lives focusing on the material aspects of this world are misguided: "One's life does not consist of possessions," Jesus proclaims. "For this reason I say to you, do not be worried about your life, as to what you will eat or what you will drink; nor for your body, as to what you will put on. Is not life more than food, and the body more than clothing?" (Matthew 6:25). Jesus emphasized the next world, the spiritual world. Bringing heaven (the immaterial world of goodness) and God to earth trumps everything. Helping the poor is noble, but it was never a sacrament. Helping the poor is morally righteous, but never at the expense of the spiritual world, because the gospel states, "People do not live by bread alone, but by every word that comes from the mouth of God" (Matthew 4:4). The spiritual world transcends everything. Jesus explicitly denies any significance to this material, earthly world by begging his followers to focus their efforts on reaching the next world, the Kingdom of God. There is even a strand of Christian thought that denies any significance whatsoever to this material world, and this gave the world monasticism and hermeticism. These ascetic movements teach that relinquishing earthly desires and material goods brings us closer to God, the ultimate good.

Reagan opposed many government means to help the poor because these programs conflicted with freedom, his highest good. All ideologies and religions have their values, which they place above everything else. For the Muslim, it is submission to Allah; for the Christian, living like Christ; for the socialist, economic equality; for the fascist, the love of nation; and for the environmentalist, living in accordance with nature. For Reagan, it's freedom. Reagan ponders, "What do we want for ourselves and our children? Is it enough to have material things? Aren't liberty and morality and integrity and high principles and a sense of responsibility more important?"[5] This is a question that has plagued philosophers since the time of Socrates. How do we live the good life? Is it by obtaining material things like money, cell phones, cars and computers? Can one live a satisfactory, fulfilling life without these things? Are they necessary for human happiness? Is freedom more important?

These are basic ethical questions that we all must answer. How to live a moral life, not how to help the less fortunate by providing them with material things, was of central importance to Reagan. He contended, "The world's truly great thinkers have not pointed us toward materialism; they have dealt with the great truths and with the high questions of right and wrong, of morality and integrity. They have dealt with the questions of man, not the acquisition of things."[6] He is mostly right. The world's great philosophers have been spiritualists like Socrates, Plato, Augustine, Kant, and Hegel, not materialists like Marx, Hobbes, and Holbach. Socrates, Plato, and Augustine were not moral relativists, and Marx, Holbach, and Hobbes were not great philosophers. Western antimaterialist conceptions of the good life actually began with the father of philosopher, Socrates, who claimed, "I spend all my time going about trying to persuade you, young and old, to make your first concern not your bodies or your possessions but the highest welfare of your souls."[7] The greatest work in Western political philosophy, Plato's *Republic*, criticized materialism. Plato insisted that truth and subsequent happiness lie in the immaterial realm, what he called the form or idea. Plato's ideas inspired many early Christian thinkers, so naturally they, and their followers, Reagan among them, minimized material concerns.

Helping the poor is good, but not if it comes at the expense of freedom.[8] One supersedes the other. For this reason many conservatives continue to push for "faith-based" poverty relief programs, which, in contrast to government-run relief programs such as welfare, do not rely on taxes and are strictly volunteer, thereby maximizing freedom while also helping the poor. Reagan advocated soup kitchens and other, similar programs to help the poor, arguing that churches had a "duty" to assist the needy.[9] Material considerations were not absent from Reagan's thought; they were just secondary. This prioritization allowed citizens to maintain their freedom while simultaneously helping meet the needs of the poor.

The Kingdom of Freedom is the end of humankind, at least until the Kingdom of God arrives. In Platonic terms, freedom, like form (idea), is something greater than any one of us. What is humanity for? Plato argued that it was for seeking the immaterial form; Christians reply it is for finding the spiritual God and His immaterial riches; and Reagan insisted that all goodness and beauty can be found in freedom. When man finds freedom, he finds the good life. Freedom transcends race, class, culture, gender, and religion. Reagan writes in a private letter to a couple who came to the United States from the Soviet Union, "I dream of a day when all of the world['s] people can know this freedom and escape from communist rule. I promise you that I shall do everything I can to preserve the freedom that you have found here."[10] Continuing the Socratic, Platonic, Ciceronian, and Christian traditions that argued for a timeless, perfect concept that transcends all cultural and temporal values, Reagan believed in one law, and this law was freedom. Like the Kingdom of God, Reagan felt, freedom is a universal realm that we must actively seek. Rich and poor, men and women, American, Russian, Pole, and Iraqi, all deserve to find this highest good. The Kingdom of Freedom does not discriminate. All are welcome to enjoy its righteousness.

Reagan's leading biographer, Lou Cannon, recognized the religious passion Reagan had for freedom when he wrote, "Reagan believed in the magic of individual freedom. He believed that the appeal of free markets and personal freedoms ultimately would prove irresistible to all people everywhere. He believed in spreading the gospel of freedom."[11] Reagan reconciled the most powerful concept of the Middle Ages, God and his Kingdom, with the dominant idea of our time: freedom. Fused together, the two form a coherent cosmology and ethical system that provides not just the foundation for Reagan's thought but the key component in conservative policy. This Hegelian interpretation that stresses synthesis insists that Reagan reconciled the two most powerful ideas in Western history, forging a cosmology that combines the best elements of Christian and modern values.

Freedom has always reigned supreme in America. "An empire of liberty" is what Jefferson desired for America, initiating America's freedom-centered cultural history. Since the founding of the republic, an influential strand of political thought has argued that a powerful government infringes on the rights and liberties of its people. During the creation of the new republic, all of the Founding Fathers agreed that some sort of constitution was necessary in order to safeguard the rights of citizens against a strong central authority, such as a hereditary king. Yet whereas Federalists believed that the original Articles of Confederation (1781) were too weak and needed a stronger central authority, anti-Federalists argued that a strong central authority would usurp both state and individual rights. They drew inspiration from two eighteenth-century British sources, *Cato's Letters* by John Trenchard and Thomas Gordon and *Political Disquisitions* by James Burgh. Both works agreed that the love of power is natural and that in order to curb it, government must be limited. An inverse relationship existed between the power of the government and freedom: the more powerful the government, the less freedom the people have. Continuing this, anti-Federalists maintained that the strong central government proposed by the Federalists fostered the tyranny that caused the Revolutionary War, so they fought for a weak central government in order to maximize individual rights and freedoms. In order to placate the fears of the anti-Federalists, the Bill of Rights was implemented, with its promise of certain rights and liberties, such as the freedom of speech and the right to bear arms, thus keeping the central government in check. If the goal of the new nation was to protect liberty, the thinking went, the constitution had to keep the central government as weak as possible. Reagan descends from this tradition.

Strong monarchs dominate European history, some of whom are glorified even today, but for the American people there are no examples of leaders who centralize control. . In contrast to most nations, American history lacks a single great king. In fact America was created as a reaction against a strong, central leader. King George III—the only king American children ever encounter in grade school—is a bête noir in American history.

The Enlightenment era saw the first debates about the proper type of government. From the dawn of civilization until the seventeenth century, most Westerners were ruled by a king or an emperor. The Sumerians, the Greeks (with the unique exception of the Athenians), the Romans, the barbarian tribes, and most European nations were ruled by a single, authoritarian ruler. In the Middle Ages this ruler reigned by "divine right." This system began to break down during the Enlightenment, however, when ideas appeared that weakened the traditional relationship between the rulers and the ruled, bringing, in theory, more freedom to society. The Scientific Revolution discredited parts the Bible as literal truth, and subsequent Enlightenment philosophers believed society could be transformed and improved by eliminating traditional Christian morality and, by extension, the idea that God had placed kings on the throne to rule over others as subjects.

The French Enlightenment began with Voltaire, and Voltaire's intellectual odyssey began in England. Admiring the freedom he found during his exile in England, Voltaire proclaimed, "An English man, as a free man, goes to Heaven by whatever way he pleases."[12] He and other Enlightenment philosophes felt that freedom needed to be contrasted with a powerful church and state. Even Rousseau, who hardly fits the Enlightenment mold and was an enemy of Voltaire, contended, "With liberty, wherever abundance reigns, well-being also reigns."[13] He also wrote, "To renounce liberty is to renounce being a man, to surrender the rights of humanity and even its duties. For he who renounces everything no indemnity is possible. Such a renunciation is incompatible with man's nature;

to remove all liberty from his will is to remove all morality from his acts."[14] Rousseau's friend David Hume wrote in his famous *History of England*, "We, in this island have ever since enjoyed, if not the best system of government, at least the most entire system of liberty that ever was known amongst mankind."[15] Attempting to summarize the entire Enlightenment era, Diderot maintained, "Every age has its own dominant idea, that of our age seems to be liberty."[16] Diderot did not celebrate justice, equality, nature, or peace; these were subordinated to freedom. The significance of the Enlightenment for Western civilization lies in the philosophes' championing of liberty.

Conceptions of and demands for liberty litter the Middle Ages— from St. Augustine's City of God to the speech by Pope Urban II that inaugurated the Crusades—but Enlightenment philosophers made liberty the foundation of their ethical philosophy. The Enlightenment elevated freedom to an ethical end. Political freedom, religious freedom, free trade, freedom of speech, and freedom of the press reign in a just world. During the Enlightenment freedom became an end in itself, a cherished noble virtue, even greater than God for some. Enlightenment thinkers argued that governments should be judged on how well they promoted freedom, not on how well they served God. This was a radical new idea. In creating a new Western culture, Enlightenment philosophes were the first freedom fighters. They attempted to rupture Western civilization from its Christian heritage by placing the freedom of man above everything else. For the philosophes, man was *Homo libertas*.

The ideas of Voltaire and his contemporaries must be contextualized by an understanding of the absolutist time period that characterized the age, proving their distaste for a strong, centralized state. Louis XIV and Louis XV were the two most absolutist monarchs in history; all power was concentrated in their hands and in the hands of their small clique of advisors. Aristocrats provided military and political support for the monarchy yet were always subordinate. This centralized system of government, a government that consolidates all power, was what most of the philosophes rejected. Montesquieu, for example, declared, "When the legislative and executive powers are united in the same person, or in the same body of magistrates, there can be no freedom."[17] They were not radical republicans (defined as those who wanted no king at all), nor did they believe in participatory democracy, but they associated a strong central government with tyranny. In order to thwart tyranny, we must weaken (the central) government.

One of the most controversial aspects of Enlightenment thought was its insistence on free trade. In contrast to the mercantilist economic philosophy, which advocated an active government that embraced tariffs in order to limit imports, leading eighteenth-century economic theorists argued that productive workers, if left alone, would create national wealth. Adam Smith preached specialization, the breaking down of large jobs into smaller components so that each worker becomes an expert in one specific area, thus increasing that worker's productivity. Wealthy nations have workers who produce goods of value. Smith's quintessential Enlightenment laissez-faire economic ideas meant that, at least in the macro economy, government interference must be limited. Smith championed a free economy, which led him to this observation: "Every workman has a great quantity of his own work to dispose of beyond what he himself has occasion for; and every other workman being exactly in the same situation, he is enabled to exchange a great quantity of his own goods for a great quantity, or, what comes to the same thing, for the price of a great quantity of theirs. He supplies them abundantly with what they have occasion for, and they accommodate him as amply with what he has occasion for, and a general plenty diffuses itself through all the different ranks of the society."[18] Never a true economic libertarian because he believed government should play a role in promoting education, Smith's ideas nonetheless laid the foundation for classical liberal economic thought, which holds that government intervention retards growth and prosperity. Herein lie the origins of "trickle-down" economics.

Smith wasn't the only laissez-faire Enlightenment thinker, just the most famous one. Montesquieu felt that commerce and free trade even promote peace, because "two nations who traffic with each other become mutually dependent . . . and thus their union is founded on their mutual necessities."[19] Anne Robert Jacques Turgot, the Enlightenment's second-most influential economic theorist, believed that economic barriers hindered progress. Economic inequality was necessary for technological innovation to occur, he contended. Smith and Turgot were particularly popular among philosophes and early revolutionary leaders, as well as economic theorists in the nineteenth century. A man who exerted influence on both sides of the Atlantic, Thomas Paine, took a similar position: "I have been an advocate for commerce, because I am a friend to its effects. It is a pacifist system, operating to unite mankind by rendering nations, as well as individuals, useful to each other. . . . If commerce were permitted to act to the universal extent it is capable of, it would extirpate the system of war and produce a revolution in the uncivilized state of government."[20] This free-market ideology gradually took the name "liberalism." It is often called "classical liberalism" today in order to distinguish it from twenty-first-century liberalism that doesn't necessary vest faith in the free market. Besides free markets, nineteenth-century classical liberals demanded freedom of speech, freedom of religion, free elections, and equality before the law. Classical liberals drew from the Enlightenment and attempt to apply Enlightenment ideas to government and society. They tried to politically implement Enlightenment ideas about the natural freedom of man. Despite the fact that liberal thinkers were blamed for the excesses of the French Revolution (tens of thousands killed in the Reign of Terror, millions more in the ensuing Napoleonic Wars), Enlightenment works exploded in popularity in the early nineteenth century, including in the United States.

The free-market liberal ideas of classical liberals like Smith and Turgot would be refined by Frederic Bastiat in the middle of the nineteenth century. Bastiat remains a favorite of American conservatives, and his 1850 work *On Law* was part of Reagan's private library. Hazlitt utilized Bastiat, probably leading to Reagan's interest in the French thinker. While reading this work, Reagan would have encountered passages like the following:

God has implanted in mankind all that is necessary for them to accomplish their destinies. He has provided a social form as well as a human form. And these social organs of persons are so constituted that they will develop themselves harmoniously in the grand air of liberty. Away, then, with quacks and organizers! Away with their rings, chains, hooks, and pincers! Away with their artificial systems! Away with the whims of governmental administrators, their socialized projects, their centralization, their tariffs, their government schools, their state religions, their free credit, their bank monopolies, their regulations, their restrictions, their equalization by taxation, and their pious moralizations! And now that the legislators and do-gooders have so futilely inflicted so many systems upon society, may they finally end where they should have begun: May they reject all systems, and try liberty; for liberty is an acknowledgment of faith in God and His works.[21]

One hundred years before Hayek and von Mises, Bastiat criticized government planning, insisting that freedom comes from God.

The spread of liberalism favored by Bastiat was uneven and inconsistent, however. On the one hand, liberals won important battles, such as universal male suffrage, which was achieved in the United States, England, and France in the first half of the nineteenth century, yet on the other hand, this was a time of tremendous social upheaval engendered by the Industrial Revolution. With the onset of the new capitalist economy favored by liberals, as prescribed by the economic theorists above, lives had not universally gotten better by the middle of the 1800s, as Smith, Condorcet, and Bastiat had promised. Instead, at least for millions of new workers, misery triumphed. Harsh working conditions and child labor characterize this age. Laissez-faire economic policies wrought great wealth for some by hastening the decline of the landed aristocracy in favor of the bourgeoisie, but this wealth remained a distant dream for workers. Enlightenment thinking had brought both success and failure, so it still needed some tinkering. The leading voices for reform came from Germany.

In Germany the seeds of anti-Enlightenment thought date back to the upheavals of the French Revolution, when, counting the victims of the Napoleonic Wars, millions lost their lives. In many respects Napoleon was a liberal, as he advocated education, constitutions, and equality under the law, but in Germany he was viewed as the anti-Christ. The French Revolution, coupled with the Industrial Revolution, spawned a new intellectual and cultural movement in Germany called romanticism. Romantics blamed Enlightenment figures and their obsession with reason and science for social chaos. They believed that reason does not create a better world, but instead stifles creativity. The maxim of the romantic movement was "I feel, therefore I am." Harkening back to the Middle Ages, romantics glorified the countryside and collectivism because to them, rampant individualism led not to freedom but to misery, as demonstrated by the hollow existence of the working class. True freedom, they felt, must be understood in relationship to other people. The concept of the *Volk* (the people) comes from this era. It explicitly asserts that the group trumps the individual. J. G. Herder, for example, minimized the importance of individuals, stressing culture instead. He argued that each culture is unique, possessing its own language, history, philosophy, and literature.

Probably the most important intellectual source of nineteenth-century anti-Enlightenment philosophy was, in fact, the Enlightenment philosophe J. J. Rousseau. Rousseau was a contrarian among contrarians, as demonstrated by his skepticism toward science and an epistemology based on emotion more than on reason. Like Nietzsche in the next century, when his philosopher brethren zigged, he zagged. Although Rousseau desired freedom and rejected many French social and political institutions that characterized the Ancient Regime he questioned the Anglo (which would become American) conceptions of freedom. Shaping the views of twentieth-century social critics like Herbert Marcuse and Theodor Adorno, Rousseau pointed out that freedom is more than voting and having freedom of speech and to worship. While his peers, especially Voltaire, celebrated the English system, with its (relative) religious tolerance and limited monarchy, Rousseau questioned this system: "The English people believes itself to be free; it is gravely mistaken; it is free only during the election of Members of Parliament; as soon as the Members are elected, the people is enslaved; it is nothing."[22] Rousseau's concept of the general will attempted to reconcile the ideal of freedom with the needs of society. The general will is the common good of society, and it should never be opposed. It curbs rampant individualism by projecting a virtue that transcends individuals. It's collectivist. Rousseau's popularity among nineteenth-century romantics and socialists, coupled with his conception that people are "forced to be free," has led some to argue that he contributed to the totalitarian systems of the twentieth century. Individual rights and liberties play a secondary role among all of Rousseau's disciples, which include most nineteenth-century German intellectuals.

This is the intellectual context for Marxism, the foremost intellectual nemesis of Reagan and American conservatives. Arguably, Marx did little more than put a material spin on Hegel's thought by adopting Hegel's dialectic, dualism, teleology, and emphasis on history. Hegel argued that history progresses due to conflict between two antagonistic ideas, the thesis and the antithesis; Marx substituted classes for ideas. The history of the world is the history of class struggle. Each era has its own ruling and ruled class, oppressor and oppressed. The ancient era witnessed the struggle between citizen and slave, the Middle Ages between lord and serf, and the modern era, Marx's era, between the bourgeoisie and the proletariat, or between the wealthy factory owners and the working class. The proletarians need the bourgeoisie for their material existence, just as the bourgeoisie rely on the workers to perpetuate the capitalist system. Neither group, contrary to what they are taught and what they believe, exercises any freedom in this ghastly system. Defying Enlightenment principles, Marx called free trade the most unconscionable of all freedoms. For Marx, all so-called freedoms, such as parliamentary forms of government, were mere pseudo-democracies, serving the interests of only the bourgeoisie class. In effect the world's most powerful socialist thinker created a New Left, a left—distinct from classical liberals—that after the social chaos wrought by the Industrial Revolution sought to temper, if not completely overthrow, the malignant capitalist system.

Marx condemned attempts to spread bourgeois freedom around the world, for example voting and free speech. He believed that all attempts to spread bourgeois freedom were economically motivated because all reality can be reduced to economics. Philosophers call the study of reality metaphysics, and Marx's metaphysics can be defined in two words: *economic determinism*. All history, political systems, ideas, morality, religion, elections, laws, wars, and vast amounts of other human behavior are guided by economics. In twenty-first-century American political discourse, this means that wars are fought for oil, the wealthy create laws in their own interests, and corporations give us the news they want us to hear. We are all slaves to the economic interests of the wealthy. America is an oligarchy, not a democracy, because the government merely represents the wealthy elite. Maybe the best way to understand economic determinism is to realize that it is merely the idea that God controls most events turned on its head: economics is providential, argue Marxists. It guides everything.

The real roots of bourgeois attempts to spread democracy lie in the desire to spread capitalism, Marx believed. The French and American revolutions must be understood as the bourgeoisie's attempts to expand their political power and create a political system that benefits them, or parliamentary democracy. World War I and World War II must be understood as conflicts between capitalists in their search for new markets. Only by eliminating bourgeois freedom, capitalism, and subsequent exploitation can we achieve real freedom. Upon the inevitable death of capitalism there will arise a new society: "In place of the old bourgeois society, with its classes and class antagonism, we shall have an association, in which the free development of each is the condition for the free development of all."[23] Marx's ultimate end is a world of utopian freedom, but not the type of freedom that those of us living in Western democracies assume. Influenced by romanticism, this freedom is not achieved by rampant individualism but must be placed within the context of the group. For Marx and many subsequent left-wing writers, freedom comes only once we have equality; freedom exists in relation to others. Marx slammed traditional Enlightenment thought and its advocacy for free trade because he believed free trade is really only free for the bourgeoisie. One of Marx's most famous disciples, the Marxist revolutionary Che Guevara, wrote, "We have already described the guerilla fighter as one who shares the longing of liberation, who once peaceful means are exhausted, initiates the fight. . . . From the very beginning of the struggle he has the intention of destroying an unjust order."[24] Thus, according to Guevara, capitalism breeds unfairness, and true liberation occurs only when capitalism and Western notions of democracy are eradicated.

Unfortunately "Marxism" has become a pejorative term, so describing the Marxist influence on our society and culture can be a sensitive subject, but whereas Enlightenment philosophes favored a free economy, after Marx leftists favored a more tempered capitalism, one concerned with the lower classes and Marx's protagonist, urban dwellers. For Marx, free-market capitalism favors the bourgeoisie, or upper classes, at the expense of the lower classes, but conservatives like Reagan begged to differ, insisting that free trade benefits all. They proudly look to Adam Smith for intellectual justification. The contemporary conservative, including Reagan, blends Enlightenment (especially its economic side) and Christian elements, while the contemporary left wing marries Enlightenment ideas (especially its social ideas) with Marxism in order to create a comprehensive cosmology and fundamental value system. Both cosmologies are ethical cosmologies as well as metaphysical systems that attempt to explain the world. They should never be underestimated when trying to understand interpretations of reality, both past and present.

How can both the American left and right draw inspiration from the same intellectual movement? The Enlightenment was the handmaiden of America, so both sides of the political spectrum have inherited some of its principles. Modern American conservatives like Reagan have grafted its free-market principles onto their conservative social values. Conservatives thus may fairly be described as "classical liberals," at least economically. Their economic thought was the original liberal philosophy, until the rise of Marxism. Modern American conservatives believe that freedom benefits everyone. Contemporary leftists, however, assert class distinction, in the tradition of Marx. This division of the world into two classes (rich and poor) descends as well from the German intellectual tradition. The German Marxist Adorno epitomizes the sentiment by contending, "People have so manipulated the concept of freedom that it finally boils down to the right of the stronger and richer to take from the weaker and poorer whatever they have left."[25] According to this view, class precedes freedom. The more freedom the rich have, the more oppressed the poor are. Yet for Reagan and conservatives, rich and poor collaborate to form society and the economy. Since the two classes are related, what is good for one is good for the other. For the left, the relationship between rich and poor is antagonistic; everything that helps the wealthy (e.g., tax cuts) hurts the poor. Since the rich keep getting richer, the poor must get poorer. Reagan's trickle-down theory asserts a direct relationship between rich and poor: whatever benefits the wealthy will ultimately help the poor too. After all, rich and poor are not separate classes. Giving one group freedom helps everyone. Republicans like to cite John F. Kennedy, who argued, "A rising tide lifts all boats."[26] These two philosophies, at their core, are merely a continuation of an economic debate between classical Enlightenment economic liberals (whom today we call conservatives) and the more socialist-minded.

Reagan and Equality

But economic freedom does create economic equality. In his biography of Reagan, John Sloan contended, "Since the quest for equality is such a vital component of the American political culture, I believe that Reagan's ridicule of attempts to promote social justice will lessen the chances of his being evaluated as a great moral leader by anyone other than his most conservative supporters."[27] Insisting that Reagan ridicules equality oversimplifies the issue because it assumes only one type of equality: economic. In fact,

Reagan's domestic philosophy is premised on the equality of all people. To be sure, equality has played a pivotal role in shaping America. I would contend that it is not the socialist equality many of Reagan's critics pine for, but another type of equality that epitomizes the Anglo-American cultural tradition: political equality.

One of the intellectual fathers of the Enlightenment and America, John Locke, argued that in the state of nature, people are free and equal: "Man being, as has been said, by nature all free, equal and independent, no one can be put out of his estate and subject to the political power of another without his own consent, which is done by agreeing with other men, to join and unite into a community for their comfortable, safe and peaceable living, one amongst another, in a secure enjoyment of their properties."[28] Equality and liberty are linked. When people impose their will on others (including in the material sphere), equality is reduced. In a system with political equality, people are not governed by an elite power (e.g., a hereditary king or a powerful government) but rather govern themselves. People are free because they are equal. Equality and freedom, therefore, are not maximized by a powerful government but rather by a weak one, where ordinary people make the decisions that shape their lives, or at least do so through their elected representatives. This position rejected Plato, who favored an aristocratic form of government because he held that people are inherently unequal.

Marx contended that freedom comes once we have equality, but for Locke, freedoms come because we are equal. Locke argued that all differences arise merely from experience, so no one person or group deserves special privileges without explicit consent. A contract exists between the governors and the governed, Locke believed, and when the governors do not live up to their end of the contract, the people have the right to break the chains that tie them to their government. Why? Because we are equal. These ideas provide the intellectual foundation for modern democracy and for limited government.

Like Locke, most Enlightenment thinkers preached some sort of primitive and theoretical equality; this was rarely extended to the economic sphere. With a couple of exceptions, most condemned any attempts to level society economically. Holbach, for one, believed that fostering economic equality would only abridge freedom. Those who worked hardest, he argued, should be rewarded the most.[29] Nothing promoted misery more than the abolition of private property for the leading Federalist, John Adams.[30] Jefferson, whose credentials as an advocate for equality are impeachable, rejected a powerful central government. Traces of socialism can be found in the works of Rousseau, but Rousseau was hardly a characteristic Enlightenment thinker. Rousseau's general will, Herder's belief in the significance of groups, and Marx's critiques of bourgeois capitalism are all anti-Enlightenment ideas, so they are on the fringes of the American cultural heritage. The intense debates between Federalists and anti-Federalists in the eighteenth century lacked socialist ideas. The Federalist Party preferred a larger and more powerful federal government because they sought to promote stability, not economic equality. This doesn't invalidate any attempts to use government to promote economic equality; it just places it outside of American traditions.

The greatest student of nineteenth-century American equality was Alexis de Tocqueville. The French aristocrat admired the equality he found in America: "The more I advanced in the study of American society, the more I perceived that this equality of condition is the fundamental fact from which all others seem to be derived."[31] It wasn't economic equality, or material condition, that defined America for Tocqueville. It was an abstract equality that precedes economic equality. It's the equality that leads to freedom, as described by Locke. When Tocqueville came to America, he was struck by the fact that no man bowed before another. Why not? Because we are all equal! More so than in European countries, Americans are equal in their relationships. No one man or group of people should govern others without their explicit consent.

This is the equality that Reagan promoted. It isn't economic equality but a belief that all people really are equal. Reagan declared in 1964, "This is the issue of this election. Whether we believe in our capacity for self-government or whether we abandon the

American Revolution and confess that a little intellectual elite in a far-distant capital can plan our lives for us better than we can plan them ourselves."[32] Equality (as opposed to elitism) is practiced by shrinking the size and scope of the federal government, creating a more equitable power distribution. The larger the government, the weaker the citizen. The government expands by taking power from the people, Reagan believed.

Some scholars have a hard time accepting that the right actually seeks power to the masses. Corey Robin begins his unsympathetic analysis of the conservative mind with this typical description of our modern era: "Since the modern era began, men and women in subordinate positions have marched against their superiors in the state, church, workplace and other hierarchal institutions . . . and shouted different slogans about freedom, equality, rights, democracy and revolution. In virtually every instance, their superiors have resisted them, violently and non-violently, legally and illegally, covertly and overtly. The march and demarche of democracy is the story of modern politics or at least one of its stories."[33] Robin reduces history to two sides: his side, the left, which believes in freedom, progress, and power for the masses, and conservatives. Robin interprets twenty-first-century conservatism through a nineteenth-century Marxist prism because he asserts the centrality of class distinction: "Historically, the conservative has favored liberty for the higher orders and constraint for the lower orders."[34] This was truer of Marx's age than it is today. Robin's account ignores twentieth-century history, specifically real experiments with socialism and economic equality. In practice, socialism leads to political power in the hands of those in government, and for conservatives, too much power in the hands of the few reduces political equality. Reagan and his disciples saw themselves as being on the side of the powerless who fight against an ever-expanding government, in the name of equality. Twenty-first-century conservatives, such as those in the Tea Party, who marched against expanding government, fight against those who wield power. Robin counters that the Tea Party protestors are related to the conservative reactionaries of the nineteenth century. And he is right. They are related, but critical differences exist too, just as a child is simultaneously related to and different from his or her parents. There are similarities and differences between nineteenth-century and twenty-first-century conservatives. Ideologies (and even religions) change over time. Some progressive beliefs change too. Early twenty-first-century progressives don't mimic all of the beliefs of their early twentieth-century progenitors. (Early twenty-first-century progressives were far more likely to adhere to Christianity, for example.) Conservatives and progressive both change over time. They are different, yet related.

Robin, following Marx, would contend there is more political equality under socialism than under capitalism because there is more economic equality. That is debatable. From the conservative perspective, socialism breeds political inequality because those few who hold the levers of power in government control the system. Conservatives contend that socialism leads to rule of the few over the many. Even Marx recognized this. Socialism, for him, was just a transitory episode that paved the way for communism, when true freedom and equality would reign.

Marx made economic equality a precondition for political equality, and it may be argued that socialism promotes equality because the poorest Americans become materially and socially equal with the wealthiest Americans, then they exert equal political power. By cutting welfare spending, these people claim, we are only giving more to those who already have material wealth. This leads to political inequality. The most contemporary proponent of the idea that freedom requires equality was the American political philosopher John Rawls. Rawls published his *Theory of Justice* in 1971 (the same year Reagan passed welfare reform in California), arguing that only in theory is one allowed to pursue freedom in an ideal society. Rawls critiqued freedom, insisting that first everyone must have an equal opportunity to achieve freedom. Moreover, he insisted, there must be limitations on freedom because if everyone freely pursues their own ends, mass inequality will ensue, denying some their rightful chance at freedom. He stressed justice and fairness. Rawls wasn't a communist, but his philosophy was more community-oriented than the classical economic approach favored by Smith, Turgot, and Montesquieu (all of whom had been influenced by Locke) and their classical liberal disciples, who by the 1970s were becoming the Republican Party.

A new twentieth-century conservatism burgeoned, reacting against Soviet socialism and other forms of state planning. Explaining his shift away from the Democratic Party, Reagan said in 1976, "I was once a Democrat myself and I believed that party represented our core values faithfully. . . . But the intellectual and political leadership of [the] Democratic Party changed. The party was taken over by elitists who believed that only they could plan properly the lives of the people."[35] Reagan was at the vanguard of a new conservative movement, one deeply committed to democracy, equality, and populism. Populism is premised on the idea that all people really are equal. These concepts were originally advanced by left-wing thinkers in the nineteenth century and opposed by traditional conservatives. But the 1960s also saw the advent of a New Right. It championed populism by contrasting itself with socialism; state planning became elitism. Reagan's new conservative populism challenged "big government" and quasi-socialist, New Left liberalism. This is how Reagan helped pave the way for Trump and his alleged populism.

Critics of conservative populism call it anti-intellectualism. There is some truth in this because populism minimizes the power of the intellectual class too. A radical idea? Not necessarily. It's completely consistent with modern democracy, wherein everyone, regardless of their intelligence level or political education (just to name one intellectual skill) get precisely one vote. The educated and uneducated, the wise person and the dunce, get the same number of votes. Why? Because we are in fact equal. Those who preach intellectualism, wittingly or not, promote a system in which power is unevenly distributed, particularly favoring those with certain intellectual credentials. Why should the intellectual classes wield more power over society? In his Pulitzer Prize–winning work, *Anti-Intellectualism in American Life* (1963), Richard Hofstadter insists, "Anti-intellectualism was not manifested in this country for the first time in the 1950s. Our anti-intellectualism is, in fact, older than our national identity, and has a long historical background."[36] Hofstadter continues that America's egalitarianism leads to a distrusting of those with alleged expertise.

At the same time Reagan was promoting this new conservative populism, Russell Kirk was preaching against it. Kirk asserted that populism is merely "a revolt against the smart guys."[37] Today it's American conservatives who more often rebel against "the smart guys." Reagan led this rebellion. Late in his life the archconservative Kirk lambasted the burgeoning neoconservative movement, wistful for a return to the old conservatism of Burke, a conservatism opposed to radical change and popular democracy. Traditional conservatives, like the nineteenth-century Austrian aristocrat Metternich, writing in the wake of the French Revolution, believed maintaining traditional social patterns was less disruptive to life. They were skeptical of change and freedom. Reagan, in contrast, sought change. Specifically he wanted more freedom for American citizens, and even for the people of Eastern Europe. Neoconservatives are heirs to this tradition. They are not traditional conservatives precisely because they reject the hierarchical and elitist values of traditional conservatives like Burke, Metternich, and Kirk.

Accordingly, Reagan quoted the nineteenth-century abolitionist Henry Ward Beecher (1867): "The real American idea is not that every man shall be on a level with every other, but that every man shall have the liberty . . . to be what God made him."[38] Beecher, one of the leading Christian proponents of equality in nineteenth-century America, believed in the equality of all men, but this didn't mean economic equality. It meant liberty. He writes about democratic American man, "There shall be no prejudice against him if he be high; and that no disgrace shall attach him if he be low; that he shall have supreme possession of what is his and what he has; that he shall have liberty to use his forces in any proper direction; that whether he be born of Caucasian, African or Indian parents, he shall have all the rights which God have him."[39] Beecher, who spent time in England defending the North's cause in the Civil War, is just one example that Henry

Steele Commager used in his work about the American mind. Commager writes, "Intellectually eighteenth century America was very much part of the European Enlightenment—particularly in its English, Scottish and French Manifestations."[40] The German intellectual movement that entered the United States after World War II was a distinct intellectual movement, one separate from America's intellectual heritage. It is more socialist, seeking more economic equality. This underscores my argument about Reagan's working within the traditional American cultural milieu, while many of his opponents are descended from a different European tradition, one at odds with America's heritage. This partly explains why self-described conservatives outnumber self-described liberals by a 3.5 to 2.5 margin in the United States.[41] Reagan's political ideas cannot be completely separated from American cultural history.

It's hard to argue against American cultural history. Twentieth-century America produced some of the greatest achievements in human history, including, but by no means limited to, rescuing Europeans from themselves in three world wars (including the cold war), putting a man on the moon, and creating the personal computer, quite possibly the most significant invention in the past five hundred years. Reagan extolled American virtues, history, and contributions: "In the past thirty years, we have fought three wars and helped rebuild the countries that were devastated by those wars. We have given more than $150 billion of our national resources to help our friends—and even some of our former enemies—to become economically self-sufficient. We have opened our own markets to imports because we believe in the principles of free trade."[42] Scholars still have not satisfactorily answered the critical question of why Germans, Italians, and the French were deluded by Nazi, fascist, socialist, and communist ideologies, while these ideas appeared only on the fringes of the American political scene. Are American voters smarter? Doubtful. The best answer comes from analyzing the Anglo-American cultural heritage, especially its emphasis on individual rights and freedoms. The radical European ideologies of socialism, communism, Nazism, and fascism all promised better worlds, as long as the people were willing to sacrifice some of their individual rights and liberties. Americans resisted.

American culture has helped make America the richest nation on earth; its middle-class citizens enjoy a wealth unknown to much of the world. Reagan explicitly rejected the idea common among Enlightenment thinkers like Montesquieu and Jefferson that climate or environment explains why some nations are richer than others, insisting in 1967 that "backward nations are backward and underdeveloped nations are underdeveloped not because of their climate and not because of their soil." Instead Reagan reduced American economic power to the American capitalist system, or freedom:

> In the United States we have been blessed, not alone by our natural resources—other nations have great resources, too—but by our people, the world's most industrious, ingenious, enterprising and inventive, and by our political system—one of the few devised by man that is both stable and free. Stable enough to let a prosperous economy evolve and free enough to allow initiative and ingenuity to triumph over the dead hand of bureaucracy and regulation. . . . Here we unleashed the genius of every man by giving him freedom to an extent never known before by man anywhere.[43]

He reiterated these ideas in a radio address nine years late:

> Our productivity is phenomenal. We raise 37% more wheat per acre than the world average. We are 6% of the world's population on only 7% of the world's land, but we produce almost half of the world's corn, 2/3 of its soy beans, 1/3 or more of the world's paper, electrical power, college graduates and 1/3 of the farm machinery. Just to round it off we make more than 2/3 of its computers & 80% of all passenger aircraft. . . . All this because our system freed the individual genius of man. Release[d] him to fly as high and as far as his own talent & energy would take him.[44]

Reagan related freedom to productivity. Productive workers, by definition, produce goods and services of value to society. They

bring wealth to a nation. Feeding soldiers and innovating tech-
nologically leads to military victory, and this is what America has
done better than any other country else in the twentieth century.
More than any other society in history, the United States has an
ample supply of guns and butter. Why is America so rich? Is it
because of its exploitative history? European countries engaged in
slavery and exploitative nineteenth-century imperialism far more
brutally than did the United States. American freedom explains
everything for Reagan:

> We have a very visible example of the contrast between the
> free market and government ownership in a household neces-
> sity we take for granted. The invention of Alexander Graham
> Bell—the telephone offers us irrefutable proof of the superi-
> ority of the free market. As recently as 1880 there were only
> 34,000 miles of telephone wires on the whole North Ameri-
> can continent. There were dozens and dozens of small tele-
> phone companies using several different kinds of equipment
> and there was no inter-connection between these different com-
> panies. The same situation prevailed in all the other so-called
> advanced nations. If someone had openly advanced a plan to
> put a phone in every home, on every farm, in every hamlet &
> city and hook them all together I'm sure someone would have
> said, "only govt. has the resources to do that."[45]

Many leftists promote public or communal ownership of what Marx
called the modes of production, or the ways human produce material goods. Reagan, on the other hand, argued for private ownership. By minimizing government influence, we promote freedom
and subsequently creativity, productivity, and ultimately national
wealth. For Reagan, history has vindicated the American capitalist system.

Some have interpreted the American capitalist system as selfish-
ness. Reagan counters, "We are generous people. We have shared
our wealth more widely among our people than any society heretofore known to man. We support more churches, more libraries,
more symphonies, and operas, and more nonprofit theaters than

any other country. We publish more books than the rest of the world put together. . . . Now all we need is to be reminded of our destiny—that God intended America to be free; to be the Golden hope of all mankind."[46] America is a beacon of hope for the rest of the world, just as it was during World War I, when Armageddon characterized the Western Front before American involvement; during World War II, as Nazism enveloped Europe; during the Korean War, when communist forces invaded the democratic south; when Stalin blockaded Berlin in 1948; and when the Berlin Wall was constructed and the West Germans pleaded for American intervention.

America was different from other nations, Reagan believed. Besides its love of God and liberty, it had another unique characteristic. He proclaimed at the end of World War II, "America stands unique in the world—founded not on a race but on a way and an ideal."[47] Decades later Reagan described a letter he received from a man who reminded him, "You can go live in France, but you cannot become a Frenchman; you can go to Germany, but you cannot become an German. . . . But anyone, from any corner of the world, can come to live in America and become an American."[48] Whereas Marxists deplored America as a force of capitalism and therefore misery in the world, Reagan had a different attitude: America, the harbinger of light and freedom, was a positive force in the world. Having defeated evil ideologies like Nazism and Japanese fascism, America even helped rebuild those countries that had tried to kill our young men and women. Tens of billions—hundreds of billions in today's dollars—were spent in hopes of improving lives ravaged by war. What better evidence for American generosity could there possibly be?

Reagan: The Amiable Dunce, or, What Did Reagan Know?

Reagan was an avid reader and writer. One of his former speechwriters who has combed through most of Reagan's pre-presidential speeches contends that Reagan wrote at least 500,000 words, or several large books. When asked about his most vivid memory of his father as a child, Michael Reagan replied, "Easy. Back before he became governor, he did a lot of work at his home [in Pacific Palisades]. When I'd get back from school in the afternoon, I'd toss my books and go into the master bedroom to say hello. Dad had a big desk there, and he was always at the desk, writing. Not almost always. Always."[49] Reagan read and wrote more than most twentieth-century presidents. Nonetheless some of his critics believe that he was as dumb as an ox. Even some of his aides disparaged his knowledge. Reagan's deputy national security advisor Robert MacFarlane and his speechwriter Peggy Noonan acknowledge that they questioned Reagan's intellectual abilities. Reagan's biographers are left with the question, What did Reagan know? The answer: way more than he let on.

His ability to convince others that he was naïve worked on many levels. It allowed him to exercise his acting skills and outsmart those who thought they were wise, while being funny and getting the last laugh. Reagan, the actor, was playing his most convincing role, feigning ignorance and disguising the true depth of his knowledge. Reagan was, first and foremost, an actor. He prided himself on this. Edmund Morris revealed that four years after leaving the Oval Office, Reagan returned to Washington to receive the Medal of Freedom. Morris, who spent several years in close proximately with Reagan during his presidency, recounted, "Afterward, in the receiving line, he [Reagan] took my hand and nodded with patent lack of recognition. . . . *Well it had to happen*, I told myself. . . . Dutch [Reagan's nickname] finally stopped recognizing me. Yet the following afternoon, Fred Ryan, his retirement Chief of Staff, called from Los Angeles to say that Reagan had remarked . . . 'I saw Edmund in the reception line this morning. . . . I think he's waiting for me to die before he publishes his book.'"[50] Reagan sometimes pretended not to recognize people. This was his sense of humor, and he was the only one who got the joke. He was one of the funniest presidents of the twentieth century. Upon seeing Nancy after getting shot in 1981, he apologized to her, saying, "Honey, I forgot to duck."[51] Alan Greenspan, a former chair of the Federal Reserve, described Reagan as "a professional comedian, a professional raconteur."[52] His sense of humor ranged from wry to raunchy. I have encountered other figures in history (and in life) who liked to play the role of the village idiot in order to fool those who think they are wise. They think it's funny. And deceiving others can make people feel powerful. It was a game Reagan liked, a game he could never lose. He may not have always been the smartest guy in the room, but by feigning ignorance, he could outsmart those who believed themselves to be superior. They didn't know as much as they thought they knew.

This may explain the oft-cited quote by Clark Clifford that Reagan was an "amiable dunce." The quote appears in many Reagan biographies and it needs to be contextualized. Clifford was the quintessential Washington insider; he advised all Democrat presidents, from Truman through Carter. He wanted to meet President Reagan, so he contacted Michael Deaver, Reagan's deputy chief of staff. Deaver writes, "[Reagan] was in a festive mood, but it soured somewhat when I brought up Clifford. 'Why would I want to meet with Clifford,' Reagan asked, somewhat bemused. . . . Reagan would normally meet with anyone, Democrat or Republican, it didn't matter to him, but some sort of warning signal seemed to go off in his brain. He didn't want to do it, but he left it to me."[53] Finally Reagan acquiesced. However, when Clifford met Reagan in the Oval Office, Deaver recounts, Reagan was subtly different with Clifford than with his hundreds of other guests. "I think he sensed that the old man [Clifford] had come to take his measure, and Reagan—a different drummer in ways both large and small—simply wasn't going to have anything to do with it."[54] As he did with Morris, Reagan may have just been playing a convincing role. It is what he liked to do best.

Reagan's sharp mind displayed itself in a debate with Robert Kennedy in 1967.[55] At the time, Reagan was California's new governor and Kennedy was a senator from New York. The event, broadcast on CBS, was not a formal debate between Reagan and Kennedy but rather a debate between Reagan, Kennedy, and a group of students, most of whom were critical of American foreign policy. Reagan impressed more than Kennedy. Suggesting the debate may be a harbinger of future contests between the two politicians, *News-*

week reported, "The political rookie Reagan . . . left old campaigner Kennedy blinking when the session ended."[56] David Halberstam wrote that the general consensus was that Reagan destroyed Kennedy in the debate.[57] Reagan's intellectual strengths were not his analytical skills, but he was very sharp. He was more intelligent than his detractors claimed.

Reagan's fear of flying meant he crossed the country on trains, an activity more conducive to reading than is flying. Many who met Reagan commented on the small library he always carried with him, filled with works on political philosophy and economics. One early biographer wrote that while interviewing Reagan in his home in 1965, he perused Reagan's personal library. The biographer, Lee Edwards, recounts, "I began pulling the books out of the shelves and looking at them. They were dog-eared. They were annotated. . . . It was clear that he had read them, had digested them, and had studied them."[58] Edwards remembers three of the authors already studied here: Chambers, Hazlitt, and Bastiat. A consultant for Reagan's first gubernatorial campaign noted that Reagan's library was stacked with books on political philosophy.[59] Larry Williams, an actor who appeared with Reagan in five films, recalled, "Statistical information of all sorts was a commodity Ron always had in extraordinary supplies, either carried in his pockets or in his head. Not only was this information abundant, it was stunning in its catholicity. . . . Ron had the dope on just about everything: this quarter's up-or-down figures on GNP growth, V. I. Lenin's grandfather's occupation, all history's baseball pitchers' ERA, the optimistic outlook for sugar-beet production in the year 2000. . . . One could not help but be impressed."[60] Reagan did have a photographic memory. David Gergen, a member of his administration, maintained that Reagan had a "steel-trap mind" for things he read.[61] Reagan wasn't intellectually curious unless he was passionate about the topic, but he was passionate about current events and politics. Milton Friedman said that Reagan "was an intellectual in the sense that he had a real interest in ideas. He read widely and was interested in what was going on."[62]

Reagan's analytical and critical thinking skills understandably left many frustrated. He believed almost everything he read, which became sacred truths for him, but these facts and figures then had to be researched for accuracy by his aides. He sometimes introduced fictional characters into real-life events, no doubt believing they were real. Reagan really did occasionally confuse what he saw in movies with real life. Morris, insisting Reagan liked numbers with lots of zeroes at the end, tells the story of how Reagan once said on TV, "I've been told that something like forty-two trillion rate decisions were given by the ICC [International Commerce Commission] in its eighty-five-year history."[63] Reagan always had facts and figures ready to support his views, and sometimes they were only half true, at best. If he had lived in the twenty-first century instead of the twentieth, one wonders how he would have grappled with the exponential increase in information available. If there were ever a person who needed to heed the adage "Don't believe everything you read on the internet," it was Reagan. Cannon postulates that Reagan never needed to develop any analytic skills early in life because he had a photographic memory that allowed him to succeed all the way through college without much intellectual effort, while his strong people skills and imagination allowed him to thrive in professional environments.[64]

Reagan had little interest in scientific or psychological issues. Intellectuals study the world around them in hopes of understanding and subsequently explaining it. Different academic paradigms offer different ways to understand the world. None of this interested Reagan. He wanted to create a wonderful new world, not understand the one in front of him. Peggy Noonan claimed, "Ronald Reagan did not have the natural talents and cast of mind of a businessman or economist or political figure, he has the natural talents and cast of an artist. . . . And indeed he went all through his life drawing faces, caricatures, designing leather crafts and memorizing poetry."[65] Reagan's intelligence was more intuitive than intellectual; he gathered knowledge by instinctively analyzing what he felt rather than synthesizing what he read. Reagan saw the world as a romantic. Instead of employing reason and logic, which nineteenth-century romantics argued was cold and lifeless, he relied on his instincts and feelings; the world could not be understood only by analysis and calculation.

Even more than his photographic memory, Reagan's greatest intellectual gift was his imagination. Knowledge is important, but it's limited. Imagination is boundless. Only imagination can lead to change and to human improvement, because before any human endeavor exists, it must be imagined. Reagan's imagination surpassed every other post–World War II president. Always more concerned with the way the world could be than with the way it actually was, he was one of the few people who could imagine a world without a Soviet Union, a world bereft of the Berlin Wall, a world without communism.

Reagan preferred concrete examples to abstract thought; as a Hollywood actor, when his personal income taxes sometimes reached 90 percent, Reagan recalled that this discouraged some actors from working, producing, and being creative. Cannon pointed out, "Reagan was an inductive thinker; as economist Annelise Anderson observed, he always thought in concrete examples."[66] In order to discover the truth, Reagan began with his own experiences. They taught him that high tax rates discourage work and creativity, and therefore, in order to increase productivity and wealth, he needed to cut taxes. Inductive thinking begins with experience, believing these experiences to represent reality. For Reagan, this meant that since in his experience a 90 percent tax rate discouraged work, all 90 percent tax rates must discourage work. The problem with this type of reasoning, of course, is that one's experience may not be universal. Just because I see one hundred white swans does not mean that all swans are white. Just because the 90 percent top marginal tax rate discouraged Reagan's peers from working does not mean that such a tax rate would produce the same result at all times.

This inductive epistemology too descends from the Anglo-American intellectual tradition. Comparing it with deductive reasoning helps illuminate why Reagan was often deemed an intellectual simpleton. Philosophers and intellectuals prefer the deductive method, especially on the European Continent, with Descartes, Leibniz, Spinoza, and Marx being the most prominent examples.

Most philosophers prefer deductive reasoning, starting with abstract, theoretical principles they have discovered, such as *Cogito ergo sum* or the idea that the history of the world is a history of class struggle. These do not necessarily derive from immediate experience; they begin with mind. Deductive reasoning allows them to construct comprehensive systems of thought, potentially capable of explaining vast amounts of observed phenomena. Cartesian metaphysics explains a remarkable array of physical, religious, and mental phenomena from the simple notion *Cogito ergo sum*. Marxism magnificently explains all historical events, from the war in Iraq to the rise of Christianity and the French Revolution with one word: economics. The explanatory powers are amazing. Intellectuals are curious people, so Descartes's and Marx's deductions prove seductive, since they provide answers to vexing questions, creating order and rationality in a world that may appear chaotic and unpredictable. Their ideas are to students of the humanities what a unified field theory is to physicists. Of course, if the fundamental principle of deductive reasoning is false, then this type of reasoning falters and everything collapses like a house of cards. What if my thinking does not prove my existence? What if the history of the world is not the history of class struggle? All beliefs, all deductions are invalidated. Basing all opinions on an opinion (regardless of how secure we find this opinion to be) is therefore epistemologically risky.

The German intellectual tradition, above all others, is far more rationalistic and deductive, meaning truth and knowledge come from the human mind. Experience is subordinated. This tradition (which contributed to the Frankfurt School, postmodernism, and other twentieth-century intellectual and cultural movements) has disproportionately shaped contemporary academia, social scientists, philosophers, and intellectuals through the works of great German thinkers like Marx, Max Weber, Freud, Horkheimer, Adorno, Marcuse, and, more recently, Jürgen Habermas. Taking a cue from Kant, all of these thinkers argued for a world beyond our experiences. Experience gets subordinated.

For example, probably the most influential left-wing academic of the second half of the twentieth century was Marcuse, often called the "guru of the New Left." Marcuse attempted to reconcile Marxist principles with the reality that the socialist Soviet Union promoted not freedom but oppression. By the time Marcuse started writing, the Soviet Union was losing credibility due to famine and purges. Did this mean that Marx, the greatest left-wing philosopher in history, had it all wrong? Not so fast. Marcuse railed against American capitalism, employing such concepts as "false consciousness." Freud, with his characteristically German emphasis on the sublime, deeply influenced Marcuse, who contended that although Americans might feel free, no truth can be gleaned from this. Only by delving beyond surface appearances can we understand the malignant capitalist system. It is hard to imagine that Marcuse's personal experiences with American capitalism were that unfortunate: one of his primary residences in the United States was in La Jolla, California, one of the wealthiest communities in Southern California. The other two members of the Marcuse-Adorno-Horkheimer trio wrote in their classic critique of capitalist society, *Dialectic of Enlightenment*, "The individual is entirely nullified in the face of economic powers."[67] They wrote this while living in Pacific Palisades, a posh region of Los Angeles. That doesn't invalidate their work; it just suggests that they didn't draw their theories from experience.

Michael Harrington's famous socialist work, *The Other America: Poverty in the United Sates*, rejected empiricism. Harrington, like many other socialist writers, condemned American capitalism by arguing that its true nature exists in areas beyond our experiences, such as poverty in the rural mountains and inner cities, places most Americans never visit. He even described "invisible Americans." Capitalism brings suffering into the world, but the suffering is beyond our experiences. American capitalism must be understood by looking beyond our senses. Harrington, like any good socialist, argued that Americans needed to invest in more areas rife with poverty.[68] According to the left, although a person's experiences with the American capitalist system may be favorable, these experiences do not sufficiently describe American capitalism. The fabric of reality lies below superficial appearance. In America, adherents to this type of reasoning believe, malignant, latent forces control the system, even for those who live posh middle-class lifestyles.

Reagan vehemently disagreed, insisting that experience best yields truth. After describing Marxism as a fanatical ideology, Reagan insisted, "Conservative wisdom and principles are derived from willingness to learn, not just from what is going on, but from what happened before. The principles of conservatism are sound because they are based on what men and women have discovered through experience in not just one generation of a dozen, but in all of the combined experiences of mankind."[69] Reagan proposed empiricism. He believed experience with the capitalist system reveals its true nature. He wanted to fly Mikhail Gorbachev, the leader of the USSR, in a helicopter over American cities, believing that after experiencing American capitalism and talking to ordinary Americans, the general secretary would abandon his socialist pretensions.[70] Direct experience with the capitalist system would yield truth. The difference between the two systems of thought can be most simply addressed with a question: Are my personal experiences as a middle-class American indicative of the true nature and reality of the American system? For conservative inductivists, the answer is yes, while for left-wing deductivists, like Marcuse and Adorno, the answer is no. For the latter, personal experiences do not necessarily yield truth. They use ideology (mind) to understand the world. These two traditions continue to battle in the culture wars and subsequently in American politics.

Reagan's faith in experience further explains why so many left-wing thinkers minimize his intelligence. Most intellectuals rely on the powers of their marvelous minds, not the external world, in order to understand reality. Socialism is more a product of the human mind (ideology) than is capitalism. This may further explain its appeal to intellectuals since they become more useful in a socialist system because people are needed to orchestrate the economic system. The advantage Reagan and conservatives have is that their method is more consistent with America's intellectual and cultural heritage. Locke, the great empiricist whose philosophy contributed to the American Revolution, castigated the deductive rationalism of Descartes and Platonists. (And subsequent German thinkers like Kant, Hegel, and Marx condemned British empiricists like Locke.) Rationalists maintained that truth could be discovered by reason (the mind) alone, a priori, or without experience. They weren't the intellectual architects of America, however. In the same immortal speech where he exclaimed "Give me Liberty or give me death," one of America's most famous patriots declared, "I have but one lamp by which my feet are guided, and that is the lamp of experience."[71] This all helped shape Reagan's own political philosophy and his rejection of abstract, metaphysical principles. It is the American Way.

These ideas led to the distinctly American philosophical movement called pragmatism. Generally, pragmatists shun the abstract reasoning favored by traditional philosophers, instead favoring a more practical, down-to-earth approach to ideas. Ideas should not be judged on their popularity nor on how rational they seem, but on how well they actually work. The idea that socialism is good because it works in theory would be rejected by the pragmatists because nothing can be deemed good until it is actually tried. Tocqueville, writing decades before the pragmatist movement crystallized, studied why Americans prefer practical to theoretical sciences and concluded, "Those who cultivate the sciences among a democratic people [Americans] are always afraid of losing their way in visionary speculation. They mistrust systems; they adhere closely to facts and study facts with their own senses."[72] Pragmatism explains why Americans are more averse to academic philosophy than are Europeans. It also explains and contributed to what has justly been called "anti-intellectualism" in America today. This, in turn, explains why Americans (and those who prefer its traditions, like conservatives) are sometimes considered to be less intelligent. In reality they are just different philosophical systems.

There have been some attempts to reduce Reagan's political success to his deft skills as a communicator and media manipulator. Pejoratively calling Reagan the "Teflon president" for his ability to deflect blame and criticism, some Democrats use this as a means to explain his political success. The Democratic congresswoman Patricia Schroeder, who coined the term, recalls, "As a young congresswoman, I got the idea of calling President Reagan the 'Teflon president' while fixing eggs for my kids. He had a Teflon coat like the pan."[73] No criticisms of Reagan stuck. From one perspective, attributing Reagan's political success and personal popularity to his communicative skills, or ability to deflect criticism, conveniently allows critics to minimize the significance of his ideas and policies. According to this reasoning, Reagan was a popular president not because of his conservative ideas but rather because of his ability to communicate. In the same way, Republicans explain Clinton's and Obama's success by maintaining that they were "great politicians." What I want to suggest is that Reagan's success can be attributed to his ability to postulate ideas concordant with America's religious and cultural heritage. His "Teflon coat" can be explained by the fact that his entire cosmology was consistent with American traditions. He spoke the American language fluently and his ideas found receptive ears.

5

...

A Moral View of the Cold War

Atheism is as much a part of communism as the GULAG. Every kind of roadblock is thrown in the way of religion up to and including imprisonment. Children in Soviet schools are indoctrinated from grade 1 with the falsehood that there is no God.

—KIRON SKINNER AND ANNELISE ANDERSON,
Reagan in His Own Hand

The Treaty of Versailles in 1919 reduced the German military to 100,000 men. This didn't stop Adolf Hitler from reconstructing the German Wehrmacht in the mid-1930s. In March 1936 Hitler again violated the Versailles Treaty by sending German troops into the Rhineland. Fearing war, international leaders' response to this invasion was muted. In March 1938 Hitler's troops invaded Austria, and again there was no response. Six months later Hitler began preaching the need to "liberate" Germans living in the Sudetenland region of Czechoslovakia. Now Western leaders decided to act—by calling a conference. Prime Minister Neville Chamberlain of Great Britain flew immediately to Munich, determined to avoid war. He succeeded, because when Hitler requested territory in exchange for the promise that his German army would stop marching, Chamberlain said yes. Chamberlain returned to England a hero, declaring that he had achieved "peace for our time." Within a year, however, Hitler unleashed the German Wehrmacht against Poland. The most devastating war in history had begun.

To many of us today, this is history, but Reagan lived through it. He believed much could be learned from the diplomatic mistakes of the 1930s. It taught him that evil cannot be negotiated with; it cannot be trusted. It taught him that curbing military expansion does not foster peace but rather instigates war, because the evil powers in the world will ignore all treaties and all laws and pursue their own ruthless expansionist agendas. These lessons were easily applied to the cold war. In Reagan's mind, American leaders were too accommodating to the Soviets, just as Western powers had been to Hitler.

Like his domestic philosophy, Reagan's geopolitical philosophy can never be separated from his theological background. The cold war was a titanic struggle, a holy war between good and evil, with the fate of humanity hanging in the balance. All our efforts, Reagan believed, had to be spent fighting the forces of evil: "We cannot buy our security, our freedom from the threat of the bomb by committing an immorality so great as saying to a billion human beings now enslaved behind the Iron Curtain, 'Give up your dreams of freedom because to save our own skins, we're willing to make a deal with your slave masters.'"[1] He knew that freedom could be obtained only with struggle and sacrifice:

> We are at war with the most dangerous enemy that has ever faced mankind in his long climb from the swamp to the stars, and it has been said if we lose that war, and in doing so lose this way of freedom of ours, history will record with the greatest astonishment that those who had the most to lose did the least to prevent its happening. Well, I think it's time we ask ourselves if we still know the freedoms that were intended for us by the Founding Fathers. . . . If we lose freedom here, there is no place to escape to. This is the last stand on Earth.[2]

The Kingdom of Freedom does not descend easily. We cannot be passive bystanders, expecting it to arrive without sacrifice. Narrow is the hallway to freedom, and broad is the path to destruction. Reagan exclaimed, "Freedom is never more than one generation away from extinction—we didn't pass it on to our children in the bloodstream. It must be fought for, protected, and handed on for them to do the same, or one day we will spend our sunset years telling our children and our children's children what it was once like in the United States when men were free."[3] These ideas explain Reagan's activist international politics in the cold war, even as a growing number of Americans embraced isolationism in the wake of Vietnam. Religious history provided a foundation for Reagan's arguments. "If nothing in life is worth dying for," he asked, "when did this begin—just in the face of this enemy? Or should Moses have told the children of Israel to live in slavery under the pharaohs? Should Christ have refused the cross?"[4] Suffering and death, Reagan believed, are sometimes needed to ensure life. The good life never passes into our hands easily. This is what the Bible, Platonic philosophy, as well as history teach us.

The cold war, after all, was merely a replay of past two world wars. Reagan insisted, "The great ideological struggle that we find ourselves engaged in today is not a new struggle. It's the same battle. We met it under Hitlerism, we met it under Kaisers."[5] Reagan's foreign policy was driven by humanitarian impulses, not economic ones, just like the American war against Nazism. The great struggles of the twentieth century were not formal religious struggles, but they were still moral struggles between right and wrong. Reagan recognized the similarities between Nazism and communism, even when many others did not. Both are collectivist movements, fundamentally opposed to individual rights and freedom. Both require their adherents to sacrifice some of their individualism in favor of something greater.

The most important source for Reagan's knowledge about Marxism and communism was Laurence Beilenson, Reagan's attorney and a Hollywood associate. Beilenson argued that since the Soviets know no morality other than advancing communism, making any sort of agreements with them is pointless. They will attempt to advance communism, regardless. How do we stop them? In his work *The Treaty Trap*, Beilenson stated simply, "The Soviet Union retreats

when faced with strength."[6] Like James Burnham he demanded
a hardline stand against the Soviet Union. Anything else meant
accommodating evil. Beilenson helped Reagan recognize the natural expansionist intentions of the evil Soviet Union, something
explicit in its Marxist foundations (as well as in past and present
Russia). Reagan stated, "Karl Marx established the cardinal principle that communism and capitalism cannot coexist in the world
together. Our way of life, our system, must be totally destroyed;
then the Communist state will be erected in its ruins. In interpreting Marx, Lenin said, 'it is inconceivable that the Soviet Republic should continue to exist for a long period side by side with the
imperialist states. One must conquer.'"[7] Marx predicted the victory
of the proletariat, insisting that the socialist revolution would engulf
capitalist nations, inaugurating a workers' paradise. Attempting to
apply Marxist theory, Stalin consolidated his control over Eastern
Europe—which he had liberated from the Nazis during World
War II—and reneged on his promises at Yalta to allow democratic
elections in this region of the world. Rather than bring his troops
home, Stalin kept them in Eastern Europe and, unlike the United
States in West Germany, denied the people legitimate elections.

The American formal response to Soviet expansion after World
War II was containment. Its architect, George Kennan, fortunately
also recognized that expansionist tendencies were part of Marxist
philosophy and Russian history. The Soviet Union would expand
unless checked by American authority. (Notably Kennan did not
argue that the United States should attempt to crush communism
in the areas where it already existed, such as Russia and Eastern
Europe. Burnham, Eisenhower's secretary of state John Foster
Dulles, Beilenson, and others did.) These ideas formed what has
been called the "cold war consensus," a policy that was in effect from
roughly 1945 to 1968, during which time Republicans and Democrats in Congress joined hands in their willingness to use whatever
means necessary to stop the spread of communism, even if it meant
resorting to war, such as in Korea and, initially, in Southeast Asia.

Vietnam changed everything, however. Undermining the ability of the American military to fight the cold war, it launched a

new era of American foreign policy, one based on negotiation and compromise. Vietnam provoked an isolationist sentiment among many Americans, that America could not, and therefore should not, attempt to spread democracy. The Vietnam War proved to be as influential in the intellectual rearing of baby boomers as World War II was for Reagan, but the lessons of history were reversed: whereas the lesson of World War II seemed to be that the United States should not back down from tyranny, the lesson of Vietnam was that the United States could not fight tyranny by military means. Antimilitarists continue to use these lessons of history today. Reagan called the Vietnam War a "noble cause," meaning that its goal—to defeat the communist Vietcong in order to ensure they did not control the country—were altruistic. Like the American invasions of France, Belgium, and West Germany and American use of force in Korea two decades earlier, America invaded a sovereign nation in an attempt to stop the spread of a malignant system of government. But although America succeeded in turning back the Nazis in Western Europe and the communists in Korea, it failed to defeat the communists in Southeast Asia.

This failure led to détente. Intended to relax tensions between the superpowers, détente, it was hoped, would allow America to stop the spread of communism without resorting to military force. Many Americans, including Republicans like Nixon, believed that America should "peacefully coexist" with the Soviet behemoth. This idea of peaceful coexistence was originally Premier Nikita Khrushchev's; like every Soviet leader, Khrushchev had to make an important choice: promote the spread of communism through military means and potential conflict, or avoid military confrontation with the United States by accepting communist limitations. American détente was the brainchild of Henry Kissinger, maybe the most famous diplomat of the twentieth century. Kissinger, of Eastern European descent, earned a Ph.D. in political science after completing a dissertation analyzing the Congress of Vienna, where European leaders promoted a balance of power among Europe's leading nations. As secretary of state, first under Nixon, then under Ford, Kissinger harkened back to the French Revolution, when the outbreak of war was caused by a country becoming too strong. The solution? A balance of power. The world's powers (at this time France, Russia, Prussia, Austria-Hungry, and England) should rival each other in strength, thus ensuring that no one country become so strong that it dominated the others. President Nixon maintained, "I think it will be a safer world and a better world if we have a strong, healthy U.S., Europe, Soviet Union, China and Japan, each balancing the other." Its hegemony vanquished, America needed to work with other nations in order to promote peace and security.

Détente resulted in two significant phenomena. First, relations between the United States and communist nations improved, so much so that the Chinese and Russians worried about each other more than they did America. The years between roughly 1973 and 1979 saw the closest relations ever between the United States and the Soviet Union. The public feared the outbreak of World War III and nuclear annihilation less during those years than in the preceding decades and in the 1980s. Second, the loss in Vietnam led to the gradual deconstruction of the American military. Adjusted for inflation, U.S. defense spending fell 42 percent during the Nixon and Ford administrations.[8] Since the Soviets continued the buildup on their side, the superiority of conventional weapons the United States had enjoyed throughout the cold war was gone. The Soviet general secretary Leonid Brezhnev had learned the lesson of the Cuban Missile Crisis, when Khrushchev negotiated from an inferior position. Brezhnev vowed to catch up, if not surpass, the United States in quantity of nuclear warheads owned, and the American government was complicit in this process because it wasn't willing to risk U.S. lives to protect the rest of the world from antidemocratic forces. It was time to look inward.

National pessimism fueled détente. Besides the tragedy of Vietnam, the oil shocks profoundly influenced the American psyche. American involvement in the Yom Kippur War prompted the Middle East's leading supplier of petroleum, OPEC, to cut oil supplies, leading to a surge in U.S. gas prices. Moreover, by 1980 inflation and unemployment hovered near 10 percent. Using these statistics, the economic crisis of 1979–82 was worse than the more recent recession of 2008–10. The American Age seemed to be over, and the future did not belong to America or its values. New Marxist regimes popped up across Southeast Asia, joining China and the Soviet Union. Daniel Patrick Moynihan, a future Democratic senator from New York, declared, "Neither liberty nor democracy seem to be prospering. . . . [They] have no relevance for the future. It is where the world was, not where it was going."[9] The Soviets, on the other hand, were optimistic. They had now at least reached military parity with the United States, leading Brezhnev to proclaim, "We are achieving with détente what our predecessors had been unable to achieve using the mailed fist. We have been able to achieve [more] in a short time with détente than was done for years pursuing a confrontation policy with NATO. Trust us, comrades, for by 1985, as a consequence of what we are now achieving with détente, we will have achieved most of our objectives in Western Europe."[10]

Reagan's optimism could not tolerate détente and its premises. He believed, despite appearances, that America's best days lay ahead. He disagreed with containment and despised détente. He quipped that détente was what a turkey and its farmer have, until Thanksgiving. Urging continued American involvement in the world, even after the Vietnam fiasco, he consistently drew parallels between the current era of détente and the era of appeasement:

> Alexander Hamilton said, "A nation which can prefer disgrace to danger is prepared for a master, and deserves one." Now let's set the record straight. There's no argument over the choice between peace and war, but there's only one guaranteed way you can have peace—and you can have it in the next second—surrender. Admittedly, there's a risk in any course we follow other than this, but every lesson of history tells us that the greater risk lies in appeasement, and this is the specter our well-meaning liberal friends refuse to face—that their policy of accommodation is appeasement, and it gives no choice between peace and war, only between fight or surrender. If we continue to accommodate, continue to back and retreat, eventually we have to face the final demand—the ultimatum.[11]

Reagan was determined to use American strength to end tyranny and promote freedom. He begged Americans, in the name of peace, not to retreat from world affairs. He scorned Democratic and Republican thinking at the time; both Ford and Carter had suppressed American power. In fact Reagan made Ford's continuation of détente one of the central themes of his 1976 campaign to unseat the incumbent president. The echoes of appeasement never left Reagan's mind. A constant lesson of history for conservatives, it taught Reagan that military spending was a way to promote peace, not war. (The generation before Reagan was reared on the idea that military spending promoted war, since World War I was preceded by an arms race across the West.)

In his quest for peace, Reagan promoted the American military. In a handwritten radio address from 1975 entitled "How Much Is It Worth Not to Have World War III?" he said, "The leaders of that generation saw the growing menace and talked of it but reacted to the growing military might of Germany with anguished passiveness. . . . World War II did not happen because the nations of the free world engaged in a massive military buildup. In most countries, including our own, 'too little too late' described the reaction to the Nazi military colossus."[12] According to Reagan, an arms race did not lead to World War II; rather a general reduction in military spending by Western powers, save Germany, did. Reagan concluded that the world is made a better, more peaceful place not by scaling back the military but by expanding it. "We want to avoid war and that is better achieved by being so strong that a potential enemy is not tempted to go adventuring."[13] It's analogous to a heavyweight boxing champion. A strong champion earns respect. A weak one, after years of atrophy, invites attack; his weakness, not his strength, encourages conflict. "Armaments do not cause war," Reagan insisted, "armaments are built and used by aggressors whose intention from the beginning is war and the threat of war. Peace loving nations must match their weaponry . . . or fall victim to the aggressor."[14]

Whereas his opponents preached disarmament as a path toward peace, Reagan maintained that peace could be accomplished by making ourselves stronger than our enemies. Peace through strength. He argued in 1972, "Despite the lessening of tensions and the hopeful signs of great power cooperation in the future, it is America's industrial and economic strength, translated into military potential, that represents the single guarantee of peace for the world."[15] Besides articulating the principles that would guide him as president, this statement recognized the relationship between the American economy and its geopolitical success. Arguing that the biggest advantage America had in the cold war was its material strength and national wealth, Reagan knew an economically prosperous America meant a strong and influential America. The goal therefore needed to be to strengthen the American economy by whatever means necessary and parlay this into military might. This is how Reagan felt we should deal with communism—through strength, both economic and military:

> Cutting $30 billion from the defense budget, dismantling great parts of our navy and air force, scaling back the space program, and ignoring technical developments, such as supersonic transport, are real issues, not subjects for a senior thesis. . . . The president [Nixon] wants to end the Cold War era of conflict and to substitute an era of negotiations and peaceful settlements of disputes before they flare into war. I am sure every American shares this goal. But are we also aware that every nation in history which has sought peace and freedom solely through negotiation has been crushed by conquerors bent on conquest and negotiation?[16]

For too long, Reagan complained, American presidents had acquiesced to the Soviets. They had been giving too much and receiving too little. When Reagan lost the Republican nomination for president in 1976, his biggest regret, he told his son Michael, was this: "That I won't get to say 'nyet' to Mr. Brezhnev."[17]

Reagan's greatest fears were realized in 1979, when the Soviets launched a full-scale invasion of Afghanistan, despite promises not to. Détente turned out to be appeasement, take two. Compromise, negotiation, and reducing military spending led to war.

Hitler and the Soviet leadership both interpreted these Western overtures as weakness, leading to aggression. President Jimmy Carter, insisting that Brezhnev had lied to him, called the Soviet invasion of Afghanistan the greatest threat to international peace since World War II. The invasion made him fully aware of the Soviet reality, and he immediately increased the American defense budget. Carter began pulling America away from détente. For the Carter administration, this meant that the ideas of hardliner National Security Advisor Zbigniew Brzezinski received precedence over those of Secretary of State Cyrus Vance, a proponent of compromise and arms reduction. Yet if we believe a hardline policy was the right approach, Reagan was the preferable candidate because there would have been no Cyrus Vances in the Reagan administration. The Soviet invasion gave credence to Reagan's ideas. Now even Democrats supported an increase in military spending, rejecting détente. It appeared that Reagan had the best grasp on the nature and reality of the Soviet system.

The Soviet invasion of Afghanistan further weakened Reagan's faith in conferences, at least until his second term as president. He was chided for not meeting with Soviet leaders early in his presidency, but from his perspective, post–World War II conferences like Yalta had advanced peace about as much as the Munich Conference did in 1938. American and Soviet leaders came together again in Geneva in 1955. This did nothing to prevent the massacre in Hungary in 1956. Kennedy and Khrushchev's meetings in Vienna were followed within months by the construction of the Berlin Wall. In 1967 American and Soviet leaders met in Glassboro, New Jersey, with the goal of improving American-Soviet relations; in 1968 the Soviet Union invaded Czechoslovakia. In June 1979 Carter and Brezhnev met and signed the Strategic Arms Limitations Treaty, restricting the number of missiles on both sides; six months later the Soviets invaded Afghanistan.

Reagan's harsh rhetoric, his refusal to compromise coupled with his military buildup made it easy for his critics to paint him as a reckless cowboy with one finger on the trigger, especially during his first term as president. Peace protesters dogged Reagan wherever he went, sometimes reaching the hundreds of thousands, especially when he went to Europe. The *Bulletin of Atomic Scientists* moved the hands of the "Doomsday Clock" to three minutes to midnight after Reagan's election in 1984, the closest the human race had come to annihilation since 1953, when both the Americans and the Soviets detonated hydrogen bombs. According to the *Bulletin*, if the clock strikes midnight, we are doomed.[18] A concerned *Bulletin* informed readers, "U.S.-Soviet relations reach their iciest point in decades. Dialogue between the two superpowers virtually stops. Every channel of communications has been constricted or shut down; every form of contact has been attenuated or cut off. And arms control negotiations have been reduced to a species of propaganda. The United States seems to flout the few arms control agreements in place by seeking an expansive, space-based anti-ballistic missile capability, raising worries that a new arms race will begin."[19] Many of his opponents believed Reagan might literally cause the end of Western civilization. Contemporary fears regarding Donald Trump's sanity and recklessness were directed at Reagan in the early 1980s.

Reagan always wanted peace, though. More recent accounts have even described him as dovish, claiming he never wanted war. In fact, these accounts say, his personal relationships and smooth talking with Soviet leaders during his second term enabled a peaceful end to the cold war. John Patrick Diggins paints this portrait of Reagan to dissociate him from twenty-first-century neoconservatives, who are too quick to use force, in Diggins's opinion.[20] Paul Lettow in *Ronald Reagan and His Quest to Abolish Nuclear Weapons* showed that Reagan always feared nuclear weapons and nuclear war.[21]

Both interpretations are correct. Reagan was a dove in the sense that he sought the peaceful dissolution of the Soviet Union, but his personal experiences of World War II and his ignorance of the fact that Soviet leaders never wanted war either led him to believe Americans had to prepare for the worst. Reagan didn't want war, but he didn't know that Soviet leaders, despite their fervent belief in the victory of the proletariat and the imminence of worldwide socialism, didn't either. He correctly interpreted Marxism as an expansionist ideology, but he was naïve when it came to understanding the realities that Soviet leaders faced, at least before he became president. Until his meetings with Gorbachev, Reagan viewed the Soviet Union through a Marxist-Leninist paradigm, as taught to him by hardliners like Burnham and Beilenson. And that was pure theory. Marxist-Leninists like Khrushchev, Brezhnev, and their successors Yuri Andropov and Konstantin Chernenko did want to overthrow American capitalism, but they first had to feed their own people. That task was challenging enough.

Reagan interpreted reality through his own religious paradigm, rooted in Scripture. The cold war conformed perfectly to Revelation: a titanic struggle between the forces of good and evil. Reagan noted in his private diary at the peak of renewed cold war tensions, "Got word of Israel bombing of Iraq—nuclear reactor. I swear I believe Armageddon is near."[22] Much to the chagrin of some of his closest advisors, Reagan was fascinated by Armageddon and the stories told in the Book of Revelation. Edmund Morris writes about a discussion he had with Reagan regarding Armageddon: "'When [Armageddon] comes,' Reagan plainly stated, 'the man who comes down from the wrong side, into the war, is the man, according to the prophecies, named Gog, from Meshech, which is the ancient name of Moscow. . . . But on the other side are ten kings from Europe. Well, the European conference, now, is ten nations. And then from the West comes a young nation, under the sign of an Eagle!'"[23] Reagan did not want war, of course, but he believed that God's will trumped everything, and if Armageddon arrived, we had to be prepared to fight. And we had to win.

This distinguishes Reagan from Nixon. Although each came to power as strident anticommunists, their policies and ideas about communism differed. Nixon lambasted communism, but upon becoming president, he launched détente. He personally despised communists, but more than Reagan he was willing to compromise with them on a political level. Nixon never viewed the cold war in the Manichaean fashion; he would never describe the Soviet Union as an "evil empire," and he never viewed the Soviet Union as a temporary entity. Part of this may stem from their differing religious backgrounds; for those shaped by evangelicalism like Reagan, the Book of Revelation plays a far more prominent role among preachers than it does for pacifist Quakers. Obviously Nixon dismissed pacifism, but the Book of Revelation never played the large role in his intellectual rearing that it did in Reagan's. Nixon never felt that Armageddon was imminent because he did not characterize the world as a struggle between good and evil. He never developed an ideology that interpreted the world as a cosmological struggle between two antagonistic concepts, each seeking world domination.

Using the Judeo-Christian paradigm to describe the world allowed Reagan to understand the cold war and so discover two related truths. First, the Soviet Union was indeed an evil empire, in essence no different from the Nazi state. Both societies minimized individual rights and liberties. Second, the Soviet Union's time on earth was short. Reagan understood both the moral and economic flaws in the Soviet Union, something those working within more secular paradigms could not do. He argued that the Soviet Union was materially weak, and he was right. He also argued that communism would disappear, and he was right. He believed that America could play a critical role in undermining communism, and he was right. A good-versus-evil interpretation of the cold war led to truth. (Of course, this paradigm also made it more difficult to interpret events in parts of Central and South America, where things were not so black and white.) This recognition of Soviet futility allowed Reagan to promote an aggressive foreign policy that ultimately sought to bring down the evil empire and help bring the Kingdom of Freedom to earth.

Modern-day secular ideologies provide prisms through which to understand current events. Those who poke fun at Reagan for his religious beliefs employ similar means to understand reality, such as the belief in exploited and exploiter classes or exploited and exploiter races. These metaphysical interpretations are, in fact, related to Reagan's cold war metaphysics; they interpret reality as a struggle between two concepts, such as rich and poor or black and white. Metaphysics is the branch of philosophy that studies the nature of reality. It is the oldest branch of philosophy, and maybe the most important, since so many philosophers build entire ethical systems based on their metaphysics. Reagan, for instance, recognized what now seem like obvious flaws in the Soviet Union:

> In size [the] Soviet Union is number 1 with 8.6 million square miles. China is next with 3.7, barely larger than our own country at 3.6. In population, China is way out in front with nearly one billion. Russia has 262 million and we number 220 million. Despite the size and population advantages, Reagan pointed out, "We have only estimates of the GNP of Russia and China and they are probably padded but ours is nearly twice Russia and nearly 5 times that of China. The percentage of our work force engaged in agriculture is only about 1/8 that of Russia and 1/26 that of China, yet both of them have to import food or starve."[24]

During détente the American government sold grain to the Soviets at a bargain-basement price. Reagan continued his remarks by describing the significant American advantage in cars and telephones, proving that the United States was materially stronger than the Soviet Union. This material strength, he realized, gave America its biggest advantage in the cold war.

A contingent of scholars questioned Reagan's interpretations of the USSR, maintaining that the Soviet Union was a viable alternative to American capitalism. The acclaimed historian Arthur Schlesinger argued, "Those in the United States who think that the Soviet Union is on the verge of economic and social collapse are wishful thinkers."[25] Analyzing and understanding the true nature of the Soviet Union is important, because if the Soviet Union is strained, we can argue for an aggressive foreign policy designed to undermine its existence. Of course, if the Soviet Union is strong, any sort of confrontation should be avoided, since it could lead to our own destruction, so conciliatory policies must prevail. Two completely different foreign policies can be deduced, depending on how we view the Soviet system. Metaphysics provides a foundation for foreign policy. What is the true nature and reality of Hitler and Nazism? Is Hitler really a man we can trust, as Chamberlain claimed? If so, we should pursue conciliatory policies with him. What about the Soviet Union and communism? What about Osama bin Laden and Al Qaeda? Are they inherently evil? Or are they, under certain conditions, malleable?

It was the philosopher Isaiah Berlin who described political leaders as foxes and hedgehogs. Foxes know many small things, while the hedgehog knows one big thing. Intellectuals tend to sympathize with the former, but Reagan was the latter. The big thing Reagan knew was that communism and the Soviet Union were flawed. Some successful presidents have been foxes, and some have been hedgehogs. One hedgehog was George Washington. Compared to most of his band of brothers, Washington was one of the least well-read, one of the least thoughtful, and one of the least intellectual. But Washington was not stupid. And he was the only real choice to be the nation's first president, a job he did better than virtually all of his followers. Historians of thought may favor Jefferson, but presidential historians favor Washington.

Recognizing the futility of the Soviet Union was the greatest knowledge of all after World War II. Reagan stepped on the gas when it came to the arms race because he knew it would strain the Soviet Union. In a 1981 interview he said, "Up until now, we have been making unilateral concessions, allowing our forces to deteriorate, and they have been building the greatest military machine the world has even seen. But now they could be faced with [the fact] that we could go forward with an arms race and they can't keep up."[26] Several years later he wrote, "If he [Gorbachev] really wants an arms control agreement, it will only happen because he wants to reduce the burden of defense spending that is stagnating the Soviet economy. This could contribute to his opposition to our SDI [Strategic Defense Initiative, Reagan's plan for a defense shield against nuclear missiles]. He doesn't want to face the cost of competing with us."[27] To those unaware of Soviet shortcomings, this seemed like a measure that would only bring the world closer to war, but since the Soviet Union was flawed and weak, Reagan wanted to destroy it. Strobe Talbott, at the time a journalist for *Time* magazine and later a senior official in the Clinton administration, argued at the time, "Reagan is counting on American technological and economic predominance to prevail in the end."[28] Andrei Gromyko, the Soviet minister of foreign affairs from 1957 to 1985, stated, "The Reagan administration wants to cause trouble. They want to weaken the Soviet System. They want to bring it down."[29] Soviet newspapers compared Reagan to Hitler, an ominous analogy considering that the Nazis invaded the Soviet Union in 1941. The Sovietologist Stephen F. Cohen wrote in 1983, "All evidence indicates that the Reagan Administration has abandoned both containment and détente for a different objective: destroying the Soviet Union as a world power and possibly even its Communist system."[30] Many understood his motives. In his private diary Reagan noted, "We are still meeting and stewing about East-West trade and now we must take on the problem of what to do or if to do something to help the Polish people. Their economy is going bust. Here is the 1st major break in the Red dike—Poland's disenchantment with Soviet Communism."[31] Reagan knew Soviet communism was doomed. He sought to expedite its collapse.

Comparing Reagan's ideas with one of his policy critics demonstrates the importance of understanding the USSR. James Galbraith, a vocal critic of the Reagan administration's military buildup, said in 1984, "That the Soviet system has made great material progress in recent years is evident both from the statistics and from the general urban scene. . . . One sees it in the appearance of well-being of the people on the streets . . . and the general aspect of restaurants, theaters, and shops. . . . Partly, the Russian system succeeds because, in contrast with the Western industrial economies, it makes full use of its manpower."[32] The Soviet Union, in contrast to the United States, had virtually no unemployment, which Galbraith considered a good thing. Today we realize this was actually a serious flaw because it makes expanding a business difficult since it's harder to find employees. Second, it breeds less productive workers because they have job security regardless of their performance. Soviet workers had less fear than American workers of losing their jobs, so their work performance was often subpar. "We pretend to work. They pretend to pay us," went one Soviet joke. Soviet industrial workers were roughly one-quarter as productive as American workers, and Soviet farmers were a staggering one-tenth as productive as American farmers.

It was not only in their economic interpretations of the Soviet Union that Reagan and Galbraith clashed. Galbraith critiqued the Reagan administration's cold war policies; not everyone eagerly sought a renewed cold war. In response to Reagan's heavy defense spending, Galbraith helped establish Economists against the Arms Race and later, after the fall of the Soviet Union, Economists Allied for Arms Reduction. Galbraith believed that military spending did not create peace but rather fostered war. He and Reagan both drew their argument from history, but they differed over which historical events mattered. This may be partly reduced to generational differences: Galbraith was born in 1952, meaning he was in his late teens when the Vietnam War peaked, so draft prospects loomed large. Begging to differ over the issue of war with Reagan, Galbraith wrote, "War is ruinous—from a legal, moral and economic point of view. It can ruin the losers, such as Napoleonic France, or Imperial Germany in 1918. And it can ruin the victors, as it did the British and the Soviets in the 20th century. Conversely, Germany and Japan recovered well from World War II, in part because they were spared reparations and did not have to waste national treasure on defense in the aftermath of defeat."[33] Galbraith's ways to prevent war differed vastly from Reagan's. The importance of World War II and Vietnam in shaping minds cannot be overestimated.

Containment's tacit acceptance of communism was unacceptable to Reagan, although this verdict is not unanimous. The historian Eric Hobsbawm wrote in his widely read *Age of Extremes*, "President Reagan himself, whatever the rhetoric put before him by his speechwriters, and whatever went on in his not always lucid mind, believed in the co-existence of the USA and USSR."[34] But how could an optimist like Reagan accept the existence of an atheist society? The Bible tells us that evil and sin exist in the world, but that doesn't mean we have to accept them. The Bible, the Word of God, according to Reagan, tells us that evil will disappear. Reagan followed this by insisting in 1975, "Communism is neither an economic or political system—it is a form of insanity—a temporary aberration which will one day disappear from the earth because it is contrary to human nature. I wonder how much more misery it will cause before it disappears."[35] These ideas preceded Reagan's speech before the British Parliament and prove that he genuinely believed in the transitory nature of communism. For any Christian, accepting the existence of the Soviet Union is deeply pessimistic, but religious and political ideologies are by nature optimistic, promising a better world. Otherwise, why believe? Why fight and struggle for a cause that can never prevail? "We will win" is a mantra shared by Christians, Marxists, Republicans, and Democrats. Eventually people will achieve Enlightenment and think as we do, despite present-day conditions. Marxists were so certain they would win (the victory of the proletariat is inevitable), they dubbed their socialism "scientific."

Just as it was Reagan's Christian millenarian cosmology that allowed him to understand the Soviet Union, for many scholars like Galbraith, their cosmologies precluded them from recognizing the inherent flaws in a socialist system where people are given "free" food, clothing, higher education, shelter, and health care. Was Reagan smarter than his critics? Were his analytic and critical thinking powers superior? Doubtful. Intelligence and education don't lead to ideologies and historical interpretations. We start with our values and ideology, and then interpret the world accordingly. In Kantian fashion, the mind (ideology) creates a rational world. Although historical interpretations begin with facts, a priori concepts determine how we organize these facts. Even for academics and intellectuals, preexisting ideology shapes how they interpret the world before us. The more the world conforms to our ideology, the better the world must be, and of course vice versa. For Reagan, a healthy and prosperous Soviet Union was fundamentally contradictory to his value system, so he could never accept it, just as those on the other side of the ideological spectrum could never imagine that a system that promoted economic equality far more than the United States does could be so rotten.

6

. . .

Promoting Freedom Abroad

All across the world today—in the shipyards of Gdansk, the hills
of Nicaragua, the rice paddies of Kampuchea, the mountains of
Afghanistan—the cry again is liberty.

—REAGAN, "Address Before a Joint Session of the
Irish National Parliament"

A Soviet official once complained, "It would evidently require a
modern computer to estimate how many times Ronald Reagan
used the term 'freedom' in his remarks."[1] Spreading freedom to
new regions of the world was the cornerstone of Reagan's foreign
policy. This distinguishes him from his predecessors in the White
House, who merely sought to protect freedom. The old cold war
attitudes of containment and détente were replaced by the far more
ambitious "rollback." When Reagan came to Washington, many
predicted that American-Soviet relations would change, and not
necessarily for the better. But Reagan never attempted to accommodate the Soviet system. He wanted to bust it and expand the
Kingdom of Freedom.

When Reagan was elected president in 1980, winning the cold
war seemed impossible. The 1970s was a bad decade for America. The United States formally lost its first war. After defeating
the Germans twice, the United States was outlasted by a ragtag
crew of guerrilla warriors in the jungles of Vietnam. Our president

resigned in disgrace. By the late 1970s and even through the early 1980s, the American economy was in shambles. Unemployment was over 10 percent. Inflation was nearing double digits too. Gas prices soared. In 1975 President Ford contended in his State of the Union address, "I must say to you that the state of the union is not good." He added, "I've got bad news, and I don't expect much, if any, applause."[2] Anyone who knows anything about the Carter presidency knows nothing got better once he took office, and he didn't get any more optimistic. Again and again Carter stressed the deep problems America faced. By 1980 national productivity, the leading economic indicator for most economists, had stagnated. Americans produced fewer goods and made less money in that era than at any time since the Great Depression.

None of this deterred Reagan. Despite internal problems, Reagan refused to make the mistakes of the appeasement era, when powerful nations turned inward during the Depression, allowing evil to fester. The president pledged to reconstruct America's military forces, effectively outspending and outlasting the Soviet Union. Shortly after entering office in 1981, Reagan invested heavily in stealth technology; submarines armed with nuclear warheads; MX, Pershing, and Tomahawk missiles; three thousand new combat aircraft; and ten thousand new tanks. It was a bonanza for the Department of Defense, totaling nearly two trillion dollars over the 1980s. Reagan even sent hundreds of missiles to Europe, to be ready for quick deployment. The cold war was renewed, but for Reagan this simply meant that the United States was one step closer to victory. The Bible is explicit: war and rumors of war precede the advent of a better world because Armageddon is followed by the return of Christ and the establishment of His kingdom on Earth.

As the cold war intensified, Reagan declared in a speech before the British Parliament:

> We're approaching the end of a bloody century plagued by a terrible political invention—totalitarianism. Optimism comes less easily today, not because democracy is less vigorous, but because democracy's enemies have refined their instruments

of repression. Yet optimism is in order, because day by day democracy is proving itself to be a not-at-all-fragile flower. . . . Must freedom wither in a quiet, deadening accommodation with totalitarian evil? In an ironic sense Karl Marx was right. We are witnessing today a great revolutionary crisis, a crisis where the demands of the economic order are conflicting directly with those of the political order. But the crisis is happening not in the free, non-Marxist West, but in the home of Marxist-Leninism, the Soviet Union. It is the Soviet Union that runs against the tide of history by denying human freedom and human dignity to its citizens. It also is in deep economic difficulty. The rate of growth in the national product has been steadily declining since the fifties and is less than half of what it was then. The dimensions of this failure are astounding: A country which employs one-fifth of its population in agriculture is unable to feed its own people.[3]

The Soviet Union was plagued by economic difficulties; it could be defeated. After intense struggle, freedom would win. The victory of democracy was inevitable:

Since the exodus from Egypt, historians have written of those who sacrificed and struggled for freedom—the stand at Thermopylae, the revolt of Spartacus, the storming of the Bastille, the Warsaw uprising in World War II. More recently we've seen evidence of this same human impulse in one of the developing nations in Central America. For months and months the world news media covered the fighting in El Salvador. Day after day we were treated to stories and film slanted toward the brave freedom-fighters battling oppressive government forces in behalf of the silent, suffering people of that tortured country.

And then one day those silent, suffering people were offered a chance to vote, to choose the kind of government they wanted. Suddenly the freedom-fighters in the hills were exposed for what they really are—Cuban-backed guerrillas who want power for themselves, and their backers, not democracy for the people. They threatened death to any who voted, and destroyed hundreds of buses and trucks to keep the people from getting to the polling places. But on election day, the people of El Salvador, an unprecedented 1.4 million of them, braved ambush and gunfire, and trudged for miles to vote for freedom.[4] Everywhere around the world, the cry is for liberty.

How could Reagan be so certain that freedom was a universal principle, one that the United States must spread, and not just another example of Western imperialism? Some criticized Reagan's actions in Central America, arguing that American involvement in these areas was no different from Soviet involvement in Eastern Europe. Why was it all right for the United States try to impose their system, they asked, but not the Soviets? These same criticisms were made against the Iraq War by those who accused the Bush administration of terrorism and imperialism. One of the principal proponents of the idea that American foreign policy is hypocritical and driven by economic interests is Noam Chomsky, whose works have condemned American "imperialism" since the 1960s. Responding to these accusations, Reagan argued, "This is not cultural imperialism, it is providing the means for genuine self-determination and protection for diversity. Democracy already flourishes in countries with very different cultures and historical experiences. Who would voluntarily choose not to have the right to vote, decide to purchase government propaganda handouts instead of independent newspapers, prefer government to worker-controlled unions, opt for land to be owned by the state instead of those who till it, want government repression of religious liberty, a single political party instead of a free choice, a rigid cultural orthodoxy instead of democratic tolerance and diversity?"[5] Reagan believed the Kingdom of Freedom was meant for all to enjoy. The failures of Nazi Germany proved that some political systems could boast the moral high ground over others. Those that promoted freedom were inherently superior to those that didn't. One did have the right to overthrow and transform the other. Economic interests didn't determine Reagan's cold war policies.

Reagan's emphasis on freedom did not make him extraordinary.

As Eric Foner shows, virtually all American social movements and political figures have argued their methods promote freedom. Both abolitionists and southern plantation owners believed they fought for freedom during the Civil War. Reagan's uniqueness as president was his belief that freedom can and should be spread to countries previously outside the scope of American influence, including Eastern Europe. A belief in freedom does not distinguish Reagan; a belief in a universal Kingdom of Freedom does. Again Reagan's Christian heritage can't be underestimated when trying to understand his desire to spread freedom: he was merely a missionary seeking to spread the Good Word. Missionaries—those who try to convert nonbelievers—are hallmarks of Christianity. Before Christianity no one in the West attempted to convert the masses to their values. Yet even secular ideologies today have adopted the missionary as an ideal type. During every presidential campaign, thousands of ordinary Americans travel to different parts of the country, attempting to the spread the Good Word and convert nonbelievers to the values of their candidate, in the name of improving humanity.

Reagan's political ecumenism has deep roots. Ecumenism, or universalism, has played a pivotal role in the shaping of Western civilization all the way back to the Greeks and Romans. It may be the one idea that transcends historical eras and intellectual contexts. The Greeks, the Romans, the Christians, Enlightenment philosophes, Marxists, and conservatives like Reagan all sought values that would bind all humanity together, ending discord caused by our differences.

Plato first gave expression to the universal. Truth and reality (the form/idea) was a universal, singular realm for Plato. There are a plurality of false appearances, but only one true form. This singular form gives birth to all truth and reality, all that is right and just. Plato even imagined an ideal society, ruled by philosopher-kings, protected by guardians, and fed by artisans. It applied to all civilizations, at all times. His antagonist Aristotle contested that myriad forms of government were valid; monarchy, aristocracy, and polity, under certain circumstances, could provide the best form of government, yet for Plato, all truth could be found in a singular, universal realm. Plato was the first thinker to assert a universal form of government.

Platonic philosophy became the foundation for succeeding Roman thought, and no one demonstrates this better than Cicero, Plato's greatest disciple in the Republican era. Cicero made no distinction between human beings because all have the ability to reason and therefore discover the universal law. Law, Cicero taught, "is not a product of human thought, nor is it an enactment of peoples, but something eternal which rules the whole universe."[6] Cicero believed that law is universal and eternal, like Plato's form. It transcends all individuals, cultures, and historical eras. We must discover the universal law through reason and live our lives according to it.

The Roman Empire was built upon the ideas (and ashes) of Cicero: it was a universal empire and it gave birth to a universal religion, Christianity. At the urging of St. Paul, the first Christian leaders deemed circumcision unnecessary, enabling the Word of God to be spread to Gentile communities. As Paul contends in Galatians 6:15–16, "It doesn't matter whether we have been circumcised or not. What counts is whether we have been transformed into a new creation. May God's peace and mercy be upon all who live by this principle; they are the new people of God." The Christian God is the God of everyone. He loves everyone equally, and we should share this love with everyone. This was a critical turning point in human history because whereas Judaism is an exclusive religion, Christianity is open to all. The word "catholic" means "universal" and is derived from the Greek word *katholikos*, meaning "according to the whole." The church's greatest philosopher, St. Augustine, argued that history as we know it ends when God's Word and the Christian Empire descended to Earth, covering all nations in God's goodness and "the perfectly ordered and harmonious communion of those who find their joy in God, and in one another in God."[7] Augustine's end of history is characterized by a pristine City of God, where the righteous live eternally. There are no geographic divisions in Augustine. The Kingdom of God is universal.

The Catholic Church intended to be a universal institution in the Middle Ages. Its influence spread across Europe, especially in the Age of Charlemagne, when Christianity reached central Europe. Aligning his empire with the Church, Charlemagne declared to the pope, "Your task, most holy father, is to lift up your hands to God, like Moses, so as to aid our troops, so that with your help the Christian people, with God as its leader and giver of victory, always and everywhere be victorious over the enemies of his holy name, so that the name of our Lord Jesus may be famous throughout the world."[8] Europe begins with Charlemagne, and the bond Charlemagne forged between his empire and the church lasted for centuries. With church help, Charlemagne succeeded in spreading Christianity across Europe. By the end of the Carolingian era, God's name was indeed famous throughout Europe.

The end of the Middle Ages and the beginning of our modern era did not curb universalist ideas. The discovery of the New World in the fifteenth century fostered the expansion of Christianity and provided new opportunities to spread this universal religion. The notion of spreading the Word of God to heathens contributed to the Age of Exploration, first among explorers, and later among missionaries. Columbus's voyages were motivated to some degree by his desire to spread the universal word of Christ. Subsequent missionary influence on early Portuguese, Spanish, and Dutch merchant ships was prominent in the New World and Asia, where missionaries like Matteo Ricci and St. Francis Xavier spread the Good News of the universal God. Western explorers looked down on the "savages" of the New World, but these people could still receive the Word of God, despite sharing nothing with Europe. Although racism permeated the early explorers' views of the new cultures they encountered, it did not permeate theological thinking. The Catholic Church never discriminates when it comes to converts. Ecumenism is its hallmark.

Church significance waned in the seventeenth and eighteenth centuries, yet the ecumenical impulse continued to dominate the minds of the creators of our modern world, dominating the Scientific Revolution and the Enlightenment. The seventeenth and eighteenth centuries were periods of tremendous intellectual foment as Western civilization began questioning its Christian heritage, transitioning to our modern world. But even when a snake sheds its skin, despite surface appearances, its vital organs remain the same. The religious ecumenism of the church paved the way for subsequent scientific, philosophical, and political ecumenism. Theology gave way to science and politics as the primary methods of intellectual discourse, but theological concepts were not completely discarded. A new worldview was created, and it was built upon the old ecumenical Catholic cosmology. The culmination of the Scientific Revolution of the seventeenth century was Isaac Newton's discovery that all earthly and heavenly bodies are governed by universal laws. The same quantifiable forces make an apple drop to earth, control the flow of the tides, and make the location of intergalactic planets predictable and sensible. As the eighteenth-century poet Alexander Pope famously exclaimed, "Nature and Nature's laws lay hid in night: God said, Let Newton be! And all was light."[9] Newtonian science turned darkness into light by demonstrating that the entire physical universal is bound together by universal, quantifiable gravity.

The Enlightenment climaxed in eighteenth-century France, but its roots lie in late seventeenth-century England, with Newton's friend John Locke. Locke analyzed how human beings existed in the state of nature, bereft of all external and cultural influences. By arguing that the mind is a blank slate, Locke suggested that there are no innate differences among men in the state of nature; rather all differences are merely the result of experiences. Locke insisted that all men are by nature free and equal, governed by the universal law of reason. In the state of nature everyone has the power to execute natural, universal laws that render all men free and equal. Like Cicero and St. Augustine, Locke never distinguished between time periods, cultures, and geographic regions.

Locke's and Newton's ideas provided the fountainhead from which all eighteenth-century Enlightenment thought flowed. With reason, one discovers the universal laws of humanity, and from these laws one creates the best political, economic, and social institutions. These ideas mark the beginning of modern political philosophy and are the foundation for modern liberal democracies that take for granted the fact that all equally have the ability to correctly reason. In arguably the final work of the French Enlightenment, Condorcet examined the human mind and envisioned a future where all beings will be free and equal:

> The aim of the work that I have undertaken, and its results will be to show by appeal to reason and fact that nature has set no term to the perfection of human faculties; that the perfectibility of man is truly indefinite; and that the progress of this perfectibility, from now on words independent of any power that might wish to halt it, has no other limits than the duration of the globe upon which nature has cast us. . . . It will be necessary to indicate by what stages what must appear to us today a fantastic hope ought in time to become possible, and even likely; to show why, in spite of the transitory successes of prejudice and the support that it receives from the corruption of governments or peoples, truth alone will obtain a lasting victory; we shall demonstrate how nature has joined together indissolubly the progress of knowledge and that of liberty, virtue and respect for the natural rights of man.[10]

Writing mostly from a prison cell, Condorcet affirmed that humanity will universally find truth, virtue, and, ultimately, freedom and happiness.

Political universalism accordingly first flared during the French Revolution. Many of the revolutionary leaders believed that their ideas, such as liberty, equality, and fraternity, were exportable. Even more so than the American Revolution, whose leaders were more provincial and modest, the French Revolution was a revolution for all men, for all times. The Declaration of the Rights of Man and of the Citizen contained rights that were applicable to all men, not just Frenchman. They are now called "human rights." Condorcet's Girondins sought to extend the ideas of the French Revolution across Europe; the Revolution, they felt, should be internationalized. The Girondins welcomed the American revolutionary Thomas Paine into their ranks. Paine's *Rights of Man* (1791) linked the American and French revolutions by asserting that each had established "universal rights of conscience, and universal rights of citizenship." Even Napoleon sought to expand liberty and equality to new regions of the world, audaciously even to Prussia.

Reagan and modern-day neoconservatives (those who believe American-style government to be "universal" in terms of its application) descend from this intellectual tradition. They are heirs to the Enlightenment too, specifically the notion that the world progresses when liberal democracy and human rights spread. They seek a cosmopolitan world where all men travel through free nations, complete with freedom of speech, press, and religion and free markets.

Events that occurred during 1989 provided evidence for liberal universalism and therefore contributed to the idea that human liberty is for everyone, including people in Iraq and Afghanistan. The year 1989 will be remembered in world history, just like 1066, 1517, 1789, and 1945. While 1989 did not mark the beginning of Soviet demands for democratization, as examples of Eastern Europeans clamoring for democracy can be found virtually since the inception of the Soviet Union, these voices, following Gorbachev's policies, were given their greatest opportunity for expression. And once they were allowed to speak, the peoples of Eastern Europe used democracy to bring down the Soviet system. Eastern Europe had no real democratic tradition. Nonetheless in 1989 democratic momentum spread across Eastern Europe like wildfire as Czechoslovakia, Hungary, Romania, and Poland all experienced turmoil. An influx of Western culture ensued—not just democracy and capitalism but also rock-and-roll music and Coca-Cola. Evidently it's not just our political and economic systems that people around the world demand but our whole way of life.

Demands for democracy spread to non-Western regions of the world in 1989, notoriously even China. As the world watched, millions of Chinese demonstrated where the communist state had been proclaimed on October 1, 1949. Prompted by the dismissal of a liberal-minded government official, Hu Yaobang, over 100,000 people participated in what were intended to be peaceful demonstrations. A statue of the "Goddess of democracy," modeled after America's Statue of Liberty, was passed among the protesters. Protestors demanded serious government reform, human rights, liberal democracy, and more freedom of speech and press. This suggested to neoconservatives that Reagan was right: all people wanted freedom, American-style freedom. These events and ideas contributed to the wars in Iraq and Afghanistan.

7

. . .

Did Reagan's Ideas Matter?

National defense is not a threat to peace; it is the guarantee of
peace with freedom.

—REAGAN, in Cannon, *President Reagan*

By contemporary standards, Ted Kaczynski is a really smart guy. He
graduated from Harvard at age twenty, earned a PhD in mathemat-
ics at twenty-four, and became a professor at Berkeley. His "Industrial Society and Its Future" is more sophisticated than anything
Reagan ever wrote. The work blends elements of Rousseau, Marx,
and Nietzsche in order to critique modern industrial and technological society. He is an insightful social critic. Kaczynski is also
popularly known as the Unabomber; his mail bombs killed several
people and wounded many more. His ideas will never be studied
like Reagan's because they have had little social and political influence. His ideas have not shaped the American political landscape
or events. Kaczynski posited some interesting ideas, but historians
have no interest in him because he has no historical importance.

How, and if, Reagan's ideas transformed the world continues
to be debated. For example, some scholars contend that Reagan's
ideas and subsequent policies had nothing to do with the collapse
of the Soviet Union. George Kennan, the architect of the containment policy Reagan refuted, asserted that Reagan's policies
played no role in ending the Soviet Union: "The claim heard in

campaign rhetoric that the United States under Republican Party leadership 'won the cold war' is intrinsically silly. The suggestion that any administration had the power to influence decisively the course of a tremendous domestic political upheaval in another great country on another side of the globe is simply childish. No great country has that sort of influence on the internal developments of any other one."[1] Kennan's biases need to be acknowledged: he actively opposed many of Reagan's cold war policies. The communist historian Hobsbawm contended, "Since the USSR was to collapse just after the end of the Reagan era, American publicists were naturally to claim that it had been overthrown by a militant campaign to break and destroy it. The USA had waged the Cold War and utterly defeated the enemy. We need not take the crusaders' version of the USA too seriously."[2] Hobsbawm reasoned that no one in the United States foresaw the fall of the Soviet Union, and the CIA naïvely believed that the Soviet economy was strong. Sean Wilentz, a historian at Princeton, wrote, "With regard to the Soviet Union, there is little credible evidence that Reagan's massive military buildup of the early 80s did anything to persuade the Soviet leaders to come to the bargaining table."[3] The Soviet Union was inherently doomed, and its fall was inevitable. Had Jimmy Carter and Walter Mondale won the 1980 and 1984 elections, the events of 1989 would still have occurred in roughly the same manner.

On the other hand, conservatives like the British prime minister Margaret Thatcher declared that Reagan "won the Cold War without firing a shot."[4] Her biases need to be recognized too. Naturally conservatives tout Reagan's foreign policy as a central force in the ending of the cold war. Like Kennan and Hobsbawm, conservatives have ideological biases.

Before examining the ways Reagan's ideas contributed to bringing down the Soviet system, however, some philosophy of history must be kept in mind. As the notable Scottish historian and philosopher David Hume pointed out, cause and effect transcend human capabilities to grasp and understand them. Hume's famous example uses billiard balls: We see billiard ball A smash into ball B. Ball B moves, so we assume the motion of ball A caused this.

But although event A may seem to cause event B, Hume argued, the assertion of cause and effect is still speculative. These ideas may be applied to history. Proving cause and effect can be really hard for historians. After all, World War I may have broken out without the assassination of the archduke; the French Revolution might have occurred if Rousseau had never lived; and America might have won World War II even if FDR had been defeated in the 1940 presidential election. What historians use in order to understand cause and effect is evidence. Is there proof that Rousseau contributed to the French Revolution? No. Is there evidence? Yes. As one example, Robespierre, one of the leading figures of the Revolution, carried copies of Rousseau's books with him. This suggests to most historians, at least to some degree, that Robespierre was influenced by Rousseau. The term "general will," a concept coined by Rousseau, also appears in the Declaration of the Rights of Man and of the Citizen, again suggesting (not proving) some sort of influence. Would the French Revolution have occurred if Rousseau had never lived? This is a tricky question, but evidence suggests that his ideas played a role.

Evidence—specifically Soviet leaders—suggests that Reagan's ideas and subsequent policies impacted the Soviets. Soviet leaders are better sources of evidence than most others, due to their proximity to the events. They are closer to primary sources than figures like Kennan, Hobsbawm, Wilentz, and Thatcher. Soviet leaders contend that for the first time in cold war history, the Soviets had trouble keeping up their end of the arms race. General Secretary Yuri Andropov stated in 1983, "The Soviet Union feels the burden of the arms race into which we are being pulled, more than anybody else does. . . . It is not a problem for Reagan to shift tens of billions of dollars of appropriations from social needs to the military industrial complex."[5] The United States could win the arms race because of its material wealth. Nothing could be more disconcerting during the cold war. Always a key component in determining cold war success and failure in the minds of leaders, arms spending was a zero-sum game. The more the Americans spent, the further the Soviets fell behind.

The further they fell behind, the weaker their system seemed, igniting a need for reform.

The arms race was taken to another level in 1983, when Reagan announced the Strategic Defense Initiative (SDI). Lou Cannon asserted, "More than any other specific program of the administration, SDI was a product of Reagan's imagination and Reagan's priorities. Another president might well have proposed an income tax reduction or a rebuilding of the defense budget, but no other prominent American politician was even talking about construction of a public space shield that would protect civilians from a nuclear holocaust."[6] SDI epitomized Reagan's originality. He pondered in a nationally televised address:

> What if free people could live secure in the knowledge that their security did not rest upon the threat of instant U.S. retaliation to deter a Soviet attack, that we could intercept and destroy strategic ballistic missiles before they reached our own soil or that of our allies? I know this is a formidable, technical task, one that may not be accomplished before the end of the century. Yet, current technology has attained a level of sophistication where it's reasonable for us to begin this effort. It will take years, probably decades of efforts on many fronts. There will be failures and setbacks, just as there will be successes and breakthroughs. And as we proceed, we must remain constant in preserving the nuclear deterrent and maintaining a solid capability for flexible response. But isn't it worth every investment necessary to free the world from the threat of nuclear war?[7]

SDI was a defensive measure, aimed at preventing nuclear attack. An antiballistic missile system that would destroy nuclear missiles using lasers in outer space, it caused a firestorm because many, if not most, physicists argued SDI was not feasible, at least not any time soon. (The physicist Edward Teller was the most notable exception.) To many, it seemed like the latest wasteful manifestation of the American military-industrial complex.

Whether SDI can ever be feasible matters little for historians because the fact is, the Soviets took SDI very seriously. Reagan's most significant military expenditure psychologically weakened the Soviets and contributed to the need for reform by demonstrating Soviet inferiority in the realm of technology. Gorbachev wondered, "Maybe we shouldn't be so afraid of SDI? Of course we cannot disregard this dangerous program. But we should overcome our obsession with it."[8] KGB General Nikolai Leonov conceded that SDI played a powerful "psychological role" by demonstrating the weakness of Soviet technology: "It underlined the need for an immediate review of our place in world technological progress."[9] It underlined a need for reform by showing Soviet technological inferiority. Another Soviet official described the Soviet reaction as "highly emotional . . . in a tone approaching hysteria."[10] The Sovietologist Martin Malia wrote, "More important is the geopolitical point that SDI posed a technological and economic challenge the Soviets could neither ignore nor match. Hence, the only way to diffuse the challenge was through negotiation, and so Gorbachev made winding down the Cold War his first priority. Many in the West would undoubtedly dispute this version of the turn towards ending the conflict, but former Soviet military personnel and political analysts agree that the Soviet Union's inability to keep up its half of the arms race, in particular with regard to SDI, was a principle factor in triggering perestroika."[11] It was a trigger for liberal reform because SDI and Reagan's military buildup showed the Soviets how far they lagged behind the United States in key cold war categories. Their system had never seemed so weak. The only way to strengthen it was through reform.

SDI's psychological impact on Soviet leadership resembled *Sputnik*'s impact on American leadership in the late 1950s. Like *Sputnik*, SDI is significant for what it suggested—in this case, that the American system had surged ahead of its Soviet antagonist in the fields of science and technology. *Sputnik* was just a satellite that orbited the Earth, but it was an important victory for the Soviets in the cold war because it meant Soviet missiles potentially could quickly reach the United States. It had a profound psychological impact on Americans that can be described as hysterical. *Sputnik* and SDI showed that one side potentially had gained a significant advantage in the arms race. sdi potentially meant all Soviet missiles were meaningless. Yes, this is in the abstract, but the cold war was often fought in the abstract, in the minds of men. The difference between sdi and *Sputnik* was that whereas the United States eventually exceeded *Sputnik* by putting a man on the moon, the Soviets could never match sdi. Gorbachev knew this. Much of the negotiation between the Soviets and the Americans during the summit meetings revolved around sdi, so much so that Gorbachev even proposed a complete elimination of nuclear weapons on both sides—as long as the Americans limited sdi research. American technological and military strength proved to the Soviets that they were losing the technological side of the arms race, and therefore were losing the cold war. By roughly 1985 the advantage had swung to the Americans. If the Soviet Union wanted to continue, something had to change.

For those who are still skeptical that Reagan's ideas had anything to do with the Soviet demise, placing Gorbachev's reforms in the broader context of Russian history illuminates how Soviet failure in key aspects of the cold war led to reform, and ultimately collapse. Gorbachev was merely the most recent example of a long line of Russian rulers who attempted reforms following defeat in war. Peter the Great, Russia's first reformer, was partly inspired by Russian attempts at war against Sweden in the seventeenth and early eighteenth centuries. Russia's next round of reforms, led by Tsar Alexander II, were provoked by the Russian debacle in the Crimean War in the 1850s. While Russian forces were able to defeat the mighty Napoleon, several decades later they were victims of the new French military technology inspired by the Industrial Revolution. In the most significant Russian reforms of the nineteenth century, Alexander II, called Tsar Liberator, subsequently freed tens of millions of Russian serfs from the land. Some transitory reforms and liberalizations followed the Russian defeat by Japan in 1905. It would take Russian failures in World War I to lead to the most radical reform, led by Lenin. Although it may seem contradictory to our twenty-first-century Western position, Lenin genuinely believed his version of communism liberated Russia, and without Russian failure in the war, communism never would have been established there. Gorbachev's policies that led to the end of the cold war were in no small part a response to the Soviets' inability to match America technological and military strength. By roughly 1986 the cold war was over and Gorbachev, following in the footsteps of Peter, Alexander II, and Lenin, demanded change.

The arms acceleration also made Reagan the stronger party when he met with Soviet leadership. Reagan, thanks to his time as SAG president, was the most experienced negotiator in presidential history. No one who studies the history of Hollywood can deny the contentious nature of the negotiation between SAG and entertainment executives during the 1950s, partly because TV stars first emerged during this period. He learned during his time as SAG president the advantages of negotiating from a position of power. And this is what he achieved as president from 1981 to 1985. Now he could negotiate. He had more chips. Some writers have credited these meetings with Gorbachev as an impetus for the end of the cold war.[12] This may lead one to see an inconsistency between the Reagan who deemed the Soviet Union an evil empire, the Reagan who sought to roll back communism, the Reagan who pointed missiles at Eastern Europe, the Reagan who invested heavily in offensive and defensive weapons, and the Reagan who befriended Gorbachev. The first Reagan was a hawk; the last, a dove. Reagan used the carrot-and-stick approach to provoke positive change. Reagan initially used threats, until the Soviets were ready to negotiate, then used rewards in order to induce change. He talked loudly and carried a big stick.

Would the Soviet Union have collapsed if Reagan never became president? Probably. But numerous primary sources suggest Reagan's ideas and policies contributed to provoking Soviet reform by demonstrating the inferiority of the Soviet system. Reagan deserves as much credit for winning the cold war as FDR does for winning World War II. A critic of Roosevelt's can plausibly declare that America still would have won World War II had Wendell Willkie won the 1940 presidential election. This is probably true, but that doesn't mean present-day historians deny Roosevelt any credit. Historians prefer to grant agency rather than contend "That would have happened anyway." It is the nature of the field.

Reagan's defense spending may have helped bring about the dissolution of the Soviet Union, but this meant that although he preached limited government, the size of the U.S. government did not significantly shrink during his presidency. This explains the ballooning budget deficits. A dizzying array of statistics can be used by either side of the political spectrum in order to suit their political purposes when it comes to Reagan and spending. Writing history can be tricky. After reviewing all of the analysis of Reagan's effect on government spending, it's hard not to agree with the adage that "there are lies, damn lies, and statistics." The conservative Mises Institute charges, "In 1980, Jimmy Carter's last year as president, the federal government spent a whopping 27.9% of national income. . . . Reagan assaulted the free-spending Carter administration throughout his campaign in 1980. So how did the Reagan administration do? At the end of the first quarter of 1988, federal spending accounted for 28.7% of national income. Even Ford and Carter did a better job at cutting government. His budget cuts were actually cuts in projected spending, not absolute cuts in current spending levels."[13] Most of Reagan's "cuts" were either cuts in projected spending or were later reversed. For example, welfare spending was cut early in Reagan's presidency, so one can justly say that he cut welfare spending. However, these cuts were reversed, so by the end of his presidency, the United States was spending more on welfare per capita (in constant 1984 dollars) than it was in 1980.[14] One biographer calls Reagan a "guns and butter president."[15]

Another variable that must be introduced is that most of Reagan's spending was for defense programs. Although it can be debated how much government grew mainly under Reagan, those who criticize him for expanding government build a straw man because they don't realize that he wanted to shrink the size of every part of the government, save the military. Defense spending was never a budget issue for Reagan because the cold war raged, a war that had to be fought, and won. The fate of humanity lay in the balance. Spend whatever you need to win the cold war, Reagan maintained. The size of government grew under Reagan not because he increased the size of domestic programs but because he revamped the American military. There is an argument that Reagan wanted to reduce the size of government; government grew under Reagan; therefore Reagan failed. This is too simplistic. Reagan never wanted to reduce the size of government when it came to defense spending, because the military was needed to preserve liberty and, more specifically, to win the cold war. Reagan maintained, "National defense is not a threat to peace; it is the guarantee of peace with freedom."[16] Yes, Reagan argued, we need taxes to have a strong defense, but this was justified. By spending heavily on the military, we preserve liberty, and therefore justify this spending.

Do Reagan's ideas about a strong military contradict Christian pacifism? A Christian who preaches war and violence is hypocritical, the argument goes. Jesus preached against violence, so any true Christian should oppose any war. Yet the Christian tradition is hardly a pacifist one. Much like in the Koran, one can find justification in the Bible for either peace or war, depending on which passages are cited. Although Jesus preaches peace in parts of Scripture, other parts are filled with violence. The Book of Jeremiah, for example, abounds with predictions and justifications of death. Jeremiah 20:4 reads, "For this is what the Lord says: 'I will send terror upon you and all your friends, and you will watch as they are slaughtered by the swords of the enemy. I will hand the people of Judah over to the king of Babylon. He will take them captive to Babylon or run them through with the sword.'" Jeremiah 48:10 says, "Cursed are those who neglect doing the Lord's work. Cursed are those who keep their swords from killing." One of Christianity's greatest icons and Jesus's most important forefather, King David, was a warrior who killed. Moses too killed. By using King David as evidence, a Christian can justify death, even if it violates the Ten Commandments. Sometimes death and destruction make the world a better place, such as with King David's slaying of Goliath. Christianity's greatest philosopher, St. Augustine, believed that if war created peace in the world, it was justified. If killing one person saves two lives, is it worth it? Christians like Reagan can justify death, destruction, and war.

The Christian future is not one without violent conflict, because, according to biblical prophecy, violence is a necessary precondition for a better world, the Reign of Saints. Jesus says in Matthew 24:3–14:

> As Jesus was sitting on the Mount of Olives, the disciples came to Him privately. "Tell us," they said, "when will this happen, and what will be the sign of your coming and the end of the age?" Jesus answered: "Watch out that no one deceives you. For many will come in my name, claiming, 'I am the Christ' and will deceive many.
>
> "You will hear of wars and rumors of wars, but see to it that you are not alarmed. Such things must happen, but the end is still to come. Nation will rise against nation, and kingdom against kingdom. There will be famines and earthquakes in various places. All these are the beginning of birth pains.
>
> "Then you will be handed over to be persecuted and put to death, and you will be hated by all nations because of me. At that time many will turn away from the faith and will betray and hate each other, and many false prophets will appear and deceive many people. Because of the increase of wickedness, the love of most will grow cold, but he who stands firm to the end will be saved. And this gospel of the kingdom will be preached in the whole world as a testimony to all nations, and then the end will come."

For Jesus, war and violence were necessary for the New Age, a better age for the righteous. Blessed are the peacemakers, but sometimes war is necessary. We do not want war, but we must be prepared, because sometimes God wills it.

For what it is worth, fewer American soldiers were killed in battle in the 1980s than in any other decade in the twentieth century, save the two decades between World War I and World War II, when Americans practiced a rigid isolationism. In fact, the number of Americans killed in war between 1981 and 2017 is approximately seven thousand (around 5,000 in Iraq, 2,000 in Afghanistan, plus some other skirmishes such as the first Gulf War of 1990–91), one of the lowest totals for a thirty-five-year epoch in modern American history. Reagan's massive military buildup was followed not by war but by relative peace for America. World War I, World War II, the Korean War, and the Vietnam War were far more deadly than any military involvement since 1980. Roughly ten times more Americans were killed in the Korean War than in Iraq and Afghanistan combined. The same statistics are true for Vietnam. America has fought wars since 1980, but they have been occurring with less frequency and with less social impact.

8

...

The Reagan Intellectual Legacy

Americans are a free people, who know that freedom is the right of every person and the future of every nation. The liberty we prize is not America's gift to the world; it is God's gift to humanity.

—GEORGE W. BUSH, "State of the Union Speech," 2003

Time magazine contended in 1975, "Republicans now must decide whether he [Reagan] represents a wave of the future or is just another Barry Goldwater calling on the party to mount a hopeless crusade against the twentieth century."[1] In hindsight Reagan represented the future of the Republican Party, and maybe even America. His 1980 election bordered on a landslide. Furthermore the 1984 election was arguably the largest landslide in American history. Never has the Electoral College voted for anyone as overwhelming as it did for Reagan in 1984. In 1994 Reagan's party took control of Congress for the first time in forty years. At the federal level, from 2002 to 2006 Republicans controlled the House, the Senate, and the presidency. They hadn't controlled this much federal government for so long since the days of Teddy Roosevelt. And the same phenomenon occurred again in the wake of the 2016 elections.

Yet few figures divide people as Reagan does. Many may not realize this, but Ronald Reagan was the Donald Trump of his day. The first real conservative to be elected an American president (Nixon and Eisenhower were moderates), he is probably to the right of Trump on the ideological spectrum. His corresponding rhetoric and policies naturally evoked anger and hatred by segments of the American population. Reagan's intellectual faculties too were questioned. He was considered dumb by some, senile by others. After he entered politics, some of his political opponents deemed him racist. And like Trump, he was called a warmonger because he postulated an aggressive foreign policy, used harsh rhetoric, and condemned arms reductions. The fate of the whole world seemed perilous during the Reagan years too.

These passions for and against Reagan naturally lead to strong biases. One biographer insists that writing about Reagan is not for the faint of heart, or the untenured.[2] For twenty-second-century Reagan specialists studying secondary sources from this era, identifying the political affiliation of the author will matter. For many academics and scholars, the issues are personal. John Patrick Diggins contended, "The election of 1984 was a referendum on the 1960s."[3] If so, how did activists of the 1960s feel about Reagan? The writing of history can be very personal, often revealing more about the writer than the subject.

Interpreting the Reagan presidency often takes center stage in the battle between the American left and right. Jerry Sloan accurately wrote, "Conservatives recognize that the stakes of this interpretive conflict are high. The battle over Reagan's legacy is really a struggle to determine America's future. If the Reagan administration is perceived by the public as being successful, that increases the possibility of the new conservative leaders inheriting Reagan's mantle and continuing his policies into the next century."[4] This is true, but it's only half of the truth. Liberals equally understand the importance of the interpretive struggle; continuing their policies into the twenty-first century means denying any success to Reagan. Democratic senator Chuck Schumer contended, "We're in better shape than [Republicans] are, because they don't realize that Reaganomics is dead, that the Reagan philosophy is dead. . . . We realize that New Deal democracy, which is still our paradigm, which [*sic*] is sort of appealing to each group."[5] If Reagan's ideas and tax cuts in fact stimulated economic growth and reduced unemployment, one of the central legs of the left-wing paradigm has been undercut. Moreover, if it becomes accepted that Reagan's massive military expenditures led to the collapse of the Soviet Union, Republicans could use these historical examples to justify a large defense budget, a liberal nightmare. If it becomes conventional wisdom that Reagan's tax cuts spurred economic growth, this would increase the appeal of Reaganesque candidates. This in turn would weaken other causes traditionally dear to liberals, such as environmentalism and abortion access. The left benefits by denying the overall success of the Reagan presidency, just as the right must promote his successes. Both sides have an equal stake in the debate.

When Obama lauded Reagan, he was instantly castigated by his fellow Democrats. The left-wing columnist Paul Krugman felt the need to tell "the truth about the Reagan presidency." "Historical narratives matter," insisted Krugman. "That's why conservatives are still writing books denouncing F.D.R. and the New Deal; they understand that the way Americans perceive bygone eras, even eras from the seemingly distant past, affects politics today." After explaining why conservatives must lambaste FDR, Krugman continued, "The Reagan economy was a one-hit wonder. Yes, there was a boom in the mid-1980s, as the economy recovered from a severe recession. But while the rich got much richer, there was little sustained economic improvement for most Americans. By the late 1980s, middle-class incomes were barely higher than they had been a decade before—and the poverty rate had actually risen." After eight years of Reagan, he argued, most Americans were not better off.[6] This narrative dominates the minds of Reagan's political critics.

Three days after Reagan's death, uc Berkeley eulogized him: "Ronald Reagan launched his political career in 1966 by targeting uc Berkeley's student peace activists, professors, and, to a great extent, the University of California itself. In his successful campaign for governor of California, his first elective office, he attacked the Berkeley campus, cementing what would remain a turbulent relationship between Reagan and California's leading institution for public higher education."[7] It's important that UC Berkeley students know the truth about Reagan. "This was not a happy relationship between the governor and the university—you have to acknowledge it," recalled Neil Smelser, a Berkeley professor of sociology. "As a matter of Reagan's honest convictions but also as a matter of politics, Reagan launched an assault on the university."[8] Reagan dished it out just as well as he took it. As governor in 1966, he called UC Berkeley "a haven for communist sympathizers, protestors and sex deviants."[9]

Conservatives have their own interpretation of Reagan, of course. Many conservatives deem him a demigod. He won the cold war, jump-started the American economy, and, most important, renewed American optimism. The conservative writer Dinesh D'Souza writes in his hagiography of Reagan that the 1980s were a time of technological innovation and advancement in the United States. Lou Cannon quantifies the period: "During the buying binge of the last six years of the Reagan administration, Americans purchased 105 million color television sets, 88 million cars and light trucks, 63 million VCRs, 62 million microwave ovens, 57 million washers and dryers, 46 million refrigerators and freezers, 31 million cordless phones and 30 million telephone answering machines."[10] Tax cuts enabled all of this, conservatives contend.

One of the greatest inventions in the history of humankind, the personal computer, proliferated, even becoming available to middle-class Americans in the mid-1980s. How does this relate to Reagan? D'Souza writes, "Where did all the venture capital for the new industries of the 1980s come from? There was a little of it around in the 1970s. George Gilder points out the number of major venture capital partnerships surged from 25 in the mid-1970s to more than 200 in the early 1980s. The total pool of venture capital nearly doubled, from $5.8 billion in 1981 to $11.5 billion in 1983."[11] This happened because Reagan poured hundreds of billions of dollars into private hands through his tax cuts, promoting investment in private companies, analogous to what today we call "start-ups." The reasoning goes that wealthy Americans had more money, which they invested in technology. Seek the Kingdom of Freedom first, conservatives say, and then your material needs will be met. Computers, televisions, and airplanes are just some examples of the material benefits of freedom, and these have benefited all strata of society. Facebook, Google, Amazon, the iPhone, and Uber have emerged from the American economic system more recently.

Besides the reduction in taxes and the lowering of inflation and unemployment that followed Reagan's tax cuts, as D'Souza contended, "when Reagan took office the poverty rate had been rising, from 11.4% to 14% in 1981. After climbing to a high of 15.2% during the recession of 1982, the poverty rate fell to 12.8% in 1989."[12] Under the Reagan presidency, the number of poor Americans declined. (This happens whenever the economy booms.) Conservatives thus believe that poverty was reduced as a result of Reagan's tax cuts. Everyone benefits from freedom.

The Reagan Foundation has its own statistics:

Twenty million new jobs were created.

Inflation fell from 13.5 percent in 1980 to 4.1 percent by 1988.

Unemployment fell from 7.6 percent to 5.5 percent.

Net worth of families earning between $20,000 and $50,000 grew by 27 percent.

Real gross national product rose 26 percent.[13]

The last two stats concerning net wealth and GDP matter because they lead to more government revenue. Generally the more money people make, the more they pay in taxes. In 1980, 4,414 Americans filed tax returns with adjusted gross income of at least one million dollars. By 1987 that number had reached 34,944.[14] Consequently, despite the fact that Reagan dramatically slashed the top marginal tax rate, the U.S. government actually collects more tax revenue per capita, adjusted for inflation, today than in 1980. Figure 1 demonstrates this.

America's population is about 1.5 times greater now than in 1980, but our federal government is poised to collect more than

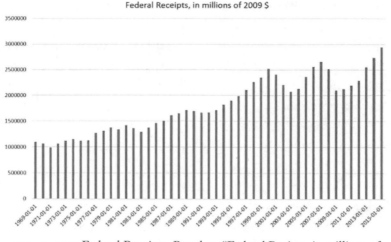

Federal Receipts, in millions of 2009 $

FIG. I. 2009 Federal Receipts. Based on "Federal Recipts, in millions of 2009 $" from the article "Flush with Cash: US Government Collects Record Taxes in 2015" by Ryan McMaken, published online by the Mises Institute, April 25, 2016.

2 times more tax revenue (receipts), despite a significantly lower top marginal tax rate.

Given all of these statistics and different interpretations, is an objective study of Reagan even possible? Sean Wilentz, in his study of Reagan, contended, "Concerning the issues of objectivity and partisanship, I firmly believe that it is possible for a historian to lay aside personal views, commitments and earlier judgments when writing about the recent past—including events in which he or she has had a small hand."[15] Yet academics, scholars, and intellectuals work within a political paradigm, no different from the scientific paradigm described by Thomas Kuhn. We maximize and celebrate evidence that conforms to our value systems, while minimizing and trivializing evidence that contradicts our deepest, most fervent opinions. When Republican economic policies are followed by economic calamity (as under Hoover), they are celebrated as lessons of history regarding why we shouldn't vote Republican. When they are followed by strong economic growth (as under Reagan), the evidence gets minimized and even dismissed, such as getting reduced to coincidence. Bias does not manifest itself through lies but rather by emphasizing evidence in such a way that it conforms to the individual person's ideology. Like lawyers in a court case, historians selectively emphasize some evidence and de-emphasize the evidence they don't like.

In his own work, for example, Wilentz denies that Reagan's conservative policies had anything to do with the economic recovery of the mid-1980s. "Several factors led to the boom. In part (as David Stockman [one of Reagan's budget directors] would later concede), the recovery was a normal phenomenon of the business cycle: the economy was bouncing back from Reagan's own recession of 1981–1982."[16] Wilentz blames Reagan for the bad economy during the first two years of his presidency but gives him no credit for the booming economy during the rest of the decade, which gets reduced to normal business cycles. Blaming Reagan for the economic realities of 1981 is a bit unfair considering he didn't even sign his tax cuts into law until August 1981, and they didn't go into effect completely until January 1982. Reagan inherited a downward-spiraling economy. Other Reagan biographers have called the recession of 1981 and 1982 the "Reagan Recession." Faulting Reagan for the recession of 1981–82 is as rational as blaming Obama for the bad economy in 2009 and 2010 (as some of those on the right did). Some analysis absolves Reagan of much of the blame for the bad economy in the first two years of his presidency, assuming historians don't blame Obama for the poor job-creation numbers and rising unemployment of 2009–10. What about Reagan's foreign policy? Wilentz lauds Reagan for successfully ending the cold war, calling it one of the great achievements in American presidential history.[17] Nonetheless he calls the Reagan foreign policy "divided and contradictory."[18] Wilentz uses Iran-contra as evidence of Reagan's foreign policy shortcomings.

When analyzing whether Reagan's tax cuts helped improve the economy, it should be remembered that even Democrats in the early 1980s pushed for tax cuts as a way to jump-start the American economy. The difference between Reagan and Democrats in the early 1980s was not whether tax cuts were needed but rather how deep the cuts should go. Democratic leaders Dick Gephardt and Bill Bradley proposed reducing the top marginal tax rate in order to foster economic growth, but whereas Democrats wanted to reduce the top marginal tax rate from 70 percent to roughly 50 percent, Reagan wanted to reduce it to between 38 and 28 percent. Even the Obama stimulus package included tax cuts, proving that he was hardly a socialist who wanted to restrict all private property. The fear was inflation and increased budget deficits. Inflation actually plummeted. The drop in inflation since the 1980s is one of the most remarkable features of the American economy. To contextualize, in 1979 inflation was at 11 percent. In 1980 it was at 13.5 percent. In 1981 it was at 10 percent. Since 1983 inflation has never been over 5 percent. Since 1992 it has never been over 4 percent. This benefits poor and middle-class Americans more than anyone else. Although deficits soared, contrary to what many reasonably feared, the budget deficits had no long-term impact on the American economy: the 1990s was another decade of strong economic growth. Unemployment was lower, inflation was lower, and GDP growth was stronger than in the 1970s, an era with smaller deficits. In the 1980s fears that budget deficits would place great strain on America seemed rational, but in hindsight they were unfounded.

No one can say with certainty whether Reagan's policies caused the drops in unemployment, surges in GDP, and reduced inflation, but historians generally grant agency to phenomena. For example, Napoleon, Lenin, and Hoover are just three of the figures in Western history to whom historians have granted agency for their economic policies, despite the fact that they had very different economic policies and different results. Historians don't like the "That would have happened anyway" argument. Even the great Abraham Lincoln fell victim to this sentiment when his opponents argued that slavery would have died out without the Civil War, so it wasn't really necessary after all. Yet historians don't like coincidences; there is little point in studying the great figures in history if all of their achievements can be reduced to other causes. Presidential historians, in particular, must be willing to grant agency to presidents; otherwise there would be no point in ranking the presidents. If it were a foregone conclusion that America would claim the Louisiana territory, remain united after the Civil War, win World War I, World War II, and the cold war, and come out of the depression and the economic malaise of the 1970s, then no president should get any credit for his or her achievements. Yet we do know that presidential historians have favorites.

Moreover, it's been over thirty years, and most of Reagan's tax cuts are still in place. This is Reagan's greatest domestic achievement. Even when Democrats have controlled the presidency and both houses of Congress, there have been no attempts to repeal Reagan's tax cuts. His opponents can criticize all the changes that have taken place in America since 1980, but like FDR's Social Security Act of 1935, Reagan's tax cuts have become an integrated feature of American political culture. Their persistence is the best testament to their success. Historians use the existence of social security and the Great Society in the United States and the persistence of the welfare state in Europe as testimony to the success of left-wing parties there, but the same must be applied to Reagan. As long as the top marginal tax rate remains significantly below the 70 percent it was at when Reagan entered office, he can claim victory on this front. Some may dismiss his tax cuts on the grounds that they didn't make America better, but Republicans maintain the same about social security and the Great Society.

In the Shadow of Reagan

Clearly Reagan cast a long shadow, longer than any other twentieth-century president, save FDR. American conservatives today descend from Reagan. And his influence has extended beyond the Republican Party. Peter Singer writes in a book on Karl Marx, "Nor has Marx's influence been limited to communist societies. Conservative governments have ushered in social reforms to cut the ground from under revolutionary Marxist opposition movements."[19] American Democrats have adopted Reagan's ideas to stop the spread of Reagan conservatives. President Bill Clinton adopted Reagan's ideas. Welfare reform, fixing social security, a low top marginal tax rate, and NAFTA were all Reagan's ideas, which many Democrats advanced in order to garner popular support. Did not President Clinton declare "The era of Big Government is over" shortly before winning reelection in 1996? Did not President Obama refuse a government takeover of the health care system, instead employing private health insurance companies to provide health insurance? Left-wing American governments have ushered in conservative ideas in hopes of curbing the influence of Reagan Republicans, or more precisely, to win back the support of Reagan Democrats, who are often swing voters. Republicans did and continue to do the same with Roosevelt.

William Leuchtenburg's *In the Shadow of FDR* provided a model for this section. Leuchtenburg showed how each of FDR's successors worked within the system FDR created. So forceful a figure was he, so powerful were his presidency and his ideas, that no one could escape his shadow. The same goes for Reagan. Presidential history following the two men's presidencies is remarkably similar: both were succeeded by their vice presidents, who served only one full-term due to their unpopularity. Then came eight years of a moderate from the other party, Eisenhower and Clinton. Next came eight years of those who at least sought discipleship, JFK-LBJ and George W. Bush (although with all three, how much discipleship is debatable). Then came eight years of rule by the other party, Nixon-Ford and Obama (all three actually showed respect). Then came someone from the same party, Carter and Trump. This can't all be coincidence.

George H. W. Bush and Reagan squared off in the contentious 1980 Republican primary. Whereas Reagan was a hardline conservative in the mold of Goldwater, Bush was a moderate, chiding Reagan's plans for tax cuts, notoriously calling the ideas "voodoo economics." Despite his experience in government and his early win in the Iowa caucus, Bush was quickly overwhelmed by the Reagan campaign. Reagan still named Bush his vice president (Ford was also considered), and the Reagan-Bush ticket convincingly won the 1980 presidential election. Bush kept a low profile as vice president and was naturally the front-runner for his party's nomination for president. His résumé for the presidency seemed unimpeachable, including stints as ambassador to the United Nations and director of the CIA. He captured the presidency in 1988, winning 53 percent of the popular vote and 426 out of 537 electoral votes. It was a natural "third term" for Reagan.

Bush had to confront the budget deficits he inherited. Cuts (or slowed growth) to social programs and increases in tax revenue generated by the booming economy from about 1983 to 1989 didn't make up for increased military spending in the early 1980s. With Democrats controlling both houses of Congress, Bush had to accept their ideas about raising the top marginal tax rate from 28 to 38 percent, thereby breaking his campaign pledge of "No new taxes." Congressional Republicans, who by now were hailing Reagan as their hero, were furious. They never trusted Bush again. No real Reagan conservative, Bush violated rule number one of the conservative agenda: he raised taxes. Politically this was fatal. Even worse, recession followed, so by the middle of 1992 unemployment edged near 8 percent. Bush had angered Republicans by reneging on a crucial campaign promise just as America faced its first recession in ten years. This perfect storm helps us understand why Bush received only 37 percent of the popular vote in a three-way race in 1992.

Internationally, like Truman, Bush asserted American hegemony, proving that America would not retreat from world affairs, as it did after World War I and Vietnam. For Truman, the occasion was Stalin's blockading of the American, French, and British sectors of Berlin in 1948. Stalin blocked Western access to Berlin by closing roads and railways in an effort to increase Soviet control of the city. Truman had to make a difficult choice: confront Stalin and risk World War III, or allow Stalin to incorporate all of Berlin into the Soviet Empire. Truman parried Stalin by orchestrating the Berlin Airlift. Demonstrating that America would not yield to Soviet pressures, the airlift was a key event in the early cold war. Berlin was distant, but America would not ignore Soviet expansion. For George H. W. Bush, the occasion was the first Gulf War. In 1991 President Saddam Hussein of Iraq launched a full-scale invasion of Kuwait, prompting the question, Should America take action and risk tens of thousands of lives or allow Saddam to control Kuwait?

Now, largely thanks to the Reagan presidency, America could act militarily. The Reagan presidency, like the FDR presidency, initiated a new era in diplomatic history, one in which America reigned supreme, willing to wield its influence across the globe. The United States, leading a multilateral force, quickly pushed Saddam out of Kuwait. Operation Desert Storm was a smashing success, leading Bush to exclaim, "The specter of Vietnam has been buried forever in the desert sands of the Arabian Peninsula"[20]

American hegemony had returned. Truman and George W. Bush provided singular global leadership, yet despite their critical international successes, contemporaries across the political spectrum were disappointed by the Truman and Bush presidencies. For the members of their own parties, these two men could never live up to the standards set by their predecessors. Reagan and Roosevelt were tough acts to follow. Economic downturns during Truman's and George H. W. Bush's presidencies led to national pessimism and frustration, much of it naturally aimed at the incumbent. Both men left office victims of the mantra that it was time for change. (A similar phenomenon occurred during the Adams presidency. Following the great George Washington was an impossible task, and Adams became the first American president voted out of office.) Change was a central theme for both Eisenhower's and Clinton's first presidential campaigns.

The time to pay the piper had come. Sure, Reagan and Roosevelt scored landslide elections, but their successes were smoke and mirrors, their critics claimed. Roosevelt and Reagan were politically successful in the short term, but their long-term legacy was malignant. The best evidence for this came from the massive budget deficits both accrued, largely the result of defense spending in the midst of war. These irresponsible fiscal policies, many of Reagan's critics pointed out, would saddle future generations with debt. Reagan's biographer John Sloan admits the initial title of his 1999 Reagan biography was "The Reagan Presidency: Political Success and Economic Decline."[21]

Reagan and FDR were suns; Truman and Bush, mere moons. Like Truman, Bush never adhered to the core principles of his predecessor; he never acquired the unmitigated support of the party of faithful because he, like Truman, was politically reared in the preceding era, so he wasn't intellectually influenced by his predecessor. Truman wasn't a Roosevelt Democrat; he was a product of the Pendergrast Machine, a powerful political organization in Missouri. And Bush, more in the mold of 1970s Republicans, was never a Reagan Republican. Nonetheless, to their opponents both men represented the colossus—a defeat of Truman meant an ex post facto defeat of FDR, while the left took the same view of the Bush administration's political failings. By 1952 Republicans controlled both houses of Congress and the White House. The Roosevelt Revolution was over. By 1992 Democrats controlled the House, the Senate, and the presidency; all that had been gained during the Reagan years was lost. There was no real Reagan Revolution, as so many conservatives had hoped. The years 1952 and 1992 were years for change, with a new party given the opportunity to govern. It was about time, many believed.

First Democratic Interlude: Bill Clinton

We meet at a special moment in history, you and I. The Cold War is over. Soviet communism has collapsed and our values— freedom, democracy, individual rights, free enterprise—they have triumphed all around the world.

—BILL CLINTON, "Address Accepting the Presidential Nomination at the Democratic National Convention in New York," 1992

The unpopularity of their successors meant that Republicans after Roosevelt and Democrats after Reagan were given a chance to rule. To their opponents this meant that the United States had finally moved away from the policies of Roosevelt and Reagan and was ready to embark on a new course. Yet those who believed America would rid itself of the key components of the presidencies of Roosevelt and Reagan were naïve. It was under Clinton that some of Reagan's ideas bloomed.

Clinton has been described as a man without a political compass, a man guided by public opinion polls. Even Clinton's biggest defenders will acknowledge that he, unlike Reagan, lacked a comprehensive, consistent vision for America. Yet Clinton was in a quandary: his biggest supporters despised Reagan, yet much of the American center—those most responsible for determining who wins and who loses elections—were Reagan Democrats. So Clinton walked a fine line. After becoming governor of the conservative state of Arkansas in 1978, he adapted to the conservative winds blowing across America by joining the newly formed Democratic Leadership Council, an organization that contended the Democrats should abandon far-left ideas. He became chairman in 1990 and campaigned in 1992 as a "New Democrat," promised to "end welfare as we know it," and stressed the need to reform social security. Apparently he had learned the lessons of the Republican victories in 1980, 1984, and 1988, the first time either side had won three straight elections since the days of FDR. Clinton won the 1992 election relatively easily, capturing 43 percent of the popular vote in a three-man race.

Clinton's acceptance speech for the Democratic nomination plagiarized some of Reagan's vision for America and the world. He contended that freedom, democracy, individual rights, and capitalism are not American values; they are universal values, applicable to all societies:

> Soviet communism has collapsed and our values—freedom, democracy, individual rights, free enterprise—they have triumphed all around the world. [Everywhere around the world, the cry is for liberty, Reagan said.]
>
> Tonight 10 million of our fellow Americans are out of work. Tens of millions more work harder for lower pay. The incumbent President says unemployment always goes up a little before a recovery begins, but unemployment only has to go up by one more person before a real recovery can begin. And Mr. President, you are that man. [Reagan joked in 1980, "Recession is when your neighbor loses his job. Depression is when you lose yours. And recovery is when Jimmy Carter loses his."]
>
> That's why we need a new approach to government, a government that offers more empowerment and less entitlement,

more choices for young people in the schools they attend—in the public schools they attend. . . . A government that is leaner, not meaner; a government that expands opportunity, not bureaucracy; a government that understands that jobs must come from growth in a vibrant and vital system of free enterprise. [Reagan said in his Inaugural Address in 1981, "Government can and must provide opportunity, not smother it; foster productivity, not stifle it."][22]

Capitalism promotes economic growth and productivity, not a government bureaucracy. The private sector and freedom create material wealth. Clinton declared that what was needed was "an America that says to entrepreneurs and businesspeople: We will give you more incentives and more opportunity than ever before to develop the skills of your workers and to create American jobs and American wealth in the new global economy. An America where we end welfare as we know it. We will say to those on welfare: You will have and you deserve the opportunity through training and education, through child care and medical coverage, to liberate yourself. But then, when you can, you must work, because welfare should be a second chance, not a way of life."[23] The far-left argued that labor creates economic growth and value, but Clinton focused on the creative classes. No Democrat would adopt so many ideas of George W. Bush, nor would a Republican mimic Clinton. However, just as no political figure in the post–World War II years could ignore FDR's shadow and legacy, the same can be said for Reagan's ideas. Even his antagonists must capitulate because his ideas have become ingrained in American political culture. Reagan's opponents criticize parts of his philosophy, but overall their attitude must be described as ambivalent.

The Democrats swept the 1992 elections, capturing key southern states that had voted for Reagan. In doing so the Democrats won the presidency for the first time since 1976 and even gained seats in the House. *Time* magazine called the results of the election "a mandate for change."[24] (Eisenhower titled his biography about his first term as president *A Mandate for Change*.) Despite Clinton's "New Democrat" pretensions, many interpreted the election as a victory for old-style liberalism and a defeat of Reaganism. The Clinton administration initially lurched far to the left. In his first two years in office, there was no effort to reform welfare. Taxes were raised, although the top marginal tax rate was only raised to 43 percent, far below where it was before Reagan took office. Clinton also introduced the holy grail of liberalism, government-run universal health care. The Health Security Act of 1993, spearheaded by Hillary Clinton, was defeated, even with a Democrat-controlled House and Senate. Clinton didn't heed Reagan's warnings about a government takeover of the entire health care system.

American voters voiced their opposition to Clinton in the 1994 midterm elections. In a mini-revolution, Republicans took control of the House of Representatives for the first time in forty years. (Democrats took back control of the House in 1954, after their 1952 fiasco.) The Reagan presidency had changed many congressional districts from blue to red. The new conservative manifesto was the "Contract for America," much of it modeled upon Reagan's 1985 State of the Union address. Specifically the contract attempted to shrink divisions between the people and their government. Term limits, reducing the size of government, and auditing fraud and waste were all part of the contract. More significant, the contract promised to cut taxes on businesses and individuals, as well as enact some sort of social security and welfare reform. After a two-year hiccup, Reagan was back.

Accordingly a new Bill Clinton emerged after 1994, a more moderate Clinton, a Clinton willing to implement some of Reagan's ideas. Like Eisenhower, Clinton attempted and succeeded at placing himself above the political fray. Now he was neither liberal nor conservative; instead he combined the best elements of each philosophy. Clinton triangulated by rising above the political extremes. Just as Ike was no FDR disciple, Clinton was no disciple of Reagan, yet each was politically astute enough not to refute certain principles. This allowed Clinton to capture the support of the American center. In his 1996 State of the Union address, Clinton famously proclaimed, "We will meet these challenges, not through big government. The era of big government is over, but we can't go back to a time when our citizens were just left to fend for themselves."[25] Government, he contended, was not the solution.

Clinton even adopted the social security position that Reagan had been arguing for decades. He recognized the inherent flaw in social security, and by the 1990s many Democrats agreed that the program needed fixing. At a speech given in Georgetown, Clinton described the impending "crisis": "If you don't do anything, one of two things will happen. Either [social security] will go broke and you won't ever get it, or if we wait too long to fix it, the burden on society . . . of taking care of our generation's social security obligations will lower your income and lower your ability to take care of your children to a degree that most of us who are parents think would be horribly wrong and unfair to you and unfair to the future prospects of the United States."[26]

Clinton embraced Reagan's ideas about welfare reform too. By the middle of the 1990s there was a concerted effort by those on both sides of the aisle to reduce the number of people on welfare. The Personal Responsibility and Work Opportunity Act of 1996 implemented many of Reagan's ideas about tightening welfare by limiting the number of years a person could receive welfare consecutively to two, and overall to five. Also, the program became more decentralized. Money was dispersed by states through block grants. The 1996 Democratic platform bragged, "Welfare rolls are finally coming down—there are 1.8 million fewer people on welfare today than there were when President Clinton took office in January 1993. . . . The new welfare plan gives America an historic chance: to break the cycle of dependency for millions of Americans, and give them a real chance for an independent future. It reflects the principles the President has insisted upon since he started the process that led to welfare reform."[27] Many liberals condemned Clinton, and even key members of his cabinet voiced opposition. But minds began to change, shifting from outright opposition to ambivalence or even modest support. The numbers of those dependent on welfare declined significantly, and there was no corresponding rise in poverty. The left-leaning *New Republic* admitted in

2006, "A broad consensus now holds that welfare reform was certainly not a disaster—and that it may, in fact, have worked much as its designers had hoped."[28] Like social security, welfare reform will always have ideological opponents, but the persistence of the program—even during times of Democratic majorities—suggests that the pros outweigh the cons.

NAFTA is another Reagan idea that Clinton embraced and ran with. This agreement, consistent with the classical economic theory favored by Reagan, eliminated trade barriers between the United States, Canada, and Mexico. It immediately eliminated tariffs on 50 percent of Mexican exports to the United States and over 30 percent of American exports to Mexico. Clinton maintained, "For decades, working men and women and their representatives supported policies that brought us prosperity and security. That was because we recognized that expanded trade benefited all of us but that we have an obligation to protect those workers who do bear the brunt of competition by giving them a chance to be retrained and to go on to a new and different and, ultimately, more secure and more rewarding way of work."[29] Some resisted NAFTA, arguing that free trade benefited only the economically powerful; instead these people yearned for "fair trade." Still, the Obama administration made no effort to renegotiate NAFTA. Trump has voiced opposition to parts of NAFTA, but it remains to be seen what changes will be made.

Internationally, Clinton sent the U.S. military globetrotting, something Ford and Carter refused to do in the wake of Vietnam. There have been four presidents since Reagan, and each has sent soldiers and dropped bombs all over the world. Whether it be the first Gulf War, Clinton's efforts in the former Yugoslavia and Somalia, wars in Iraq and Afghanistan, or more recent efforts by Obama in Syria and Libya, Reagan enabled this. Whereas the post-Vietnam years saw a reluctance to use the American military to fight the evils of the world, after Reagan both Democrat and Republican presidents have used the military that Reagan reconstructed to help solve the world's problems. Vietnam syndrome is dead. And Reagan killed it.

Finally, and maybe most significant of all, Clinton embraced Reagan's ideas about the universal applicability of American democracy, even to Iraq. Clinton maintained in 1998, "The United States wants Iraq to rejoin the family of nations as a freedom-loving and law-abiding member. This is in our interest and that of our allies within the region. The United States favors an Iraq that offers its people freedom at home. I categorically reject arguments that this is unattainable due to Iraq's history or its ethnic or sectarian makeup. Iraqis deserve and desire freedom like everyone else."[30] Reagan's influence is obvious; such ideas would have been impossible before his presidency or the fall of the Soviet Union. Clinton's role in creating a political climate conducive to war in Iraq has been underestimated, probably because the war's biggest critics voted for him. But Clinton plays an intermediary role between Reagan's belief that all people of the world deserved freedom and that America must promote this, and George W. Bush's attempt to apply this to Iraq. It was Clinton who in 1998 signed the "Iraq Liberation Act," making regime change the official U.S. policy toward Iraq. By the end of that year Clinton had ordered a sustained bombing campaign of Iraq, insisting that Iraq's weapons of mass destruction threatened American security.[31] Clinton argued, "The hard fact is that so long as Saddam remains in power, he threatens the well-being of his people, the peace of his region, the security of the world. . . . If Saddam defies the world and we fail to respond, we will face a far greater threat in the future. Saddam will strike again at his neighbors. He will make war on his own people."[32] Clinton and Reagan both helped pave the road that George W. Bush traveled. The stage was now set for an invasion of Iraq under the auspices of national security, partly inspired by the desire to spread the Kingdom of Freedom.

George W. Bush and the War in Iraq: Betrayal or Continuance?

By the mid-1990s Reagan, the man accurately described as a "one-man think tank," became intellectually impaired. Alzheimer's disease robbed him of most of his cognitive faculties, so he could no longer speak about national and foreign issues, as he had for the preceding fifty years. Now those who followed Reagan, his disciples, were left on their own to interpret his thought. Like all significant intellectual figures, Reagan has heirs and divisions exist among them; they even consider themselves rivals. In Reagan's case, the divisions are between neoconservatives and more traditional conservatives, sometimes called "paleoconservatives." Reagan inspired both; each claim to be his true heirs. This is normal in the history of thought.

Neoconservatism is sort of an inverted Marxism. It tries to export democracy instead of socialism. Whereas Marx viewed the advent of world socialism to be inevitable, neoconservatives similarly view Western-style democracy. In fact, some early neoconservatives were weaned on Marxist or, more precisely, Trotskyist dogma, which promoted worldwide or ecumenical worker revolution, as opposed to the more provincial "socialism in one country" preached by Stalin. In the 1920s Stalin argued that the Soviet Union needed to strengthen itself before promoting worldwide revolution, but Trotsky argued for "permanent revolution," or the belief that socialists needed to promote revolution everywhere, even in countries with primitive economic systems. Neoconservatives merely substitute democracy for socialism. Marxism-Leninism-Trotskyism descends from Christianity, so the fact that many figures on the right, like Reagan, can recast these ideas as their own is reasonable.[33]

Neoconservatism needs to be contextualized. It emerged after World War II, after the destruction of Nazism, largely thanks to the American military. Neoconservatives were anticommunist and believed that America needed to take an active role in the world in order to stop the spread of communism, as America did with Nazism, so they are hawks. Taking its cue from the first two world wars, American international activism defines neoconservatism, as opposed to the isolationism that America practiced between the two world wars. Neoconservatives thus hail Truman as one of their own. After World War II, Truman ensured that the United States would not revert back to the isolationist period of the 1920s and 1930s. Against popular opinion, he argued that American involvement was needed in Greece, lest communism spread there. Freedom was the issue for Truman, and he felt it was America's responsibility to "support free peoples who are resisting attempted subjugation by armed minorities or by outside pressures," such as the Soviet Union. He continued, "If we falter in our leadership we may endanger the peace of the world—and we shall surely endanger the welfare of our nation."[34] "Americans," Truman declared at another time, would use "our military strength solely to preserve the peace of the world. For we now know that this is the only sure way to make our own freedom secure."[35] In 1950, after North Korean communists crossed the thirty-eighth parallel into democratic South Korea, Truman ordered hundreds of thousands of American servicemen to Korea, starting the Korean War. Over fifty thousand Americans perished.

Nonetheless, neoconservatives hail Truman's activism and adopt Reagan's faith in the military, something Republicans were less inclined to do before Reagan. In the twenty-first century the Republican Party is associated with defense spending, but that hasn't always been the case. A Democrat brought America into World War I. FDR engaged in the largest peacetime military buildup in American history, earning him criticism from Republicans for being a warmonger. Roosevelt's leading congressional opponent was Republican Robert Taft, an isolationist who opposed any American involvement in Europe during World War II, until Pearl Harbor. After FDR's death, Taft tried to thwart Truman's attempt to bring America into the NATO Alliance. Truman remains the only leader in history to use the most deadly weapon in world history, the atomic bomb. Truman started the Korean War. It was ended by Eisenhower, the same Republican who coined the term "military-industrial complex" because he feared the cost of an arms race. What prompted him to make such statements as he left office? His successor, John F. Kennedy, insisted during the 1960 presidential campaign that the Eisenhower-Nixon administration had allowed a "missile gap" to develop between the United States and the Soviet Union, something he vowed to erase. LBJ greatly escalated American involvement in Vietnam. After initially expanding the Vietnam War, his Republican successor wound it down. Nixon and Ford both cut military spending in the post-Vietnam years. Senator Scoop Jackson, an ardent cold warrior militarist during the 1960s and 1970s, was a Democrat. The point is, the Republican Party hasn't always been the hawkish party that invests more heavily in the military. This demonstrates Reagan's influence on the contemporary conservative mind: the American military can and must be used to make the world a better place. These efforts are always noble and, if successful, never in vain.

Neoconservatism gained more traction after the fall of the USSR. One of the lessons of the most historically significant event of the second half of twentieth century is that geography doesn't restrict freedom and democracy. The fall of the Soviet Union gave neoconservatives great confidence in their core values, since it suggested that they had been right all along: America must play a key role in exporting democracy, a universal principle. To neoconservatives Reagan's hawkish foreign policy played a direct role in undermining the Soviet system. A cursory overview of the second half of the twentieth century reveals that America successfully promoted democracy in Germany, Japan, and Eastern Europe. The Middle East was next. Neoconservatives found safe haven in the George W. Bush administration. At first blush, Bush's presidency merely continued Reagan's: a foreign policy aimed at liberating people from tyrants and spreading Western notions of freedom, an economic policy focused on tax cuts, and a socially conservative, theologically inspired agenda. Who else would W look to as a model? Certainly not his father, a one-term president. The political debt that George W. Bush owes to Reagan scarcely needs to be mentioned; had there been no Reagan, there would have been no George W. Bush presidency.

After winning one of the most hotly contested elections in American history, Bush initially focused on domestic issues, mostly out of necessity because he inherited a struggling economy as the dot-com bubble burst. Bush responded by signing the Economic Growth and Tax Relief Reconciliation Act of 2001. In accordance with Reagan's policies, it tried to jump-start the American economy through tax relief. Tax rates for all classes were reduced. Unrelatedly, in the summer of 2001 the No Child Left Behind bill was signed into law. Passed with lots of Democratic support, it aimed at incentivizing and increasing federal spending on education, particularly among poor and minority students. Contra Reagan, it expanded the role the federal government played in education. Bush's focus on domestic issues was short-lived, however.

The attacks on September 11, 2001, led to a new American foreign policy. As commander in chief of the U.S. Armed Forces, President Bush swore that America would respond. His initial rhetoric emulated Reagan's interpretation of the cold war: "Tomorrow, when you get back to work, work hard like you always have. But we've been warned. We've been warned there are evil people in this world. We've been warned so vividly. . . . My administration has a job to do and we're going to do it. We will rid the world of the evil-doers."[36] The enemy seemed different, but the perpetual conflict of good versus evil remained. Communism, Nazism, and Al Qaeda might seem like entirely different entities, but they really aren't, Bush held, because they all descend from the same source. The "War on Terror," in essence, was merely the latest manifestation of the conflict between good and evil. It was as old as humanity. The United States responded by invading Afghanistan because it provided safe haven for the mastermind of the 9/11 attack, Osama bin Laden. Within days and with broad support, American military forces pounded the Taliban regime for its complicity in the attack. Yet 9/11 revealed America's vulnerability. The world contained unimaginable threats, and dictatorships in distant lands did, in fact, threaten the peace and security of the United States. America had forgotten the lessons of appeasement and paid the price, again. In hindsight the United States should have taken a more active role in Afghanistan, doing whatever it could to overthrow the regime that abetted Al Qaeda prior to 9/11. President Bush learned the lessons of history and would not make the same mistake in Iraq. Iraq repeatedly violated international law, practiced an expansionist foreign policy, and its leader committed acts of genocide when sarin gas was used against the Kurds in 1988.

The Bush administration, with the support of roughly one-third of the world and slight majorities in Congress and the American public, launched an invasion of Iraq in March 2003.

In the tradition of Reagan, Bush argued that those who oppose the war had not learned the lessons of history, namely appeasement. Bush's critics argued that he did not learn the lessons of history, specifically Vietnam. The issue is, which lesson of history matters? The Bush administration mimicked the Reagan administration by warning against appeasement to buttress its case for war in Iraq. Finding analogies between Hitler and Saddam was easy: besides being brutal tyrants who sought territorial aggrandizement, both flagrantly violated and ignored international law following their nation's defeat in war. After World War I, Hitler disregarded the Versailles Treaty by reconstructing the Nazi Wehrmacht. Following defeat in the first Gulf War, the United Nations imposed restrictions on Iraq, which Saddam disregarded. Resolution 1441 was passed unanimously in November 2002; everyone agreed that Iraq had violated resolutions 686, 687, 688, 707, 715, 986, and 1284. If Iraq did not comply, Resolution 1441 promised "serious consequences," which most knew meant war. One of the reasons the Bush administration publicly used Resolution 1441 to justify invading Iraq is because it conformed perfectly with the appeasement era of the 1930s.

Inspired by the success of Reagan's foreign policy, Bush's foreign policy aimed at defeating evil and spreading democracy to oppressed peoples. Continuing Reagan's idea about the moral supremacy of freedom, Bush argued that spreading freedom was a strategic move: "The United States has no quarrel with the Iraqi people; they've suffered too long in silent captivity. Liberty for the Iraqi people is a great moral cause, and a great strategic goal. The people of Iraq deserve it; the security of all nations requires it. Free societies do not intimidate through cruelty and conquest, and open societies do not threaten the world with mass murder. The United States supports political and economic liberty in a unified Iraq."[37] Seek the Kingdom of Freedom first, and all your earthly desires will be met.

For Bush, freedom and religion are not distinct concepts; one logically follows from the other. They are inexorably bound. He declared, "I have a message for the brave and oppressed people of Iraq: Your enemy is not surrounding your country, your enemy is ruling your country. And the day he and his regime are removed from power will be the day of your liberation. . . . Americans are a free people, who know that freedom is the right of every person and the future of every nation. The liberty we prize is not America's gift to the world; it is God's gift to humanity."[38] The Kingdom of Freedom will continue to march triumphantly. The "enemies of freedom" will have their moments—the Kingdom of Freedom never arrives without struggle and conflict—but in the end, we will win. Hitler spread evil from 1933 through 1945. Initially violence, death, and destruction overwhelmed Germany, but ultimately this yielded a better Germany, a Germany with more freedom. The American Revolution and the French revolutions of 1789, 1830, and 1848 were all violent struggles, but they led to freedom. The birth of freedom in Japan was preceded by the dropping of two atomic bombs on the island nation. History teaches us that death and destruction are sometimes necessary preconditions to freedom.

Despite demands for freedom in Eastern Europe and China and freedom's success in Muslim Indonesia, some still rejected Reagan's and Bush's idea that freedom and democracy are universal values. A writer in the the *New Yorker*, for example, contends:

> Democracy is a wonderful idea, but none of the countries in the Middle East, except Israel and Turkey, resemble anything that would look like a democracy to Americans. Some Middle Eastern countries are now and have always been ruled by monarchs. Some are under the control of an ethnic or religious group that represents a minority of the population. Saudi Arabia and the Hashemite Kingdom of Jordan are the world's only major nations named after a single family, and in Saudi Arabia the royal family functions as, in effect, the country's owner. Most Middle Eastern countries don't even make the pretense of having freely elected parliaments; in Iran, for example, candidates have to be approved by the mullahs.[39]

Applying postmodernist arguments, they asserted cultural relativity and appreciation. Bush countered, "There was a time when many said that the cultures of Japan and Germany were incapable of sustaining democratic values. Well, they were wrong. Some say the same of Iraq today. They are mistaken. The nation of Iraq, with its proud heritage, abundant resources and skilled and educated people, is fully capable of moving toward democracy and living in freedom."[40] Japan, Russia, and East Germany prove that freedom is not a Western value but a universal value, longed for and deserved by all people of the world. If democracy can succeed in East Germany and Japan, it can flourish anywhere, including Iraq. Ecumenism permeates neoconservatism. Bush asserted in 2006:

> Five years ago, Iraq's seat in this body [United Nations Assembly] was held by a dictator who killed his citizens, invaded his neighbors and showed his contempt for the world by defying more than a dozen U.N. Security Council resolutions. Now Iraq's seat is held by a democratic government that embodies the aspirations of the Iraq people. It is represented today by President (Jalal) Talabani. With these changes, more than 50 million people have been given a voice in this chamber for the first time in decades. Some of the changes in the Middle East are happening gradually, but they are real. Algeria has held its first competitive presidential election, and the military remained neutral. The United Arab Emirates recently announced that half of its seats in the Federal National Council will be chosen by elections. Kuwait held elections in which women were allowed to vote and run for office for the first time. Citizens have voted in municipal elections in Saudi Arabia and parliamentary elections in Jordan and Bahrain and in multiparty presidential elections in Yemen and Egypt. These are important steps, and the governments should continue to move forward with other reforms that show they trust their people.[41]

Everywhere around the world, the cry was for liberty. Reiterating Condorcet's ideas, Bush asserted that no nation transitions easily to democracy: "Every nation that travels the road to freedom moves at a different pace, and the democracies they build will reflect their own culture and traditions."[42] Bush was not naïve to cultural differences; he just subordinated them to freedom. For better or worse, even in the midst of violence, there was no equivocation. Political pundits may conveniently portray Bush and Obama as adversarial figures, yet spreading democracy to the Middle East has played an important role in both of their presidencies. Like Reagan, Bush and Obama have asserted that the victory of democracy is inevitable.

Naturally President Bush hoped history remembers him as a liberator: "I'd like to be a president [known] as somebody who liberated 50 million people and helped achieve peace."[43] An entire chapter of the Iraqi Constitution (2005) is dedicated to "Liberties." Parts of it read: "The liberty and dignity of man are safeguarded."

Article 37:

First: The freedom of forming and of joining associations and political parties is guaranteed. This will be organized by law.

Article 38:

The freedom of communication, and mail, telegraphic, electronic, and telephonic correspondence, and other correspondence shall be guaranteed and may not be monitored, wiretapped or disclosed except for legal and security necessity and by a judicial decision.

Article 39:

Iraqis are free in their commitment to their personal status according to their religions, sects, beliefs, or choices. This shall be regulated by law.

Article 40:

Each individual has freedom of thought, conscience and belief.

Article 42:

First: Each Iraqi enjoys the right of free movement, travel, and residence inside and outside Iraq.

Second: No Iraqi may be exiled, displaced or deprived from returning to the homeland.

Article 43:

There may not be a restriction or limit on the practice of any rights or liberties stipulated in this constitution, except by law or on the basis of it, and insofar as that limitation or restriction does not violate the essence of the right or freedom.[44]

Foner wrote in 1998, "The United States fought the Civil War to bring about a new birth of freedom, World War II for the Four Freedoms and the Cold War to defend the free world."[45] To this one may now add the Iraq War, to spread freedom. The Iraq War could be interpreted as a logical continuation of American and Western history: American freedom triumphed in World War II and the cold war, so in our age of unprecedented hegemony, spreading these ideas, using our seemingly unlimited power to spread our values, is hardly a big leap. It may be the nature of powerful civilizations to export their culture, irrespective of any human desire. Bush may represent the most powerful person in the world spreading its most powerful idea. Hegel maintained that every age has its ideas and individuals who spread them, and they are unconscious of their deeper motivations. This isn't a coronation of President Bush because Hegel contended these figures don't have to be loved.

Wars in Afghanistan and Iraq highlighted a divide between Reagan Republicans, those who fashion themselves as neoconservatives and paleoconservatives. Both claim to be Reagan's true heirs. Despite the fact that Bush used Reagan's ideas to justify the war in Iraq, paleoconservatives assert that he misinterpreted Reagan. More isolationist in nature, they argue that Reagan would have opposed the invasion of Iraq. Every dollar spent on Iraq—and the number of dollars spent exceeded one trillion—is a dollar that could be put back in the pockets of regular Americans. Reagan avoided using force to accomplish his diplomatic goals. The defeat of the Soviet Union did not follow a military conflict. Kirk, for example, wrote regarding the first Gulf War, "Unless the Bush administration abruptly reverses its fiscal and military course, I suggest, the Republican Party must lose its former good repute for frugality, and become the party of profligate expenditure, 'butter and guns.' And public opinion would not long abide that. Nor would America's world influence and America's remaining prosperity."[46]Lamenting the material costs of the first Gulf War and the rise of neoconservatism, Kirk supported Pat Buchanan in his 1992 primary challenge against George H. W. Bush

Was Reagan an inchoate neocon? Diggins didn't think so. He lauded Reagan, calling him, along with Lincoln and Roosevelt, one of the three great liberators in American history. Diggins believed Reagan played a pivotal role in orchestrating the collapse of the Soviet Union and ultimately the American victory in the cold war, but how he achieved this liberation was key for Diggins. While Lincoln and Roosevelt resorted to violence and ultimately the deaths of hundreds of thousands of Americans in order to achieve liberation, Reagan, to his credit, won the cold war peacefully, specifically through his personal negotiations with Gorbachev. Reagan, unlike modern neoconservatives, did not use war to bring down the Soviet Union, nor did he want war. He abhorred nuclear weapons and insisted that a nuclear war could never be fought. The Strategic Defense Initiative, after all, was a defensive measure aimed at preventing nuclear attack. His personal meeting with Gorbachev, not his military buildup, created favorable conditions for Soviet reform and ultimately Soviet collapse. Diggins quoted from an essay claiming there was "not a shred of evidence" that the U.S. military buildup had anything to do with Soviet reform.[47] This was designed to undermine neoconservatism.

Cannon was unequivocal. "So no, Reagan wouldn't have gone into Iraq," he declared in his study of the relationship between Bush and Reagan.[48] I really don't know if he is correct, but to play devil's advocate, Reagan did argue, "There is a profound moral difference between the use of force for liberation and the use of force for conquest," so clearly the invasion of Iraq is not akin to Hitler's invasion of Poland.[49] The problem with communism from Reagan's perspective was that it denied freedom, and this can be applied to

Iraq. And if Reagan called Vietnam a "noble cause," then isn't Iraq also a noble cause? Iraq was less costly to the United States than Vietnam. At least Bush succeeded in toppling tyranny and establishing democracy, something the architects of the Vietnam War never achieved. It remains to be seen whether democracy will succeed in Iraq, but the effort in Vietnam failed.

And Reagan was willing to use force and violence to spread freedom, albeit on a much smaller scale. The island of Grenada became another hot spot in the cold war and really gave Reagan his first chance to apply his ideas to the world. In October 1983 the United States invaded Grenada in an effort to overthrow a Marxist government. It succeeded, with nineteen Americans killed in action. It was America's first military victory since Vietnam, and it was the first time that a Marxist government had been replaced by a pro-American one. Reagan did maintain that freedom is worth dying for. Moreover those who say that Reagan would have opposed the Iraq War ignore that no international event shaped his geopolitical philosophy more than the appeasement era and that the similarities between Iraq and Nazi Germany were clear.

How would Reagan have handled the situation in Iraq? This is like asking, "Would Marx have supported the Russian and Chinese revolutions?" Lenin and Mao thought so. Would JFK have escalated American involvement in Vietnam? Johnson certainly believed so. After all, didn't Kennedy promise to bear any burden to defend liberty? Would Reagan have supported the Iraq War? The true answer is, who knows? The biographer cannot answer a question that the subject of the biography has not even remotely addressed. Reagan's ideas certainly contributed to these events, even if they have been misinterpreted. Iraq did not deviate from Reagan's geopolitical philosophy, namely the idea that America should seek to spread freedom around the world. Any history of the idea that America has a right and an obligation to overthrow tyranny and spread liberty must include Reagan.

Many scholars draw parallels between American conservatives and Jefferson's ideas about limited government, but Jefferson's ideas about freedom and the broader world historical picture helped shaped supporters of the Iraq War. Jefferson, in the midst of the outlandish violence that characterized the "Reign of Terror" phase of the French Revolution, nonetheless defended the Revolution. This was a bold stand in 1794, but Jefferson insisted, "The liberty of the whole of earth was depending on the issue of that contest." Jefferson didn't support the violence, but the French Revolution, like the American Revolution, attempted to overthrow tyranny and replace it with republicanism, so it was an encore to the American Revolution. Death, destruction, and violence were necessary preludes, he felt, for a better world. He believed that American principles could be transplanted to other parts of the world. He predicted, "This ball of liberty, I believe most piously, is now so well in motion that it will roll around the globe."[50] Jefferson's intellectual kinsman, Thomas Paine, also drew connections between the American and French revolutions, insisting each had established "universal rights of conscience, and universal rights of citizenship." Paine emphasized a "school of freedom" that originated in the Enlightenment and was now blooming in these democratic and republican revolutions, even going so far as to argue that hereditary governments would one day disappear from the earth, replaced with republican forms of government, as mankind becomes more enlightened. Paine, in accordance with Enlightenment principles, insisted that one day all of the world would live in freedom.[51] Iraq can be placed in this context.

Paine partly attempted to refute the most famous and influential opponent of the French Revolution, Edmund Burke. In 1790, one year after the French Revolution, Burke, a father of traditional conservatism, wrote a very early history of the Revolution entitled *Reflections on the Revolution in France*. He argued that by creating a society based on abstract principles, the leaders of the French Revolution were ignoring the complexities of human nature. Fundamentally he was an empiricist, castigating the rationalist underpinnings of the French Revolution. Like many critics of Iraq, Burke did not oppose liberty or even the spread of liberty to France; rather he opposed how the French went about achieving their freedom. The works of the philosophes provided an unstable foundation for the project. Burke predicted collapse. In the short term Burke was right, and near his death Jefferson acknowledged this. It should be pointed out that the "short term," in this case, was about twenty-five years. In the long run, Jefferson was right: the French people thrive under republicanism, based on the theory that all men are equal and entitled to freedom.

Jefferson's foremost antagonist, John Adams, never saw a relationship between the French revolutionaries and the crew of 1776. Siding with Burke, Adams argued that American principles could never succeed in France. He insisted that a republican form of government had the same chance of succeeding as a snowball in the Philadelphia sun.[52] As it did so often, round 1 went to Adams, but Jefferson ultimately prevailed because today, historians lump the American and French revolutions together. History books describe these tumultuous events in the same chapter, a victory for Jefferson.

What about George W. Bush's domestic policy? Did this descend from Reagan, in means and ends? Some leading conservatives argued Bush has betrayed Reagan in this realm too. He has been classified as a "Big Government Republican" because he expanded every federal department. Pat Buchanan complained:

> What killed the first Bush presidency and is ruining the second is the abandonment of Reaganism and his embrace of the twin heresies of neo-conservatism and Big Government Conservatism, as preached by the resident ideologues at *The Weekly Standard* and *Wall Street Journal*. Under Bush I, taxes were raised, funding for HUD [U.S. Department of Housing and Urban Development] and Education exploded, and a quota bill was signed under which small businesses, accused of racial discrimination, were made to prove their innocence, or be punished, in true Soviet fashion. . . . Under Bush II, social spending has exploded to levels LBJ might envy, foreign aid has been doubled, pork-at-every-meal has become the GOP diet of choice, surpluses have vanished, and the deficit is soaring back toward 5% of GDP. Bill Clinton is starting to look like Barry Goldwater. . . . When Ronald Reagan went home to California,

his heirs said, "Goodbye to all that" and embraced Big Government conservatism, then neo-conservatism. If they do not find their way home soon, to the principles of Taft, Goldwater and Reagan, they will perish in the wilderness into which they have led us all.[53]

In his work *Imposter: How George W. Bush Bankrupted America and Betrayed the Reagan Legacy* (2006), Bruce Bartlett wrote, "Traditional conservatives [e.g., Reagan] view the federal government as being untrustworthy and undependable. They use it for only necessary functions like national defense. . . . George W. Bush, by contrast, often looks first to government to solve societal problems without considering other options."[54] The budget for the Department of Education, for example, rose from $38 billion in 2001 to $68 billion in 2008.[55] For Buchanan, Bartlett, and millions of other conservatives, Bush and the neoconservatives have hijacked Reagan's vision for America by increasing government spending, whether it be for the war in Iraq or for other entitlements. Paleoconservatives seek a return to the "real" conservatism of Reagan, the conservatism of limited government. Reagan preached limited government, but his pseudo-disciples have ignored this by increasing education spending, as, for example, the No Child Left Behind Act. This program has given billions of dollars to the Department of Education in an effort to set national teaching standards as well as provide tutoring for poor children, but the Department of Education was barely necessary for Reagan. Whereas Reagan sought to curb the influence of government programs, Bush expanded their role, making them an active force in American life through the No Child Left Behind Act. Reagan explicitly said education should be left to the states, not the federal government. By the time the act was signed, Reagan could no longer comment on political issues, but his son Michael lambasted NCLB in his work *The New Reagan Revolution*, declaring, "Bottom line: No Child Left Behind is a centrally planned, Big Government invasion of the private rights of educators and parents."[56] Even the National Endowment for the Arts was enlarged. Bush was a false prophet. The revolution was betrayed.

Yet Bush wasn't always about Big Government. When he vetoed a bill that would have provided health insurance for children who were too wealthy for Medicare but didn't have private insurance, Democrats were outraged. "The president and Republicans in Congress say that we can't afford this bill, but where were the fiscal conservatives when the president demanded hundreds of billions of dollars for the war in Iraq?" asked Representative Jan Schakowsky (D-IL).[57] The answer is simple: one expands freedom, the other restricts it. If successful, the war in Iraq would bring free speech, freedom of the press, freedom of religion, free elections, and free trade to Iraq. The war in Iraq spread the Kingdom of Freedom. Expanding government-run health insurance only stretches the reaches of government, restricting freedom. The billions of dollars that would be needed to pay for expanded health care would come from the American taxpayer. "I believe in private medicine, not the federal government running the health care system," stated Bush.[58] We must vest our faith in the free, private sector. There are no inconsistencies. Freedom is the highest concept, the greatest value, which transcends all other values.

Although they are never linked, understanding Reagan's and Bush's positions on the universal applicability of American values can explain another controversial position as well: the 1986 Amnesty Act. If we view Reagan as a man committed to bringing the Kingdom of Freedom to everyone, his highly controversial position about immigration becomes more rational. Reagan attempted to allow non-Americans to experience the American dream and freedom. Reagan and Bush both rejected hardline conservative ideas about illegal immigration. Whereas some (if not most) conservatives seek to expel illegal immigrants, Reagan and Bush embraced more liberal immigration policies, opening the door to American freedom to several million illegal immigrants. If there is one issue that frustrates conservatives about the Reagan presidency, it's this one. The Immigration and Reform Control Act of 1986 granted amnesty for undocumented workers who arrived in the United States prior to 1982. Edwin Meese, Reagan's attorney general, opined, "The lesson from the 1986 experience is that such an amnesty did not solve the problem. There was extensive document fraud, and the number of people applying for amnesty far exceeded projections."[59] A conservative criticizing Reagan? Blasphemy. But Reagan's and Bush's liberal amnesty policies come from their desire to extend freedom to people who hitherto had been denied such privileges, because by liberalizing our immigration laws, we further open the doors to the Kingdom of Freedom. This is consistent with their ecumenical principles. Freedom should be open to everyone, regardless of the material consequences. As Cannon put it, "Reagan was a democratic internationalist. He believed that those who did not live in America were equally entitled to the blessings of freedom and material prosperity."[60] The Kingdom of Freedom is meant for everyone.

Bush and the neoconservatives have learned the lessons of history from the Reagan years when it comes to budget deficits. In Reagan's case, the budget deficits had minimal economic impact. Reagan and Roosevelt were the two biggest deficit builders in American history, but their budget-deficit-ridden eras were economically more prosperous than the preceding eras. Both of them justified huge deficits as a means to improve the economy and fight war. Both succeeded. And despite the deficits they left their successors, the ensuing eras of the 1950s and 1990s were some of the most prosperous in American history, certainly more prosperous than the eras that preceded theirs when deficits were smaller.

This may be called an unintended consequence of the Reagan presidency. Before his presidency he was a deficit hawk. In fact before becoming president, Reagan worried about budget deficits nearly as much as he did about Soviet communism and government intervention in the economy. He lamented in 1964, "Our government continues to spend $17 million a day more than the government takes in. We haven't balanced our budget 28 out of the last 34 years. We have raised our debt limit three times in the last twelve months, and now our national debt is one and a half times bigger than all the combined debts of all the nations in the world."[61] Yet today conservatives accept the mass budget deficits of the Bush administration. Whereas pre-Reagan Republicans were deficit hawks, post-Reagan neoconservatives are deficit defenders.

Second Democratic Interlude: Barack Obama

I think Ronald Reagan changed the trajectory of America in a way that Richard Nixon did not and in a way that Bill Clinton did not. He put us on a fundamentally different path because the country was ready for it.

—BARACK OBAMA

Reagan and Obama were thrust into office due to an economic crisis and arguably low points in American history.[62] Both saw plunges in GDP growth and declining job creation in the midst of their election. The American people sought change and renewal. Reagan and Obama promised this. Who had it worse upon entering office? That depends on which stats you emphasize. Unemployment was roughly the same when both men entered office. It rose to roughly 10 percent by the second years of their presidencies, then began to slide. In fact graphing unemployment shows remarkable similarities. Of course, Obama inherited a housing and credit crisis, which Reagan did not. The collapse of the housing market in 2008 had ripple effects across the world. Record foreclosures meant losses for the banks, which were passed on to those seeking credit, dramatically slowing the flow of money in the American economy. But soaring interest rates meant that money was stagnant when Reagan took office. They soared to 20 percent in 1981. And Reagan had to deal with double-digit inflation, which Obama did not. In 1980, when Reagan was elected, inflation was a staggering 13.5 percent. In 2008 it was a modest 4 percent.

In most respects the economy that Obama left us is better than the one he inherited. Conservatives counter that the Obama recovery has been the worst recovery from recession in modern times. Despite the fact that America has been out of recession since 2010, economic growth has averaged roughly 2 percent. To put this number in perspective, Obama is the first modern president to have zero years with at least 3 percent economic growth. Even George

H. W. Bush and Jimmy Carter, neither renowned for the economic prosperities of their eras, had multiple years of 3 percent growth, in four-year presidencies. Whereas the American economy expanded at roughly a 2 percent rate under Obama, it surged under Reagan at an average of over 4 percent. This helps explain why middle-class Americans were more frustrated after eight years of Obama than after eight years of Reagan.

GDP matters more than any other statistic because it measures the wealth of an economy. Recessions are defined by a shrinking GDP; they have nothing to do with unemployment and job creation. Citizens in nations with high GDP have higher wages and incomes. This means they have access to more tax revenue, meaning more money for schools, teachers, health care, the social safety net, infrastructure, and military. Imagine two societies, each with equal populations, each taxing their citizens at a 20 percent rate. One has a $10 trillion GDP, the other $5 trillion. The former will collect $2 trillion in tax revenue; the other, $1 trillion. Even if the former has higher unemployment, it can afford to pay its unemployed workers more in unemployment insurance, for example. Unemployed Americans make more money than employed people in many parts of world. During the most recent recession, an American concept called "fun-employed" emerged. Why can unemployed Americans have so much fun? Because America has the highest GDP in the world.

Obama followed the Reagan administration's policies in regard to budget deficits. The Obama presidency demonstrated that it may not even be possible to bring America out of "the worst economic crisis since the Depression" without running up large budget deficits. FDR couldn't do it. Reagan couldn't do it. And Obama couldn't do it either. The Obama administration insisted that the first and foremost task was restoring the American economy in those dire times. Once economic stability was achieved, then we could worry about alleviating budget deficits. The national debt rose from approximately $1 trillion to $2.7 trillion under Reagan. It rose from approximately $11 trillion to $19 trillion over the Obama years. Future historians will probably be more forgiving about Reagan's budget deficits than his contemporaries were.

Obama learned lessons from the Clinton health care fiasco and heeded Reagan's warnings too. Although his health care plan mostly eliminated the uninsured (at least in theory since not having health insurance was illegal), it didn't use strictly government means. Rather the government worked with private insurance companies to expand health care. The Affordable Care Act didn't eliminate private health insurers; it worked with them. The private sector still played a central role in the American health care system. Obama used Reaganite means (private insurance companies) to achieve liberal ends: health insurance for everyone. Since "Obamacare" employed elements from both left and right, both sides found fault with it. Conservatives didn't like that the act impinged on freedom by requiring everyone to buy health insurance from government-approved agencies. Liberals loathed the fact that the act relied on the free market instead of government to provide insurance.

CONCLUSION

They called it the Reagan revolution. Well, I'll accept that, but for me it always seemed more like the great rediscovery, a rediscovery of our values and our common sense. Common sense told us that when you put a big tax on something, the people will produce less of it. So, we cut the people's tax rates, and the people produced more than ever before. The economy bloomed like a plant that had been cut back and could now grow quicker and stronger. Our economic program brought about the longest peacetime expansion in our history: real family income up, the poverty rate down, entrepreneurship booming, and an explosion in research and new technology. Common sense also told us that to preserve the peace, we'd have to become strong again after years of weakness and confusion. So, we rebuilt our defenses, and this New Year we toasted the new peacefulness around the globe. Not only have the superpowers actually begun to reduce their stockpiles of nuclear weapons—and hope for even more progress is bright—but the regional conflicts that rack the globe are also beginning to cease. . . . Countries across the globe are turning to free markets and free speech and turning away from the ideologies of the past. For them, the great rediscovery of the 1980's has been that, lo and behold, the moral way of government is the practical way of government: Democracy, the profoundly good, is also the profoundly productive.

—REAGAN, "Farewell Address to the Nation"

Pope Gregory the Great is a critical figure in Catholic history because he was one of the architects of the medieval church. The good news is that he stressed education. Deeply learned himself, Gregory genuinely believed that all Christian children should be able to read and write. The problem (from the secular perspective) is that Gregory's version of education stressed only works that conformed to Christian principles, like the Bible and the writings of St. Augustine. These were the foundation of Gregory's education and ultimately became the foundation of Western civilization for nearly one thousand years. Works that did not support Christian cosmology at best were read with suspicion and at worst were discarded, so that Cicero, Sophocles, and Homer—all deemed pagans whose works offered no real wisdom—were marginalized because many intelligent people believed studying sources outside our belief system can only yield ignorance. Why study ideas that don't conform to our values and therefore distract us from real knowledge, wisdom, and virtue? Gregory suffered from the natural human tendency to ignore and dismiss ideas that he believed harmed the world.

Those who ignore Reagan's ideas make the same mistake. These ideas include the theoretical social benefits of a low top marginal tax rate, beliefs about a providential God, the importance of freedom, and how a military buildup can promote peace. If nothing else, examining Reagan's thought facilitates understanding of the contemporary conservative mind, something that can be considered an end in itself.

Decades and even centuries from now, when "liberal" and "conservative" have different connotations than they do today, historians will look back and try to understand what conservatives believed, just as historians look back at all "isms," even those long passed, such as Stoicism, Scholasticism, and Jansenism. Who will future historians look to as the leading expositors of modern American conservativism? I believe Reagan will be one of those figures, and the writings presented in this work will be the evidence.

A Time for Choosing

**Speech to supporters of the Goldwater Campaign,
Los Angeles, October 27, 1964**

Thank you. Thank you very much. Thank you and good evening. The sponsor has been identified, but unlike most television programs, the performer hasn't been provided with a script. As a matter of fact, I have been permitted to choose my own words and discuss my own ideas regarding the choice that we face in the next few weeks.

I have spent most of my life as a Democrat. I recently have seen fit to follow another course. I believe that the issues confronting us cross party lines. Now, one side in this campaign has been telling us that the issues of this election are the maintenance of peace and prosperity. The line has been used, "We've never had it so good."

But I have an uncomfortable feeling that this prosperity isn't something on which we can base our hopes for the future. No nation in history has ever survived a tax burden that reached a third of its national income. Today, 37 cents out of every dollar earned in this country is the tax collector's share, and yet our government continues to spend 17 million dollars a day more than the government takes in. We haven't balanced our budget 28 out of the last 34 years. We've raised our debt limit three times in the last twelve months, and now our national debt is one and a half times bigger than all the combined debts of all the nations of the world. We have 15 billion dollars in gold in our treasury; we don't own an ounce. Foreign dollar claims are 27.3 billion dollars. And we've just had announced that the dollar of 1939 will now purchase 45 cents in its total value.

As for the peace that we would preserve, I wonder who among us would like to approach the wife or mother whose husband or son has died in South Vietnam and ask them if they think this is a peace that should be maintained indefinitely. Do they mean peace, or do they mean we just want to be left in peace? There can be no real peace while one American is dying some place in the world for the rest of us. We're at war with the most dangerous enemy that has ever faced mankind in his long climb from the swamp to the stars, and it's been said if we lose that war, and in so doing lose this way of freedom of ours, history will record with the greatest astonishment that those who had the most to lose did the least to prevent its happening. Well I think it's time we ask ourselves if we still know the freedoms that were intended for us by the Founding Fathers.

Not too long ago, two friends of mine were talking to a Cuban refugee, a businessman who had escaped from Castro, and in the midst of his story one of my friends turned to the other and said, "We don't know how lucky we are." And the Cuban stopped and said, "How lucky you are? I had someplace to escape to." And in that sentence he told us the entire story. If we lose freedom here, there's no place to escape to. This is the last stand on earth.

And this idea that government is beholden to the people, that it has no other source of power except the sovereign people, is still the newest and the most unique idea in all the long history of man's relation to man.

This is the issue of this election: Whether we believe in our capacity for self-government or whether we abandon the American Revolution and confess that a little intellectual elite in a far-distant capitol can plan our lives for us better than we can plan them ourselves.

You and I are told increasingly we have to choose between a left or right. Well I'd like to suggest there is no such thing as a left or right. There's only an up or down—[up to] man's old, old-aged dream, the ultimate in individual freedom consistent with law and order, or down to the ant heap of totalitarianism. And regardless of their sincerity, their humanitarian motives, those who would trade our freedom for security have embarked on this downward course.

In this vote-harvesting time, they use terms like the "Great Society," or as we were told a few days ago by the President, we must accept a greater government activity in the affairs of the people. But they've been a little more explicit in the past and among themselves; and all of the things I now will quote have appeared in print. These are not Republican accusations. For example, they have voices that say, "The cold war will end through our acceptance of a not undemocratic socialism." Another voice says, "The profit motive has become outmoded. It must be replaced by the incentives of the welfare state." Or, "Our traditional system of individual freedom is incapable of solving the complex problems of the 20th century." Senator Fulbright has said at Stanford University that the Constitution is outmoded. He referred to the President as "our moral teacher and our leader," and he says he is "hobbled in his task by the restrictions of power imposed on him by this antiquated document." He must "be freed," so that he "can do for us" what he knows "is best." And Senator Clark of Pennsylvania, another articulate spokesman, defines liberalism as "meeting the material needs of the masses through the full power of centralized government."

Well, I, for one, resent it when a representative of the people refers to you and me, the free men and women of this country, as "the masses." This is a term we haven't applied to ourselves in America. But beyond that, "the full power of centralized government"—this was the very thing the Founding Fathers sought to minimize. They knew that governments don't control things. A government can't control the economy without controlling people. And they know when a government sets out to do that, it must use force and coercion to achieve its purpose. They also knew, those Founding Fathers, that outside of its legitimate functions, government does nothing as well or as economically as the private sector of the economy.

Now, we have no better example of this than government's involvement in the farm economy over the last 30 years. Since 1955, the cost of this program has nearly doubled. One-fourth of farming in America is responsible for 85 percent of the farm surplus. Three-fourths of farming is out on the free market and has known a 21 percent increase in the per capita consumption of all its produce. You see, that one-fourth of farming—that's regulated and controlled by the federal government. In the last three years we've spent 43 dollars in the feed grain program for every dollar bushel of corn we don't grow.

Senator Humphrey last week charged that Barry Goldwater, as President, would seek to eliminate farmers. He should do his homework a little better, because he'll find out that we've had a decline of 5 million in the farm population under these government programs. He'll also find that the Democratic administration has sought to get from Congress [an] extension of the farm program to include that three-fourths that is now free. He'll find that they've also asked for the right to imprison farmers who wouldn't keep books as prescribed by the federal government. The Secretary of Agriculture asked for the right to seize farms through condemnation and resell them to other individuals. And contained in that same program was a provision that would have allowed the federal government to remove 2 million farmers from the soil.

At the same time, there's been an increase in the Department of Agriculture employees. There's now one for every 30 farms in the United States, and still they can't tell us how 66 shiploads of grain headed for Austria disappeared without a trace and Billie Sol Estes [American businessman convicted of fraud] never left shore.

Every responsible farmer and farm organization has repeatedly asked the government to free the farm economy, but how—who are farmers to know what's best for them? The wheat farmers voted against a wheat program. The government passed it anyway. Now the price of bread goes up; the price of wheat to the farmer goes down.

Meanwhile, back in the city, under urban renewal the assault on freedom carries on. Private property rights [are] so diluted that public interest is almost anything a few government planners decide it should be. In a program that takes from the needy and gives to the greedy, we see such spectacles as in Cleveland, Ohio, a million-and-a-half-dollar building completed only three years ago must be destroyed to make way for what government officials call a "more compatible use of the land." The President tells us he's now going to start building public housing units in the thousands, where heretofore we've only built them in the hundreds. But FHA [Federal Housing Authority] and the Veterans Administration tell us they have 120,000 housing units they've taken back through mortgage foreclosure. For three decades, we've sought to solve the problems of unemployment through government planning, and the more the plans fail, the more the planners plan. The latest is the Area Redevelopment Agency.

They've just declared Rice County, Kansas, a depressed area. Rice County, Kansas, has two hundred oil wells, and the 14,000 people there have over 30 million dollars on deposit in personal savings in their banks. And when the government tells you you're depressed, lie down and be depressed.

We have so many people who can't see a fat man standing beside a thin one without coming to the conclusion the fat man got that way by taking advantage of the thin one. So they're going to solve all the problems of human misery through government and government planning. Well, now, if government planning and welfare had the answer—and they've had almost 30 years of it—shouldn't we expect government to read the score to us once in a while? Shouldn't they be telling us about the decline each year in the number of people needing help? The reduction in the need for public housing?

But the reverse is true. Each year the need grows greater; the program grows greater. We were told four years ago that 17 million people went to bed hungry each night. Well that was probably true. They were all on a diet. But now we're told that 9.3 million families in this country are poverty-stricken on the basis of earning less than 3,000 dollars a year. Welfare spending [is] 10 times greater than in the dark depths of the Depression. We're spending 45 billion dollars on welfare. Now do a little arithmetic, and you'll find that if we divided the 45 billion dollars up equally among those 9 million poor families, we'd be able to give each family 4,600 dollars a year. And this added to their present income should eliminate poverty. Direct aid to the poor, however, is only running only about 600 dollars per family. It would seem that someplace there must be some overhead.

Now—so now we declare "war on poverty," or "You, too, can be a Bobby Baker [associate of Lyndon Johnson who was suspected of bribery]." Now do they honestly expect us to believe that if we add 1 billion dollars to the 45 billion we're spending, one more program to the 30-odd we have—and remember, this new program doesn't replace any, it just duplicates existing programs—do they believe that poverty is suddenly going to disappear by magic? Well, in all fairness I should explain there is one part of the new program that isn't duplicated. This is the youth feature. We're now going to solve the dropout problem, juvenile delinquency, by reinstituting something like the old ccc [Civilian Conservation Corps] camps, and we're going to put our young people in these camps. But again we do some arithmetic, and we find that we're going to spend each year just on room and board for each young person we help 4,700 dollars a year. We can send them to Harvard for 2,700! Course, don't get me wrong. I'm not suggesting Harvard is the answer to juvenile delinquency.

But seriously, what are we doing to those we seek to help? Not too long ago, a judge called me here in Los Angeles. He told me of a young woman who'd come before him for a divorce. She had six children, was pregnant with her seventh. Under his questioning, she revealed her husband was a laborer earning 250 dollars a month. She wanted a divorce to get an 80 dollar raise. She's eligible for 330 dollars a month in the Aid to Dependent Children Program. She got the idea from two women in her neighborhood who'd already done that very thing.

Yet anytime you and I question the schemes of the do-gooders, we're denounced as being against their humanitarian goals. They say we're always "against" things—we're never "for" anything.

Well, the trouble with our liberal friends is not that they're ignorant; it's just that they know so much that isn't so.

Now—we're for a provision that destitution should not follow unemployment by reason of old age, and to that end we've accepted Social Security as a step toward meeting the problem.

But we're against those entrusted with this program when they practice deception regarding its fiscal shortcomings, when they charge that any criticism of the program means that we want to end payments to those people who depend on them for a livelihood. They've called it "insurance" to us in a hundred million pieces of literature. But then they appeared before the Supreme Court and they testified it was a welfare program. They only use the term "insurance" to sell it to the people. And they said Social Security dues are a tax for the general use of the government, and the government has used that tax. There is no fund, because Robert Byers, the actuarial head, appeared before a congressional committee and admitted that Social Security as of this moment is 298 billion dollars in the hole. But he said there should be no cause for worry because as long as they have the power to tax, they could always take away from the people whatever they needed to bail them out of trouble. And they're doing just that.

A young man, 21 years of age, working at an average salary—his Social Security contribution would, in the open market, buy him an insurance policy that would guarantee 220 dollars a month at age 65. The government promises 127. He could live it up until he's 31 and then take out a policy that would pay more than Social Security. Now are we so lacking in business sense that we can't put this program on a sound basis, so that people who do require those payments will find they can get them when they're due—that the cupboard isn't bare?

Barry Goldwater thinks we can.

At the same time, can't we introduce voluntary features that would permit a citizen who can do better on his own to be excused upon presentation of evidence that he had made provision for the non-earning years? Should we not allow a widow with children to work, and not lose the benefits supposedly paid for by her deceased husband? Shouldn't you and I be allowed to declare who our beneficiaries will be under this program, which we cannot do? I think we're for telling our senior citizens that no one in this country should be denied medical care because of a lack of funds. But I think we're against forcing all citizens, regardless of need, into a compulsory government program, especially when we have such examples, as was announced last week, when France admitted that their Medicare program is now bankrupt. They've come to the end of the road.

In addition, was Barry Goldwater so irresponsible when he suggested that our government give up its program of deliberate, planned inflation, so that when you do get your Social Security pension, a dollar will buy a dollar's worth, and not 45 cents worth?

I think we're for an international organization, where the nations of the world can seek peace. But I think we're against subordinating American interests to an organization that has become so structurally unsound that today you can muster a two-thirds vote on the floor of the General Assembly among nations that represent less than 10 percent of the world's population. I think we're against the hypocrisy of assailing our allies because here and there they cling to a colony, while we engage in a conspiracy of silence and never open our mouths about the millions of people enslaved in the Soviet colonies in the satellite nations.

I think we're for aiding our allies by sharing of our material blessings with those nations which share in our fundamental beliefs, but we're against doling out money government to government, creating bureaucracy, if not socialism, all over the world. We set out to help 19 countries. We're helping 107. We've spent 146 billion dollars. With that money, we bought a 2 million dollar yacht for Haile Selassie. We bought dress suits for Greek undertakers, extra wives for Kenya[n] government officials. We bought a thousand TV sets for a place where they have no electricity. In the last six years, 52 nations have bought 7 billion dollars worth of our gold, and all 52 are receiving foreign aid from this country.

No government ever voluntarily reduces itself in size. So governments' programs, once launched, never disappear.

Actually, a government bureau is the nearest thing to eternal life we'll ever see on this earth.

Federal employees—federal employees number two and a half million; and federal, state, and local, one out of six of the nation's work force employed by government. These proliferating bureaus with their thousands of regulations have cost us many of our constitutional safeguards. How many of us realize that today federal agents can invade a man's property without a warrant? They can impose a fine without a formal hearing, let alone a trial by jury? And they can seize and sell his property at auction to enforce the payment of that fine. In Chico County, Arkansas, James Wier overplanted his rice allotment. The government obtained a 17,000 dollar judgment. And a U.S. marshal sold his 960-acre farm at auction. The government said it was necessary as a warning to others to make the system work.

Last February 19th at the University of Minnesota, Norman Thomas, six-times candidate for President on the Socialist Party ticket, said, "If Barry Goldwater became President, he would stop the advance of socialism in the United States." I think that's exactly what he will do.

But as a former Democrat, I can tell you Norman Thomas isn't the only man who has drawn this parallel to socialism with the present administration, because back in 1936, Mr. Democrat himself, Al Smith, the great American, came before the American people and charged that the leadership of his Party was taking the Party of Jefferson, Jackson, and Cleveland down the road under the banners of Marx, Lenin, and Stalin. And he walked away from his Party, and he never returned til the day he died—because to this day, the leadership of that Party has been taking that Party, that honorable Party, down the road in the image of the labor Socialist Party of England.

Now it doesn't require expropriation or confiscation of private property or business to impose socialism on a people. What does it mean whether you hold the deed to the—or the title to your business or property if the government holds the power of life and death over that business or property? And such machinery already exists. The government can find some charge to bring against any concern it chooses to prosecute. Every businessman has his own tale of harassment. Somewhere a perversion has taken place. Our natural, unalienable rights are now considered to be a dispensation of government, and freedom has never been so fragile, so close to slipping from our grasp as it is at this moment.

Our Democratic opponents seem unwilling to debate these issues. They want to make you and I believe that this is a contest between two men—that we're to choose just between two personalities.

Well what of this man that they would destroy—and in destroying, they would destroy that which he represents, the ideas that you and I hold dear? Is he the brash and shallow and trigger-happy man they say he is? Well I've been privileged to know him "when." I knew him long before he ever dreamed of trying for high office, and I can tell you personally I've never known a man in my life I believed so incapable of doing a dishonest or dishonorable thing.

This is a man who, in his own business before he entered politics, instituted a profit-sharing plan before unions had ever thought of it. He put in health and medical insurance for all his employees. He took 50 percent of the profits before taxes and set up a retirement program, a pension plan for all his employees. He sent monthly checks for life to an employee who was ill and couldn't work. He provides nursing care for the children of mothers who work in the stores. When Mexico was ravaged by the floods in the Rio Grande, he climbed in his airplane and flew medicine and supplies down there.

An ex-GI told me how he met him. It was the week before Christmas during the Korean War, and he was at the Los Angeles airport trying to get a ride home to Arizona for Christmas. And he said that [there were] a lot of servicemen there and no seats available on the planes. And then a voice came over the loudspeaker and said, "Any men in uniform wanting a ride to Arizona, go to runway such-and-such," and they went down there, and there was a fellow named Barry Goldwater sitting in his plane. Every day in those weeks before Christmas, all day long, he'd load up the plane, fly it to Arizona, fly them to their homes, fly back over to get another load.

During the hectic split-second timing of a campaign, this is a man who took time out to sit beside an old friend who was dying of cancer. His campaign managers were understandably impatient, but he said, "There aren't many left who care what happens to her. I'd like her to know I care." This is a man who said to his 19-year-old son, "There is no foundation like the rock of honesty and fairness, and when you begin to build your life on that rock, with the cement of the faith in God that you have, then you have a real start." This is not a man who could carelessly send other people's sons to war. And that is the issue of this campaign that makes all the other problems I've discussed academic, unless we realize we're in a war that must be won.

Those who would trade our freedom for the soup kitchen of the welfare state have told us they have a utopian solution of peace without victory. They call their policy "accommodation." And they say if we'll only avoid any direct confrontation with the enemy, he'll forget his evil ways and learn to love us. All who oppose them are indicted as warmongers. They say we offer simple answers to complex problems. Well, perhaps there is a simple answer—not an easy answer—but simple: If you and I have the courage to tell our elected officials that we want our national policy based on what we know in our hearts is morally right.

We cannot buy our security, our freedom from the threat of the bomb by committing an immorality so great as saying to a billion human beings now enslaved behind the Iron Curtain, "Give up your dreams of freedom because to save our own skins, we're willing to make a deal with your slave masters." Alexander Hamilton said, "A nation which can prefer disgrace to danger is prepared for a master, and deserves one." Now let's set the record straight. There's no argument over the choice between peace and war, but there's only one guaranteed way you can have peace—and you can have it in the next second—surrender.

Admittedly, there's a risk in any course we follow other than this, but every lesson of history tells us that the greater risk lies in appeasement, and this is the specter our well-meaning liberal friends refuse to face—that their policy of accommodation is appeasement, and it gives no choice between peace and war, only between fight or surrender. If we continue to accommodate, continue to back and retreat, eventually we have to face the final demand—the ultimatum. And what then—when Nikita Khrushchev has told his people he knows what our answer will be? He has told them that we're retreating under the pressure of the Cold War, and someday when the time comes to deliver the final ultimatum, our surrender will be voluntary, because by that time we will have been weakened from within spiritually, morally, and economically. He believes this because from our side he's heard voices pleading for "peace at any price" or "better Red than dead," or as one commentator put it, he'd rather "live on his knees than die on his feet." And therein lies the road to war, because those voices don't speak for the rest of us.

You and I know and do not believe that life is so dear and peace so sweet as to be purchased at the price of chains and slavery. If nothing in life is worth dying for, when did this begin—just in the face of this enemy? Or should Moses have told the children of Israel to live in slavery under the pharaohs? Should Christ have refused the cross? Should the patriots at Concord Bridge have thrown down their guns and refused to fire the shot heard 'round the world? The martyrs of history were not fools, and our honored dead who gave their lives to stop the advance of the Nazis didn't die in vain. Where, then, is the road to peace? Well it's a simple answer after all.

You and I have the courage to say to our enemies, "There is a price we will not pay." "There is a point beyond which they must not advance." And this—this is the meaning in the phrase of Barry Goldwater's "peace through strength." Winston Churchill said, "The destiny of man is not measured by material computations. When great forces are on the move in the world, we learn we're spirits—not animals." And he said, "There's something going on in time and space, and beyond time and space, which, whether we like it or not, spells duty."

You and I have a rendezvous with destiny.

We'll preserve for our children this, the last best hope of man on earth, or we'll sentence them to take the last step into a thousand years of darkness.

We will keep in mind and remember that Barry Goldwater has faith in us. He has faith that you and I have the ability and the dignity and the right to make our own decisions and determine our own destiny.

Thank you very much.

NOTES

Introduction

1. Nash, *Conservative Intellectual Movement*, xi.
2. Hitchens, *Quotable Christopher Hitchens*, 233.
3. Kopplenberg, *Reading Obama*, 152.
4. Heclo, "Ronald Reagan and the American Public Philosophy," 18.
5. Diggins, *Ronald Reagan*, 37.

1. Religious Roots

1. Kengor, *God and Ronald Reagan*, 13.
2. Reagan, *American Life*, 22.
3. Wills, *Reagan's America*, 24.
4. Skinner et al., *Reagan*, 6.
5. Lobkowicz, *Theory and Practice*, 160.
6. Brown, *Faith of Ronald Reagan*, 56.
7. Kengor, *God and Ronald Reagan*, 32. All bible quotes are from the New Living Translation.
8. Ronald Reagan, "My Faith," *Modern Screen*, June 1950.
9. *The Complete C. S. Lewis Signature Classics*, 538.
10. Reagan, "My Faith."
11. Diggins, *Ronald Reagan*, 14.
12. Reagan and Hubler, *Where's the Rest of Me?*, 7.
13. Cannon, *Governor Reagan*, 19.
14. Morris, *Dutch*, 117.
15. Reagan, *Where's The Rest of Me?*, 66.
16. Morris, *Dutch*, 128.
17. During a flight to Catalina Island, Reagan's plane nearly crashed, leading to a fear of flying that lasted for decades. From about 1937 to 1967 Reagan took trains across America. He overcame this fear only because being governor of California required it.

18. Reagan notoriously didn't recognize people, including a cabinet member and even his own son. One explanation may be that he was blind as a bat without his glasses. I advance another explanation below.

19. Edwards, *Early Reagan*, 16.

20. Hume, *Essays*, 135.

21. Holbach, *Christianity Unveiled*, 147.

22. Kengor, *God and Ronald Reagan*, 225.

23. Skinner and Anderson, *Reagan in His Own Hand*, 257.

24. Kengor, *God and Ronald Reagan*, 225.

25. Reeves, *Ronald Reagan*, 342.

26. Winthrop, *Dominion of Providence over the Passions of Men*, 36–37.

27. Tocqueville, *Democracy in America*, vol. 2, 150.

28. Reagan "American the Beautiful."

29. Kengor, *God and Ronald Reagan*, 98.

30. Kengor, *God and Ronald Reagan*, 99.

31. Kengor, *God and Ronald Reagan*, 99.

2. From Liberal to Conservative

1. Reagan, *Where's the Rest of Me?*, 139.

2. Reagan, *Where's the Rest of Me?*, 140.

3. Reagan, *Where's the Rest of Me?*, 140.

4. Edwards, *Ronald Reagan*, 45.

5. Edwards, *Early Reagan*, 355.

6. "Reagan Campaigns for Truman."

7. "Mr. Reagan Airs His Views," *Chicago Tribune*, May 18, 1947.

8. "Mr. Reagan Airs His Views."

9. Reagan, "Testimony before the House Un-American Activities Committee."

10. M. Reagan, *Twice Adopted*, 28.

11. Edmund Morris wrote *Dutch* in memory of Christine Reagan, suggesting the importance of this incident in Reagan's life.

12. Crossman, *The God That Failed*, 4.

13. Reagan, "Remarks at Eureka College."

14. A Marxist rejecting dialectical materialism is like a Christian renouncing a providential God. It means rejecting everything.

15. Burnham, *The Struggle for the World*, 59.

16. Burnham was also one of the leading proponents of the ideas that Truman's foreign policy was responsible for "losing" China to communism.

17. Burnham, *Coming Defeat of Communism*, 24.

18. Kirk, *Conservative Mind*, 8.

19. Kirk, *Conservative Mind*, 8.

20. At the end of his life, Kirk opposed NAFTA, a Reaganesque idea.

21. Reagan, "The Defense of Freedom and Metaphysics of Fun."

22. Burnham, "The Week," 3.

23. Meyer, "The Twisted Tree of Liberty," 25–26.

24. Reagan, *Speaking My Mind*, 96.

25. Mises, *Planning for Freedom*, 218.

26. Hayek, "The Use of Knowledge in Society."

27. Hayek, *The Road to Serfdom* (1945), in *Collected Works of F. A. Hayek*, 126–217.

28. Friedman, *Capitalism and Freedom*, 50.

29. Ibn Khaldun, *Muqaddimah*, 231.

30. Skinner and Anderson, *Reagan in His Own Hand*, 274.

31. Reagan, *American Life*, 129.

32. Reagan, *Where's the Rest of Me?*, 257.

33. Evans, *Education of Ronald Reagan*, 76.

34. Hazlitt, *Economics in One Lesson*, 23–24.

35. Yager, *Ronald Reagan's Journey*, 39.

36. Reagan, "Testimony before House Ways and Means Committee," 10.

37. Houck, *Ronald Reagan*, 12–13.

38. Ronald Reagan, "Business, Ballots and Bureaus," May 6, 1959, Gubernatorial Papers Collection, 1966–74, Ronald Reagan Presidential Library.

39. Morgan, *Reagan*, 68.

40. Cannon, *Governor Reagan*, 94.

41. Reagan, *American Life*, 132.

42. Yager, *Ronald Reagan's Journey*, 19.

43. Reagan, "Testimony before the House Un-American Activities Committee."

44. Reagan, *A Life in Letters*, 705.

45. Goldwater, *Conscience of a Conservative*, 63–64.

46. Reagan, "Losing Freedom by Installments," 2.

47. Reagan, "Losing Freedom by Installments," 2.

48. Houck, *Ronald Reagan*, 28.

3. Fostering Freedom at Home

1. Anderson, "Self-Reliance," 23.

2. Lettow, *Ronald Reagan*, 18.

3. Ulam, *Ideologies and Illusions*, 68.

4. Skinner et al., *Reagan*, 266.

5. Roosevelt, "Address to the International Labor Organization."

6. Reagan, "A Time for Choosing."

7. Reagan, "A Time for Choosing."

8. Reagan, "The Creative Society," in *A Time for Choosing*, 64.

9. Reagan, "Ronald Reagan Speaks Out against Socialized Medicine."

10. Reagan, "A Time for Choosing."

11. Cannon, *President Reagan*, 243.

12. Reagan, "Creative Society."

13. As hard as it is for many of us to accept, education is a value. It wasn't until the 1800s that education became widespread. During the Middle Ages intelligent people saw little need for compulsory education.

14. Reagan, "Government and the Family," 171.

15. Reagan, "The Creative Society."

16. Leuchtenburg, *In the Shadow of FDR*, 209–17.

17. Hayward, *Age of Reagan*, 452.

18. Hayward, *Age of Reagan*, 453.

19. Coll, *Safety Net*, 199.

20. Patterson, *America's Struggle against Poverty*, 171.

21. During the 1970s Great Society spending levels remained constant or were increased by Presidents Nixon and Carter, depending on the program.

22. Roosevelt, "Annual Message to Congress."

23. Reagan, *American Life*, 67.

24. Students for a Democratic Society, "Port Huron Statement."

25. Reagan, "The Value of Understanding the Past."

26. Wills, *Reagan's America*, 382.

27. Wilson, *A Guide to Reagan Country*.

28. New, "Morning in California."

29. Collins, *Transforming America*, 41–42.

30. Morgan, *Reagan*, 106.

31. Internet Archive, "1971–1972 Governors Budget Summary," A28, Chart 8.

32. Morgan, *Reagan*, 102.

33. Cannon, *Governor Reagan*, 213.

34. Reagan, *Speaking My Mind*, 53.

35. Reagan, *Speaking My Mind*.

36. M. Reagan, *Twice Adopted*, 42.

4. Understanding Reagan

1. Cannon, *President Reagan*, 9.

2. Diggins, *Ronald Reagan*, 26.

3. Hayward, *Age of Reagan*, 203.

4. Reagan, "Losing Freedom by Installments," 8.

5. Reagan, "The Value of Understanding the Past."

6. Reagan, "The Value of Understanding the Past."

7. Cited in Hamilton and Huntington, *The Complete Dialogues of Plato*, 16.

8. Depending on how "giving to the poor" is measured, some studies show conservatives give more to the poor; others show giving is more equal between conservatives and liberals.

9. Kengor, *God and Ronald Reagan*, 179.

10. Skinner and Anderson, *Reagan in His Own Hand*, 260.

11. Cannon, *President Reagan*, 11.

12. Voltaire, *Philosophical Letters*, 15.

13. Rousseau, *Politics and the Arts*, 126.

14. Rousseau, *Social Contract and Discourses*, 10.

15. Hume, *History of England*, 535.

16. Diderot, letter to Princess Dashoff, April 3, 1771, in Warman, *Tolerance*, 74.

17. Montesquieu, *Spirit of Laws*, 151.

18. Smith, *Wealth of Nations*, 52.

19. Montesquieu, *Spirit of Laws*, 316.

20. Paine, *Rights of Man*, 448. Paine, like Smith, argued that the government had a place in the economy, with allowances for poor children being an example of such a place.

21. Bastiat, *The Law*, 76.

22. Rousseau, *Social Contract*, 141.

23. Marx and Engels, *Communist Manifesto*, 491.

24. Guevara, *Guerrilla Warfare*, 72.

25. Foner, *Story of American Freedom*, xvi.

26. Kennedy, "Remarks of Senator John F. Kennedy."

27. Sloan, *The Reagan Effect*, x.

28. Locke, *Two Treatises on Government*, 330–31.

29. Israel, *Revolution of Mind*, 97.

30. John Adams, letter to Thomas Jefferson, July 16, 1814, in Bergh, *The Writings of Thomas Jefferson*, 104.

31. Tocqueville, *Democracy in America*, vol. 1, 1.

32. Reagan, "A Time for Choosing."

33. Robin, *Reactionary Mind*, 3.

34. Robin, *Reactionary Mind*, 8.

35. Reagan, "Government and the Family," 176.

36. Hofstadter, *Anti-Intellectualism in America*, 6.

37. Kirk, *Politics of Prudence*, 144.

38. Reagan, *The Notes*, 59.

39. Beecher, *The Sermons of Henry Ward Beecher*, 31.

40. Commager, *Jefferson, Nationalism and the Enlightenment*, 3.

41. Saad, "U.S. Conservatives Outnumber Liberals."

42. Reagan, "The Obligation of Liberty."

43. Reagan, "Speech to the Merchants and Manufacturers Association Annual Banquet."

44. Skinner and Anderson, *Reagan in His Own Hand*, 13.

45. Skinner and Anderson, *Reagan in His Own Hand*, 228.

46. Skinner et al., *Reagan*, 259.

47. Morris, *Dutch*, 228.

48. Reagan, "Remarks at the Presentation Ceremony for the Presidential Medal of Freedom."

49. Robinson, *How Ronald Reagan Changed My Life*, 114.

50. Morris, *Dutch*, 656.

51. Lynn Rosellini, "'Honey, I Forgot to Duck,' Injured Reagan Tells Wife," *New York Times*, March 31, 1981, http://www.nytimes.com/1981/03/31/us/honey-i-forgot-to-duck-injured-reagan-tells-wife.html.

52. Cannon, *President Reagan*, 97.

53. Deaver, *A Different Drummer*, 112.

54. Deaver, *A Different Drummer*, 112–13.

55. "CBS News: Town Meeting of the World," May 15, 1967, YouTube, https://www.youtube.com/watch?v=I1g8HaE4ArI.

56. Hayward, *Age of Reagan*, 169.

57. Hayward, *Age of Reagan*, 169.

58. Lewis, *Too Dumb to Fail*, 29.

59. Evans, *Education of Ronald Reagan*, 9.

60. Evans, *Education of Ronald Reagan*, 75.

61. Gergen, *Eyewitness to Power*, 152.

62. Murdoch, "Egghead Reagan."

63. Morris, *Dutch*, 598.

64. Cannon, *President Reagan*, 112.

65. Noonan, *When Character Was King*, 38.

66. Cannon, *Governor Reagan*, 117.

67. Horkheimer and Adorno, *Dialectic of Enlightenment*, xvii.

68. Harrington, *The Other America*, 14–18.

69. Reagan, "Speech to the Conservative Political Action Conference."

70. Cannon, *President Reagan*, 711.

71. Henry, "Give Me Liberty."

72. Tocqueville, *Democracy in America*, vol. 2, 523.

73. Patricia Schroeder, "Nothing Stuck to Teflon President," *USA Today*, June 6, 2004.

5. A Moral View of the Cold War

1. Reagan, "A Time for Choosing."

2. Reagan, "A Time for Choosing."

3. Reagan, "A Time for Choosing."

4. Reagan, "A Time for Choosing."

5. Reagan, "America the Beautiful."

6. Evans, *The Education of Ronald Reagan*, 120.

7. "Reagan Warns U.S. Is in War," *Bartlesville (OK) Examiner Enterprise*, March 1, 1962.

8. Hayward, *The Age of Reagan*, 417.

9. Hayward, *The Age of Reagan*, 141.

10. Emmett Tyrrell, "Such Good Friends," *New York Times*, June 18, 1977.

11. Reagan, "A Time for Choosing."

12. Skinner and Anderson, *Reagan in His Own Hand*, 8.

13. Skinner and Anderson, *Reagan in His Own Hand*, 102.

14. Houck and Kiewe, *Ronald Reagan*, 113.

15. Reagan, "The Obligation of Liberty."

16. Reagan, "The Obligation of Liberty."

17. M. Reagan and Denney, *The New Reagan Revolution*, 5.

18. Donald Trump poses a slightly greater risk to humanity, according to the scientists. After his election, the *Bulletin* moved the hand to two minutes and thirty seconds from human extinction, explaining, "The probability of global catastrophe is very high." "Timeline: It Is 2 Minutes to Midnight," *Bulletin of the Atomic Scientists*, 2018, http://thebulletin.org/timeline.

19. "Timeline: It Is 2 Minutes to Midnight."

20. Diggins, *Fate, Freedom and History*, ch. 10.

21. Lettow, *Ronald Reagan*.

22. Brinkley, *Reagan Diaries*, 24.

23. Morris, *Dutch*, 632–33.

24. Skinner and Anderson, *Reagan in His Own Hand*, 228.

25. Ragone, *Presidential Leadership*, 267.

26. Schweizer, *Reagan's War*, 141.

27. Morris, *Dutch*, 544.

28. D'Souza, *Ronald Reagan*, 3.

29. Seth Mydans, "Gromyko Predicts Space Arms Talks Will Not Be Held," *New York Times*, July 30, 1984.

30. Stephen Cohen, "Sovieticus," *The Nation*, April 9, 1983.

31. Brinkley, *The Reagan Diaries*, 30.

32. D'Souza, *Ronald Reagan*, 2.

33. Galbraith, "The Unbearable Costs of Empire," 73.

34. Hobsbawm, *Age of Extremes*, 249.

35. Skinner and Anderson, *Reagan, in His Own Hand*.

6. Promoting Freedom Abroad

1. Kengor, *God and Ronald Reagan*, 224.

2. Ford, "Address before a Joint Session of the Congress Reporting on the State of the Union."

3. Reagan, "Address to Members of the British Parliament."

4. Reagan, "Address to Members of the British Parliament."

5. Reagan, "Address to Members of the British Parliament."

6. Reale, *A History of Ancient Philosophy*, 281.

7. Augustine, *City of God*, 217.

8. Davis, *A History of Medieval Europe*, 136.

9. Pope, "Epitaph on Sir Isaac Newton."

10. Condorcet, *Sketch for a Historical Picture*, 4, 9–10, 92.

7. Did Reagan's Ideas Matter?

1. George Kennan, "The G.O.P. Won the Cold War? Ridiculous," *New York Times*, October 28, 1992.

2. Hobsbawm, *Age of Extremes*, 249.

3. Wilentz, *The Age of Reagan*, 280.

4. Thatcher, "Eulogy for President Reagan."

5. Schweizer, *Reagan's War*, 214.

6. Cannon, *President Reagan*, 288.

7. Reagan, "Address to the Nation on Defense and National Security."

8. Chernyaev, *My Six Years with Gorbachev*, 56.

9. Schweizer, *Reagan's War*, 242.

10. Collins, *Transforming America*, 203.

11. Malia, *The Soviet Tragedy*, 414.

12. See Matlock, *Reagan and Gorbachev*.

13. Richman, "The Sad Legacy of Ronald Reagan," 386.

14. Davies, "The Welfare State," 212.

15. Cannon, *President Reagan*, 239.

16. Cannon, *President Reagan*, 70.

8. The Reagan Intellectual Legacy

1. Hayward, *Age of Reagan*, 454.

2. Troy, *Morning in America*, 349.

3. Diggins, *Ronald Reagan*, 320.

4. Sloan, *The Reagan Effect*, 10.

5. Charles Schumer, "Reaganism Is Dead," *Daily News*, November 29, 2006.

6. Paul Krugman, "Debunking the Reagan Myth," *New York Times*, January 21, 2008.

7. Jeffrey Kahn, "Ronald Reagan Launched Political Career Using the Berkeley Campus as a Target," UC *Berkeley News*, June 8, 2004, http://www.berkeley.edu/news/media/releases/2004/06/08_reagan.shtml.

8. Kahn, "Ronald Reagan Launched Political Career Using the Berkeley Campus as a Target."

9. Voyce, *Poetic Community*, 93.

10. Cannon, *President Reagan*, 8.

11. D'Souza, *Ronald Reagan*, 124.

12. D'Souza, *Ronald Reagan*, 112.

13. "The Second American Revolution."

14. Cannon, *President Reagan*, 8.

15. Wilentz, *Age of Reagan*, 10.

16. Wilentz, *Age of Reagan*, 170.

17. Wilentz, *Age of Reagan*, 281.

18. Wilentz, *Age of Reagan*, 284.

19. Singer, *Marx*, 1.

20. Bush, "Radio Address to United States Armed Forces Stationed in the Persian Gulf Region."

21. Sloan, *The Reagan Effect*, ix.

22. Clinton, "Address Accepting the Presidential Nomination."

23. Clinton, "Address Accepting the Presidential Nomination."

24. *Time*, November 16, 1992, cover.

25. Clinton, "Address before a Joint Session of the Congress on the State of the Union."

26. Clinton, "Remarks at Georgetown University."

27. "Political Party Platforms."

28. "Fared Well," *New Republic*, September 4, 2006, 7.

29. Clinton, "Remarks at the Signing Ceremony."

30. Clinton, "Statement on Signing the Iraqi Liberation Act."

31. Clinton's critics argued this was a ruse to distract Americans from the Monica Lewinsky scandal that concurrently engulfed the administration.

32. Clinton, "Address to the Nation Announcing Military Strikes on Iraq."

33. See Byrne, "The Victory of the Proletariat Is Inevitable."

34. Truman, "Address of the President to Congress."

35. Truman, "Address on Foreign Policy."

36. Bush, "Remarks on 9/11 Attacks."

37. Bush, "Address to the United Nations."

38. Bush, "State of the Union Speech."

39. Nicholas Lemann. "After Iraq," *New Yorker*, February 17 and 24, 2003, https://www.newyorker.com/magazine/2003/02/17/after-iraq.

40. Bush, "Address to the American Enterprise Institute."

41. Bush, "Remarks before United Nations Assembly."

42. Bush, "Remarks before United Nations Assembly."

43. Bush, "Interview Excerpts."

44. Constitute Project, Iraq's Constitution of 2005.

45. Foner, *Story of American Freedom*, xii.

46. Kirk, "Political Errors at the End of the 20th Century."

47. Diggins, *Ronald Reagan*, 405.

48. Cannon and Cameron, *Reagan's Disciple*, 213.

49. Reagan, "Remarks at a Ceremony Commemorating the 40th Anniversary of the Normandy Invasion, D-day."

50. Jefferson, letter to Tench Coxe.

51. Paine, *Political Writings of Thomas Paine*, vol. 2, 91–92.

52. Chernow, *Alexander Hamilton*, 548.

53. Buchanan, "Bush Leaves GOP in Crisis."

54. Bartlett, *Imposter*, 2.

55. U.S. Department of Education, "Education Department Budget by Major Program."

56. Reagan and Denney, *New Reagan Revolution*, 188.

57. "The President's Veto of the Schip Extension."

58. *Public Papers of Presidents of the United States: George W. Bush*, 1261.

59. Meese, "Reagan Would Not Repeat Amnesty Mistake."

60. Cannon, *President Reagan*, 404.

61. Reagan, "A Time for Choosing."

62. The Obama quote is in Sam Stein, "Obama Compares Himself to Reagan, JFK . . . but Not Bill Clinton," *Huffington Post*, March 8, 2018, https://www.huffingtonpost.com/2008/01/16/obama-compares-himself-to_n_81835.html.

BIBLIOGRAPHY

Published Works

Anderson, Martin. "Self-Reliance." In *Why I Am a Reagan Conservative*, ed. Michael Deaver. New York: Harper Paperbacks, 2006.

Bartlett, Bruce. *Imposter: How George W. Bush Bankrupted America and Betrayed the Reagan Revolution*. New York: Doubleday, 2006.

Bartley, Robert. "The Dread Deficit." In *The NeoCon Reader*, ed. Edwin Stelzer. New York: Grove Press, 2006.

Bastiat, Frédéric. *The Law: A Classic Blueprint for Society*. Trans. Dean Russell. New York: Foundation for Economic Education, 1996.

Beecher, Henry Ward. *The Sermons of Henry Ward Beecher*. Vol. 9. Boston: Pilgrim Press, 1873.

Bergh, Albert, ed. *The Writings of Thomas Jefferson*. Vol. 13. Washington DC: Thomas Jefferson Memorial Foundation, 1907.

Brinkley, Douglas, ed. *The Reagan Diaries*. New York: Harper Perennial, 2007.

Brown, Mary Beth. *The Faith of Ronald Reagan*. Nashville TN: Thomas Nelson, 2011.

Brownlee, Elliot W., and Hugh David Graham, eds. *The Reagan Presidency: Pragmatic Conservatism and Its Legacies*. Lawrence: University of Kansas Press, 2003.

Buchanan, Patrick J. "Bush Leaves GOP in Crisis." *Human Events*, November 5, 2010. http://www.uvm.edu/~dguber/POLS125/articles/buchanan2.htm.

Burnham, James. *The Coming Defeat of Communism*. New York: John Day, 1950.

———. *The Struggle for the World*. New York: John Day, 1947.

———. "The Week." *National Review*, July 18, 1956.

Bush, George H. W. "Radio Address to United States Armed Forces Stationed in the Persian Gulf Region." March 2, 1991. American Presidency Project. http://www.presidency.ucsb.edu/ws/index.php?pid=19355.

Bush, George W. "Address before a Joint Session of the Congress on the United States Response to the Terrorist Attacks of September 11." September 20,

2001. American Presidency Project. http://www.presidency.ucsb.edu/ws/ ?pid=64731.

———. "Address to the American Enterprise Institute." February 27, 2003. https://www.theguardian.com/world/2003/feb/27/usa.iraq2.

———. "Address to the United Nations." September 12, 2002. http://www.cnn .com/2002/US/09/12/bush.transcript/.

———. "Interview Excerpts of President Bush and First Lady Laura Bush by Doro Bush Koch for StoryCorps." November 28, 2008. White House. https://georgewbush-whitehouse.archives.gov/news/releases/2008/11 /20081128.html.

———. "Remarks before United Nations Assembly." September 19, 2006. http://www.washingtonpost.com/wp-dyn/content/article/2006/09/19 /AR2006091900720.html.

———. "Remarks on 9/11 Attacks." CNN, September 11, 2001. http://edition .cnn.com/2001/US/09/11/bush.speech.text/.

———. "State of the Union Speech." CNN, January 28, 2003. http://www.cnn .com/2003/ALLPOLITICS/01/28/sotu.transcript/.

Cannon, Lou. *Governor Reagan: His Rise to Power*. New York: Public Affairs, 2003.

———. *President Reagan: Role of a Lifetime*. New York: Public Affairs, 2000.

Cannon, Lou, and Carl Cameron. *Reagan's Disciple: George W. Bush and His Troubled Quest for a Presidential Legacy*. New York: PublicAffairs, 2007.

Chernow, Ron. *Alexander Hamilton*. New York, Penguin, 2004.

Chernyaev, Anatoly. *My Six Years with Gorbachev*. Ed. and trans. Robert English and Elizabeth Tucker. University Park: Pennsylvania State University Press, 2000.

Clinton William J. "Address Accepting the Presidential Nomination at the Democratic National Convention in New York." July, 16, 1992. American Presidency Project. http://www.presidency.ucsb.edu/ws/?pid=25958.

———. Address before a Joint Session of the Congress on the State of the Union." January 23, 1996. American Presidency Project. http://www.presidency .ucsb.edu/ws/?pid=53091.

———. "Address to the Nation Announcing Military Strikes on Iraq." December 16, 1988. American Presidency Project. http://www.presidency.ucsb .edu/ws/?pid=55414.

———. "Remarks at Georgetown University." February 9, 1998. American Presidency Project. http://www.presidency.ucsb.edu/ws/?pid=55348.

———. "Remarks at the Signing Ceremony for the Supplemental Agreements to the North American Free Trade Agreement." September 14, 1993. American Presidency Project. http://www.presidency.ucsb.edu/ws /?pid=47070.

———. "Statement on Signing the Iraqi Liberation Act of 1998." October 31, 1998. American Presidency Project. http://www.presidency.ucsb.edu/ws /?pid=55205.

Coll, Blanche. *Safety Net: Welfare and Social Security, 1929–1979*. New Brunswick NJ: Rutgers University Press, 1995.

Collins, Michael. *Transforming America: Politics and Culture during the Reagan Years*. New York: Columbia University Press, 2007.

Commager, Henry Steele. *Jefferson, Nationalism and the Enlightenment*. New York: George Braziller, 1975.

Condorcet. *Sketch for a Historical Picture of the Progress of the Human Mind*. Trans. June Barraclough. New York: Noonday Press, 1955.

Constitute Project. Iraq's Constitution of 2005. January 17, 2018. https://www.constituteproject.org/constitution/Iraq_2005.pdf?lang=en.

Crossman, Richard, ed. *The God That Failed: A Confession*. New York: Harper & Brothers, 1949.

Danziger, Sheldon, and Robert Haveman. "The Reagan Administration's Budget Cuts: Their Impact on the Poor." Institute for Research on Poverty, n.d. https://www.irp.wisc.edu/publications/focus/pdfs/foc52b.pdf.

Davies, Gareth. "The Welfare State." In *The Reagan Presidency: Pragmatic Conservatism and Its Legacies*, ed. W. Eliot Brownlee and Hugh David Graham. Lawrence: University of Kansas Press, 2003.

Davis, R. H. C. *A History of Medieval Europe, from Constantine to St. Louis*. New York: Longman, 1988.

Deaver, Michael K. *A Different Drummer: My Thirty Years with Ronald Reagan*. New York: HarperCollins, 2009.

Diggins, John P. *Fate, Freedom and History*. New York: Norton, 2007.

———. *Ronald Reagan: Fate, Freedom and the Making of History*. New York: Norton, 2007.

D'Souza, Dinesh. *Ronald Reagan: How an Ordinary Man Became an Extraordinary Leader*. New York: Free Press, 1999.

Edwards, Anne. *Early Reagan: The Rise to Power*. New York: Taylor Trade, 2012.

Edwards, Lee. *Ronald Reagan: A Political Biography*. Houston: Nordland, 1981.

Evans, Thomas W. *The Education of Ronald Reagan: The General Electric Years*. New York: Columbia University Press, 2007.

Foner, Eric. *The Story of American Freedom*. New York: Norton, 1998.

Ford, Gerald. "Address before a Joint Session of the Congress Reporting on the State of the Union." January 15, 1975. American Presidency Project. http://www.presidency.ucsb.edu/ws/index.php?pid=4938.

Friedman, Milton. *Capitalism and Freedom*. Chicago: University of Chicago Press, 2002.

Galbraith, John Kenneth. "The Unbearable Costs of Empire." *Prospect*, November 2002, 72–75.

Gergen, David. *Eyewitness to Power: The Essence of Leadership*. New York: Simon & Schuster, 2000.

Goldwater, Barry. *The Conscience of a Conservative*. Washington DC: Regnery Gateway, 1990.

Guevara, Che. *Guerrilla Warfare*. New York: SR Books, 1997.

Hamilton, Edith, and Cairns Huntington, eds. *The Complete Dialogues of Plato*. Princeton NJ: Princeton University Press, 2005.

Harrington, Michael. *The Other America: Poverty in the United States*. New York: Macmillan, 1962.

Hayek, Friedrich. *The Collected Works of F. A. Hayek*. Vol. 2. Ed. Bruce Caldwell. Chicago: University of Chicago Press, 2007.

———. "The Use of Knowledge in Society." *American Economic Review* 35, no. 4 (1945): 519–30.

Hayward, Steven. *The Age of Reagan and the Fall of the Liberal Order, 1964–1980*. Vol. 1 of *The Age of Reagan*. New York: Prima, 2001.

Hazlitt, Henry. *Economics in One Lesson*. Auburn AL: Ludwig von Mises Institute, 2008.

Heclo, Hugh. "Ronald Reagan and the American Public Philosophy." In *The Reagan Presidency: Pragmatic Conservatism and Its Legacies*, ed. W. Eliot Brownlee and Hugh David Graham. Lawrence: University of Kansas Press, 2003.

Henry, Patrick. "Give Me Liberty or Give Me Death." March 23, 1775. Avalon Project. http://avalon.law.yale.edu/18th_century/patrick.asp.

Hitchens, Christopher. *The Quotable Christopher Hitchens: From Alcohol to Zionism*. Ed. Windsor Mann. Boston: Da Capo Press, 2011.

Hobsbawm, Eric. *Age of Extremes: A History of the World, 1914–1991*. New York: Vintage Press, 1996.

Hofstadter, Richard. *Anti-Intellectualism in America*. New York: Knopf, 1963.

Holbach, Paul-Henri Thiry. *Christianity Unveiled: An Examination of the Principles and Effects of the Christian Religion*. Trans. W. M. Johnson. New York: Gordon Press, 1835.

Horkheimer, Max, and Theodor Adorno. *Dialectic of Enlightenment*. Ed. Gunzelin Schmid Noerr. Trans. Edmund Jephcott. Stanford CA: Stanford University Press, 2002.

Houck, Davis, and Amos Kiewe, eds. *Ronald Reagan: Actor, Ideologue, Politician. The Public Speeches of Ronald Reagan*. Westport CT: Greenwood Press, 1993.

Hume, David. *Essays: Moral, Political and Literary*. Vol. 1. Ed. T. H. Green and T. H. Grose. London: Longman, Green, 1889.

———. *A History of England*. Halifax, UK: William Milner, 1840.

Hume, James. *The Wit and Wisdom of Ronald Reagan*. Washington DC: Regnery, 2007.

Ibn Khaldun. *The Muqaddimah: A History*. Trans. Franz Rosenthal. Ed. N. J. Dawood. Princeton NJ: Princeton University Press, 1967.

Internet Archive. "1971–1972 Governors Budget Summary." https://archive.org/stream/governor7172unse#page/n35/mode/2up/search/mental+health.

Israel, Jonathan. *Revolution of Mind: Radical Enlightenment and the Intellectual Origins of Modern Democracy*. Princeton NJ: Princeton University Press, 2009.

Jefferson, Thomas. Letter to Tench Coxe. June 1, 1795. National Archives, Founders Online. https://founders.archives.gov/documents/Jefferson/01 -28-02-0282.

Johnson, Haynes. *Sleepwalking through History: America in the Reagan Years*. New York: Norton, 1991.

Kengor, Paul. *God and Ronald Reagan: A Spiritual Life*. New York: HarperCollins, 2005.

Kennedy, John F. "Remarks of Senator John F. Kennedy, Municipal Auditorium, Canton, Ohio." September 27, 1960. American Presidency Project. http://www.presidency.ucsb.edu/ws/?pid=74231.

Kirk, Russell. *The Conservative Mind: From Burke to Santayana*. Washington DC: Regnery, 2016.

———. "Political Errors at the End of the 20th Century." Heritage Foundation, February 27, 1991. http://www.heritage.org/political-process/report /political-errors-the-end-the-20th-century.

———. *The Politics of Prudence*. Bryn Mawr PA: Intercollegiate Studies Institute, 1993.

Koestler, Arthur. *Darkness at Noon*. New York, Macmillan, 1940.

Kloppenberg, James T. *Reading Obama: Dreams, Hope, and the American Political Tradition*. Princeton NJ: Princeton University Press, 2011.

Lettow, Paul. *Ronald Reagan and His Quest to Abolish Nuclear Weapons*. New York: Random House, 2005.

Leuchtenburg, William. *In the Shadow of FDR: From Harry Truman to Bill Clinton*. Ithaca NY: Cornell University Press, 1993.

Lewis, C. S. *The Complete C. S. Lewis*. New York: HarperCollins, 2002.

Lewis, Matt K. *Too Dumb to Fail: How the GOP Betrayed the Reagan Revolution to Win Elections*. New York: Hachette Books, 2016.

Lobkowicz, Nicholas. *Theory and Practice: History of a Concept from Aristotle to Marx*. South Bend IN: Notre Dame Press, 1967.

Locke, John. *Two Treatises on Government*. Ed. Peter Laslett. Cambridge, UK: Cambridge University Press, 1994.

Lowry, Rich, ed. *Tear Down This Wall: The Reagan Revolution. A National Review History*. New York: Continuum, 2004.

Malia, Martin. *The Soviet Tragedy: A History of Socialism in Russia, 1917–1991*. New York: Free Press, 1995.

Marx, Karl, and Friedrich Engels. *The Communist Manifesto*. In *The Marx-Engels Reader*, ed. Robert C. Tucker. New York: Norton, 1978.

Matlock, Jack F., Jr. *Reagan and Gorbachev: How the Cold War Ended*. New York: Random House, 2005.

Meese, Edwin. "Reagan Would Not Repeat Amnesty Mistake." *Human Events*, December 13, 2006. http://humanevents.com/2006/12/13/reagan-would -not-repeat-amnesty-mistake/.

Meyer, Frank. "The Twisted Tree of Liberty." *National Review*, January 16, 1962.

Mises, Ludwig von. *Planning for Freedom.* South Holland IL: Libertarian Press, 1980.

Montesquieu, Charles. *Spirit of Laws.* New York: Prometheus Books, 2002.

Morgan, Iwan. *Reagan: An American Icon.* New York: I. B. Tauris, 2016.

Morris, Edmund. *Dutch: A Memoir of Ronald Reagan.* New York: Random House, 1999.

Murdoch, Deroy. "Egghead Reagan." *National Review,* June 15, 2004.

Murray, Charles. *Losing Ground: American Social Policy 1950–1980.* New York, Basic Books, 1984.

Nash, George. *The Conservative Intellectual Movement in America, since 1945.* New York: Basic Books, 1976.

New, Michael. "Morning in California." *National Review,* June 10, 2004. https://www.nationalreview.com/2004/06/morning-california-michael-j-new/.

Noonan, Peggy. *When Character Was King: A Story of Ronald Reagan.* New York: Penguin, 2001.

Paine, Thomas. *Political Writings of Thomas Paine.* 2 vols. New York: George H. Evans, 1835.

———. *The Rights of Man.* New York: Dolphin Press, 1961.

Patterson, James T. *America's Struggle against Poverty in the Twentieth Century.* Cambridge MA: Harvard University Press, 1989.

"Political Party Platforms: 1996 Democratic Party Platform." August 26, 1996. American Presidency Project. http://www.presidency.ucsb.edu/ws/index.php?pid=29611.

Pope, Alexander. "Epitaph on Sir Isaac Newton," March 21, 1727. www.bartleby.com/297/154.html.

"The President's Veto of the Schip Extension." *Congressional Record* 5.153, part 19, October 3, 2007.

Public Papers of Presidents of the United States: George W. Bush. Book 2. Washington DC: Government Printing Office, 2011.

Ragone, Nick. *Presidential Leadership: 15 Decisions That Changed the Nation.* New York: Prometheus Books, 2011.

Rawls, John. *Theory of Justice.* Cambridge MA: Belknap Press, 1971.

Reagan, Michael. *Twice Adopted.* Nashville TN: Broadman and Holmes, 2004.

Reagan, Michael, with Jim Denney. *The New Reagan Revolution: How Ronald Reagan's Greatness Can Restore America.* New York: St. Martin's Press, 2012.

Reagan, Ronald. *An American Life.* New York: Simon and Schuster, 1990.

———. "Losing Freedom by Installments." *General Contractor,* November, 1961.

———. *The Notes: The Wit and Wisdom of Ronald Reagan.* Ed. Douglas Brinkley. New York: HarperCollins, 2011.

———. *Speaking My Mind.* New York: Simon & Schuster, 1989.

———. "Testimony before House Ways and Means Committee." Washington DC. January 27, 1958. In *Ronald Reagan: Actor, Ideologue, Politician. The Public Speeches of Ronald Reagan,* ed. Davis Houck and Amos Kiewe. Westport CT: Greenwood Press, 1993.

———. "Testimony before the House Un-American Activities Committee." Washington DC. October 25, 1947. http://wps.prenhall.com/wps/media /objects/108/110880/ch26_a5_d1.pdf.

———. *A Time for Choosing: The Speeches of Ronald Reagan.* Chicago: Regnery Gateway, 1983.

Reagan, Ronald, with Richard Hubler. *Where's the Rest of Me?* New York: Duell, Sloan and Pearce, 1965.

Reale, Giovanni. *A History of Ancient Philosophy III: The Systems of the Hellenistic Age.* Albany: State University of New York Press, 1985.

Reeves, Richard. *Ronald Reagan: The Triumph of Imagination.* New York: Simon and Schuster, 2005.

Richman, Sheldon L. "The Sad Legacy of Ronald Reagan." In *The Free Market Reader*, ed. Llewellyn H. Rockwell. Burlingame CA: Ludwig von Mises Institute, 1988.

Robin, Corey. *The Reactionary Mind: From Burke to Sarah Palin.* Oxford: Oxford University Press, 2011.

Robinson, Peter. *How Ronald Reagan Changed My Life.* New York: Harper Perennial, 2004.

Roosevelt, Franklin Delano. "Address to the International Labor Organization." November 6, 1941. American Presidency Project. http://www.presidency .ucsb.edu/ws/index.php?pid=16037.

———. "Annual Message to Congress." January 4, 1935. American Presidency Project. http://www.presidency.ucsb.edu/ws/index.php?pid=14890.

Rousseau, J. J. *Politics and the Arts.* Trans. Allan Bloom. New York: Free Press, 1960.

———. *The Social Contract and Discourses.* Trans. G. D. H. Cole. New York: E. P. Dutton, 1913.

Saad, Lydia. "U.S. Conservatives Outnumber Liberals by Narrowing Margin." *Gallup*, January 3, 2017. http://news.gallup.com/poll/201152/conservative -liberal-gap-continues-narrow-tuesday.aspx.

Schweizer, Peter. *Reagan's War: The Epic Story of His Forty Year Struggle and Final Triumph over Communism.* New York: Doubleday, 2002.

"The Second American Revolution: Reaganomics." Ronald Reagan Presidential Foundation and Institute, n.d. https://www.reaganfoundation.org/ronald -reagan/the-presidency/economic-policy/.

Singer, Peter. *Marx: A Very Short Introduction.* Oxford: Oxford University Press, 2001.

Skinner, Kiron, and Annelise Anderson, eds. *Reagan in His Own Hand.* New York: Free Press, 2001.

Skinner, Kiron, Annelise Anderson, and Martin Anderson, eds. *Reagan: A Life in Letters.* New York: Free Press, 2004.

Sloan, John. *The Reagan Effect: Economics and Presidential Leadership.* Lawrence: University Press of Kansas, 1999.

Smith, Adam. *Wealth of Nations*. New York: P. F. Collier & Son, 1902.

St. Augustine. *City of God*. Trans. Gerald G. Walsh and Daniel J. Honan. Washington DC: Catholic University Press of America, 1954.

Students for a Democratic Society. "Port Huron Statement." June 15, 1962. Sixties Project. http://www2.iath.virginia.edu/sixties/HTML_docs/Resources/Primary/Manifestos/SDS_Port_Huron.html.

Thatcher, Margaret. "Eulogy for President Reagan." June 11, 2004. Margaret Thatcher Foundation. https://www.margaretthatcher.org/document/110360.

Tocqueville, Alexis de. *Democracy in America*. Vol 1. Trans. Henry Reeve. Boston: John Allyn, 1876.

——— *Democracy in America*. Vol 2. Trans. Henry Reeve. New York: D. Appleton, 1899.

Troy, Gil. *Morning in America: How Ronald Reagan Invented the 1980s*. Princeton NJ: Princeton University Press, 2005.

Truman, Harry. "Address on Foreign Policy at the Navy Day Celebration in New York City." October 27, 1945. American Presidency Project. http://www.presidency.ucsb.edu/ws/?pid=12304.

———. "Address of the President to Congress, Recommending Assistance to Greece and Turkey." March 12, 1947. Elsey Papers, Harry S. Truman Administration. March 12, 1947. https://www.trumanlibrary.org/whistlestop/study_collections/doctrine/large/documents/index.php?documentdate=1947-03-12&documentid=5-9&pagenumber=1.

Ulam, Adam. *Ideologies and Illusions: Revolutionary Thought from Herzen to Solzhenitsyn*. Cambridge MA: Harvard University Press, 1976.

U.S. Department of Education. "Education Department Budget by Major Program." October 13, 2017. https://www2.ed.gov/about/overview/budget/history/edhistory.pdf.

Voltaire. *Philosophical Letters*. Trans. Ernest Dilworth. Indianapolis IN: Hackett, 2007.

Voyce, Stephen. *Poetic Community: Avante Garde Activism and Cold War Culture*. Toronto: University of Toronto Press, 2013.

Warman, Caroline, ed. *Tolerance: The Beacon of the Enlightenment*. Cambridge, UK: Open Book, 2016.

Wilentz, Sean. *The Age of Reagan: A History, 1974–2008*. New York: Harper Perennial, 2009.

Wills, Garry. *Reagan's America: Innocents at Home*. New York: Doubleday, 1987.

Wilson, James Q. "A Guide to Reagan Country: The Political Culture of Southern California." *Commentary*, May 1, 1967.

Winthrop, John. *The Dominion of Providence over the Passions of Men: A Sermon Preached at Princeton on the 17th of May, 1776*. Philadelphia: Fielding and Walker 1778.

Yager, Edward. *Ronald Reagan's Journey: Democrat to Republican*. Lanham MD: Rowman and Littlefield, 2006.

Reagan Speeches

"Address before a Joint Session of the Congress on the Program for Economic Recovery." February 18, 1981. American Presidency Project. http://www.presidency.ucsb.edu/ws/index.php?pid=43425.

"Address before a Joint Session of the Irish National Parliament." June 4, 1984. American Presidency Project. http://www.presidency.ucsb.edu/ws/index.php?pid=40011.

"Address to Members of the British Parliament." June 8, 1982. Reagan Library. https://www.reaganlibrary.gov/sites/default/files/archives/speeches/1982/60882a.htm.

"Address to the Nation on Defense and National Security." March 23, 1983. American Presidency Project. http://www.presidency.ucsb.edu/ws/?pid=41093.

"America the Beautiful." Commencement address. William Woods College, Fulton MO, June 2, 1952. http://reagan.convio.net/site/DocServer/Echoes_from_the_Woods_America_the_Beautiful_Article_0652.pdf?docID=785.

"A Time for Choosing." Televised address on Behalf of Barry Goldwater. October 27, 1964. Los Angeles. American Rhetoric. http://www.americanrhetoric.com/speeches/ronaldreaganatimeforchoosing.htm.

"The Creative Society." Campaign speech at University of Southern California, Los Angeles, April 19, 1966. http://reagan.convio.net/site/DocServer/ReaganMomentsFeb-_3_-The_Creative_Society_-_April_19__19.pdf?docID=583.

"The Defense of Freedom and Metaphysics of Fun." Speech delivered at *National Review*'s thirtieth anniversary dinner. December 5, 1985. In *Tear Down This Wall: The Reagan Revolution. A National Review History*, ed. Rich Lowry. New York: Continuum, 2004.

"Farewell Address to the Nation." January 11, 1989. American Presidency Project. http://www.presidency.ucsb.edu/ws/?pid=29650.

"Government and the Family." National television address, July 6, 1976. In *A Time for Choosing: The Speeches of Ronald Reagan*. Chicago: Regnery Gateway, 1983.

"The Obligation of Liberty." Speech before the World Affairs Council, Los Angeles, October 12, 1972. In *A Time for Choosing: The Speeches of Ronald Reagan*. Chicago: Regnery Gateway, 1983.

"Reagan Campaigns for Truman." Radio address, 1948. YouTube. https://www.youtube.com/watch?v=uJDhS4oUm0M.

"Remarks at a Ceremony Commemorating the 40th Anniversary of the Normandy Invasion, D-day." June 6, 1984. American Presidency Project. http://www.presidency.ucsb.edu/ws/index.php?pid=40018.

"Remarks at Eureka College." Eureka IL, February 6, 1984. https://www.reaganlibrary.gov/sites/default/files/archives/speeches/1984/20684b.htm.

"Remarks at the Presentation Ceremony for the Presidential Medal of Freedom." January 19, 1989. American Presidency Project. http://www.presidency.ucsb.edu/ws/?pid=35402.

"Ronald Reagan Speaks Out against Socialized Medicine." Radio address, 1961. American Rhetoric. http://www.americanrhetoric.com/speeches /ronaldreagansocializedmedicine.htm.

"Speech to the Conservative Political Action Conference." Washington DC. February 6, 1977. In *A Time for Choosing: The Speeches of Ronald Reagan*. Chicago: Regnery Gateway, 1983.

"Speech to the Merchants and Manufacturers Association Annual Banquet." Los Angeles, May 16, 1967. Vertical file, Ronald Reagan Presidential Library, Simi Valley CA.

"A Time for Choosing." Los Angeles, October 27, 1964. In *A Time for Choosing: The Speeches of Ronald Reagan*. Chicago: Regnery Gateway, 1983.

"The Value of Understanding the Past." Eureka College, Eureka IL, September 29, 1967. In *A Time for Choosing: The Speeches of Ronald Reagan*. Chicago: Regnery Gateway, 1983.

INDEX